Existential
Counselling &
Psychotherapy
in Practice

About the Author

Emmy van Deurzen is Director of the New School of Psychotherapy and Counselling, London and Co-Director of the Centre for the Study of Conflict and Reconciliation at the University of Sheffield. She is also a partner in Dilemma Consultancy in Human Relations, which provides existential psychotherapy, supervision and consultancy.

SECOND EDITION

Existential
Counselling &
Psychotherapy
in Practice

Emmy van Deurzen

SAGE Publications
London • Thousand Oaks • New Delhi

First published 2002

Reprinted 2002

 SAGE Publications Ltd
6 Bonhill Street
London EC2A 4PU

SAGE Publications Inc
2455 Teller Road
Thousand Oaks, California 91320

SAGE Publications India Pvt Ltd
32, M-Block Market
Greater Kailash – I
New Delhi 110 048

British Library Cataloguing in Publication data
A catalogue record for this book is available from the British Library

ISBN 0 7619 6223 9
ISBN 0 7619 6224 7 (pbk)

Library of Congress Control Number available

Typeset by M Rules
Printed in Great Britain by Biddles Ltd, *www.biddles.co.uk*

To my children and stepchildren:
Benjamin, Sasha, Robert and Grace.

Contents

Preface

I first wrote this book in the middle of the nineteen eighties, when counselling and psychotherapy were rapidly developing in the United Kingdom. I had been teaching the subject for nearly ten years and had suffered from the lack of any text that made direct and practical connections between existential philosophy and counselling. I had worked in psychiatric hospitals before becoming a trainer and had developed a personal way of working based more on my philosophical than on my psychological training. I had certainly drawn on the continental methods of Binswanger and Boss, and had been greatly inspired and encouraged by Laing's work, which had brought me to this country ten years previously to work in a therapeutic community. I had come to the conclusion that I had to formulate and develop on my own what I had looked for in others and I had already published a brief account of my way of working in the early nineteen eighties. Finding a publisher for a book was more difficult, and it was thanks to Farrell Burnett, who was an editor with Sage Publications at the time, that the project got under way. It was a great challenge and a great comfort finally to write the book that had been germinating in my mind for such a long time. The challenge was to dare write down what it was that I actually believed in and practised, rather than hide behind other people's findings or research. The comfort was to find that it was possible to make sense of such a personal approach and communicate it effectively.

My ideas had been generated through living, studying, working with clients, teaching, supervising and training. This continues to be true today. It goes without saying that I am therefore indebted to all those people who have been there with me in that process. When I first wrote the book I thought of this account of my position as but a fragment of what was possible and I knew that much would be needed to complete and amend it. Little did I know that the book would give me the courage to found the Society for Existential Analysis and to develop widely the training courses in existential psychotherapy and counselling that I had already established. I had no idea that all this would attract so much interest in the existential approach and put it on the map in the UK. People began to dialogue about the approach through the conferences and discussion groups of the Society for Existential Analysis and also in its Journal. Many capable counsellors and therapists joined the existential movement or were trained in the approach. There is now a well-established place for the existential approach in the UK and it is possible to train and become registered as an existential psychotherapist through a number of different organizations. The movement has its own history of splitting and fighting and there is a healthy disagreement about what existential work should be. One can only hope that such tensions will be allowed to continue and that they may be used creatively. It would be a great shame if the existential approach became rigidified and reduced to yet another technology and fixed dogma. It is the freedom and the openness of the approach that I have always valued and I think it is this that has attracted many readers to this book.

It has been wonderful to find that the existential ideas are relevant and useful to counsellors and psychotherapists of all orientations. The existential approach does not seek to be a technique or a school but rather a different way of viewing the world and human living. Those who are prepared to take it seriously usually find something in it that speaks to them directly. Frequently people feel that the approach expresses what they have thought themselves for a long time but could not quite articulate. Quite often people feel that their outlook and attitudes are drastically and definitively transformed as a result of finding a framework for living. The same process occurs with clients who too find that they can begin to think about themselves differently and in a more open way as they allow themselves to focus on those things that really matter to them rather than remaining trapped in their intra-psychic prisons.

The ideas in the book are taken from many sources but I have intentionally kept this book simple and uncluttered with references. My own background and early development have contributed just as much to my existential view of the world as my formal education and training. Anna and Arie, my parents, have certainly contributed much to my way of looking at the world. I am grateful for what they taught me about life. Much else was inspired by the works of some of my favourite philosophers, including Socrates, Spinoza, Kierkegaard, Nietzsche, Heidegger and Sartre. It will be obvious that I take the contributions of many practitioners for granted although I seldom refer to them specifically. Freud, Binswanger, Boss, Jaspers, Laing and May were a few of the most influential ones at the time I wrote the book.

There is no doubt that having been able to exchange ideas, experience and insights with those close to me has been a crucial factor in the clear formulation and critical consideration of my work. You can only write about reality if you let yourself be challenged by it. My changing and growing family have always been a source of inspiration, challenge and support in coming to terms with the tasks of life that this book is concerned with. The transformations in my own family life over the decades have made me aware of the importance of formulating steadily what is learned in one generation and pass it on to the next. Therefore I have now dedicated the book to my children and stepchildren. Not only have they been my touchstones of reality, they have helped me keep my eye on what matters and they have forced me to keep my mind open and clear. But I also want to acknowledge the support I was given by David Smith at the time I first wrote this book. Our paths have since parted, but his contribution to my early work remains intact. However, the vigorous challenges and support of my husband, Digby Tantam, have been what I needed to push me through the difficult task of re-editing this book. The closeness of our relationship has sustained me through some amazing crises, some of which were strangely prefigured in this book. It has taught me that it really is possible to keep exploring and learning even when life is at a low. It has also shown me that love is by far the best antidote to fear.

Finally, it is necessary and fitting to mention the students who encouraged me in the writing of this book, since it is their enthusiasm that spurred me on to complete this project in the first place. The many students and trainees who have since commented on it have kept my thinking alive and focused. I thank them for it.

In the revision of the book for the new edition I had originally intended to make drastic changes. Upon re-reading the text it seemed to me that it would be better to retain most of its original simplicity even though my way of working has matured and acquired greater complexity over the years. I felt that the book speaks of the beginnings of an approach and it would be wrong to want to alter it too much and change its tone. I have however extended the original counselling focus to include psychotherapy, since the existential approach and this book are relevant to the entire therapeutic endeavour. I have also added concise summaries of what has been discussed at the end of each chapter, in the hope of making the book more accessible to trainees and teachers in particular. The message of the existential approach that comes through this most loudly and clearly is that the fundamental objective of the approach is to enable people to rediscover their own values, beliefs and their life's purpose. The goal of existential therapy is to experience oneself as real again, or perhaps for the first time. This means that you come to know yourself in light of human limitations and possibilities and that you engage wholeheartedly with life in the way that is most satisfactory to you. I hope that this book will continue to show counsellors and psychotherapists how to apply such ideas in practice so that they can become more effective at helping people to find purpose and meaning in their lives which they had not been able to find before.

Introduction

This book is predominantly intended for counsellors and psychotherapists, both those already practising and those still in training. It outlines specific methods of working with people from an existential perspective. As this perspective is philosophical in addition to being therapeutic, the book is, in a wider sense, relevant to anyone interested in exploring existential concerns. The focus throughout is on practical application.

The type of counselling and therapy proposed involves assisting people to come to terms with the dilemmas of living. Issues are addressed in moral and human terms rather than in terms of sickness and health. The frame of reference is philosophical rather than medical, social or psychological. The assumption is that people need to find ways of making sense of life before they can make sense of their problems and of themselves.

It is often only at times of crisis that people become aware of the emptiness and ignorance of their lives. At these moments there can be a sudden urge to understand life better and to find meaning amid chaos and confusion. All too often people are at a loss for a place or a person to turn to for assistance in the process of clarification and discovery that they long for. Some may still find it through a church, others through medical care or psychotherapy. Few people are lucky enough to find a professional who can help them to sort out these issues without also putting them through religious, medical or psychological hoops.

A simple and down-to-earth method for helping ordinary people to get on with daily existence in a meaningful way is long overdue. This book is an attempt to provide a first outline of such a method. It has evolved from a long process of practical application of the ideas of existential philosophers. The wealth of insight into human nature and understanding of life from that source has so far largely remained untapped. The various schools of existential analysis and psychotherapy have remained secluded, exclusive and very theoretical. The language of these approaches moreover has usually been highly intellectual, abstract and enigmatic; enough so to put most therapists and counsellors off. Some other existential approaches have emphasized the political and social dimensions and have failed to propose an actual framework for practice.

Humanistic methods, seen by some as a practical application of existential ideas, unfortunately often involve distortion and misinterpretation of the most fundamental concepts. Humanistic forms of counselling and therapy are frequently highly technique-oriented or aim for quick solutions and magical cures. Their emphasis is on self-realization and personal growth, attained through the pursuit of individual choice and freedom. They are the product of the American human potential movement.

The European existential philosophers never suggested such simple solutions and they examined the complexities of human living rather more carefully. They never intended to create the illusion of being able to solve the human dilemma. There is nothing in their writing that suggests the prospect of a paradise on earth, inhabited by self-actualizing individuals. Their aim has been to gain insight into the unavoidable paradoxes that life presents and to gain strength from that knowledge. This book is firmly based on the European tradition. It provides a framework and a method for tackling problems in living. It proposes a way of thinking and working rather than a technique and a list of skills.

The first chapter describes this particular method of working as an art and the therapeutic session is likened to a tutorial. The assumptions and goals of the approach are defined and the practitioner's task is outlined.

The second chapter looks at the actual interactions between therapist and client and traces the process of existential counselling and therapy in terms of the impact on the client.

In the third chapter the basic model of working with the four levels of human experience is presented. I show how the different challenges on each dimension can be recognized and faced.

The fourth chapter goes on to explain the importance of helping people to take stock of their present mode of living. I pay attention to the way in which people's assumptions can be defined and taken into account as the indicators of their basic values and talents.

In the fifth chapter I explore various ways in which the therapeutic process can be enlivened and made more creative. This includes work with emotions, meaning, dreams and imagination.

The final chapter considers how people can be encouraged to come to terms with life, not through changing but through facing themselves against the background of their lives as they are. Making commitments in action and communicating with other people are also considered as part of the progress that people will make towards the creation of a fulfilling life.

Throughout the book ample illustrations are given of how the ideas can be practically applied. These pages are firmly based on work with clients, supervisees, students and trainees. But in the final analysis it is the product of a continuing personal search for a meaningful way of living. As such it can only be the first step on a long road into the future.

Everything has been figured out,
except how to live.

JEAN-PAUL SARTRE

1

Aim and Framework

Basic assumptions

Basic assumptions are those ideas that people hold to be true without questioning them. Every approach to counselling and psychotherapy is founded on a set of beliefs and ideas about life, about the world and about people. These notions are so essential to the approach that they can easily be overlooked. Basic assumptions are implicit rather than explicit. Every intervention that a therapeutic practitioner makes expresses some of her basic assumptions, in a subtle or in a less subtle way.

Some basic assumptions, such as the belief in the fundamental possibility of understanding another person, are shared by all therapeutic approaches. Other basic assumptions are specifically related to particular perspectives in counselling and psychotherapy. No approach is without assumptions. No approach can be practised without conveying its assumptions in the process.

Clients can only benefit from an approach in so far as they feel able to go along with its basic assumptions. It is a well-documented fact that clients will generally not gain anything from working in a psychoanalytic way until they are willing to examine their resistance. This implies acceptance of one of the basic assumptions of the analytic approach, which is that all attitudes and thoughts should be made freely available for scrutiny, because of their significance in terms of the underlying psychological process. To the extent that the client does not fall in with the idea that her thoughts and actions are unconsciously determined, she cannot be helped by a psychoanalytic approach.

In the same way clients cannot be helped by cognitive or behavioural methods unless they acknowledge the importance of acquiring new skills or thought-patterns and until they begin actively to practise these. In other words, to benefit from the cognitive-behavioural approach clients have to fall in with the assumption that people learn to think and act in certain ways and that they can therefore also relearn and correct these patterns.

Clients can only benefit from person-centred work to the extent that they agree with the assumption that people can and should take responsibility for themselves. Furthermore, they will have to agree with the idea that expressing their feelings is beneficial and necessary. Clients who are assuming that it is up to the practitioner or therapist to provide a solution for them while they can themselves remain reserved and passive are unlikely to gain much from a person-centred approach.

From an existential perspective awareness of basic assumptions is therefore deemed to be crucial for both practitioner and client. Clients can only engage fully with the therapeutic process if they have confidence in its principles. They cannot be expected to co-operate wholeheartedly until they have had a chance to understand what is supposed to happen and until they have made up their mind about the rightness of the procedure.

Some clients are keen to adopt their therapist's implicit assumptions through osmosis and through imitation of her attitudes and expressions. From an existential point of view this is not considered helpful unless the client has some idea about possible alternatives. The existential approach assumes the importance of the client's capacity for making well-informed choices about her own life and her attitude towards it.

This places great emphasis on the need for the practitioner to be acutely aware of her professional and personal assumptions. Philosophical clarity is the most basic requirement for the existential approach. If the practitioner is to help clients to clarify their attitudes and goals, she must first examine her own with the greatest care.

In practice, all too often, practitioners do not have this kind of clarity about their own intentions and assumptions. They may find themselves operating with methods that they absorbed simply because they were on offer during their initial training. They know that they want to help their clients and therefore they often accumulate a variety of techniques which seem appealing and efficient. In the hope of becoming as professionally flexible as possible they may adopt an eclectic or integrative stance. Unfortunately, the basic assumptions of the different strands of the approaches they try to integrate may be diametrically opposed.

Following the lead of the client one minute and giving her some homework the next is clearly inconsistent. In the first instance the underlying assumption is that of the value of the client's autonomy, whereas in the second the necessity of the client's obedience is assumed. In the same way, encouraging the client to express her feelings of anger most forcefully in a counselling session may clash with a subsequent interpretation of the same client's incessant rows with her partner as an expression of emotional immaturity. In this case there is a blatant contradiction between the initial assumption of the healing power of emotional expression and the eventual assumption of the superior power of reasoning and control.

Unless the practitioner is experienced and creative enough to meld different approaches and assumptions into a new and consistent synthesis, the result may be extremely confusing. Clients may pick up the message that life is confusing and that the practitioner does not really have a clue about which direction to follow. Another basic assumption often conveyed in this way is that counselling and life are random and that the best one can do is to go along with whatever appeals or seems to be in vogue at a particular time.

Clients will only benefit from this type of eclecticism to the extent that they can have peace with a view of life so basically casual and incidental.

The existential approach to counselling and therapy is in many ways the opposite of the eclectic one and yet it is a form of therapeutic integration. Not only is it assumed that a diversity of techniques, tricks and gimmicks can in itself often be more harmful than helpful, it is also considered of the greatest importance that the practitioner has a clear sense of her own direction and of the laws of life that form the basis of the integration of the work. The starting point of an existential way of working is for the practitioner to clarify her views on life and living. Taking stock of one's basic assumptions will usually involve acquaintance with possible alternatives. A practitioner can be existential only if she makes understanding life her priority. The existential view is that clients are entitled to a practitioner who has grappled with the essential issues and questions that life raises. She should have reached sufficient clarity to be able to assist other people in making sense of their own lives. She should have gained a sufficiently broad perspective to be able to allow for different points of view while making sense of each.

Of all the assumptions of the existential approach, this is the most basic one that it is possible to make sense of life and that doing so makes good sense. To put it in even stronger terms, it is considered essential for people to have a consistent framework of reference with which to reflect on their lives and organize their experience.

People who come for counselling or therapy are often confused because they cannot make sense of life or of some aspects of living. They are frequently struggling to accommodate two or more conflicting views on life. They may have just discovered that the ways in which they used to make sense of life are no longer valid in the face of a new development or crisis. Existential counselling or therapy can be seen as a process of exploration of what can make life meaningful. The despair and the sense of futility that clients start out with is construed as a necessary first step in a quest for meaning. This quest can only be undertaken if the client is ready to examine the crucial issues and question her own basic assumptions.

Clients can therefore only benefit from an existential approach in so far as they come to the sessions with a fundamental commitment to sorting out vital issues and coming to terms with life. If all they want is to be rid of a specific symptom or solve a particular problem without this further touching on the rest of their existence, clients will not be well served by an existential approach. Of course, it is also implied that clients need to come to do the work of their own accord and by their free choice. The existential method presupposes the client's full engagement and her honest intention to face herself and her life more completely than she has so far been able to do on her own.

An illustration of the appropriateness and inappropriateness of the existential approach can be seen in the experience of Leonard and James. While Leonard was advised not to venture into counselling, he was himself entirely committed to sorting things out. The urgency of his motivation and the strength of his commitment were such that he gained much from an existential approach. With James the opposite was true. He was referred to a counsellor though he had no desire for self-examination. Though he had many reasons for needing assistance, he did not wish to consider this situation as a problem in living. The existential approach was not indicated for him.

Leonard was a forty-seven-year-old man who was dying of cancer. His relatives were keeping the medical diagnosis from him and wanted him to act as if everything was going to be all right again. Leonard, however, was not fooled for very long and he decided that he needed to survey and evaluate his life before he would be able to accept his imminent death. He had little religious faith left and he therefore did not consider confession an option. In response to Leonard's great insistence on getting some lay help to make sense of what seemed like an absurd life, he was finally put in touch with a counsellor.

There was not much time left to reconsider or make changes, it was not possible to make a dramatically new start. Leonard had less than three months left to live. All that he wanted was to find some explanation for his having squandered so much time. He desperately wanted to grasp what seemed to have totally eluded him throughout his life: the fact that he had indeed been alive. With hindsight it appeared that all his efforts had gone into pretending that life was just some kind of roller-coaster, on which you took a seemingly endless ride, trying to enjoy yourself as much as possible. The actual enjoyment now seemed futile to him, especially as it had mostly consisted of the sort of things that he now knew to have contributed to his illness. His busy lifestyle, the smoking, the drinking now just seemed like an excuse for not having to commit himself to life.

It was, as Leonard put it, as if he had all those years lived in his own shadow. His 'larger than life' lifestyle had stood in the way of any close encounter with himself. He had never really asked himself whether what he was doing was right or wrong. It was just so. He had lived the life of Leonard and only now that he was about to die did he wonder whether this was how he wanted to have spent his life.

Although he was glad that his illness had helped him to question the things that had previously seemed unquestionable, he was inclined to flounder in a sense of total despair and pointlessness. He despised the hypocrisy of his friends and relatives who wanted to continue pretending that all would be well. This exemplified his own former attitude of forced optimism and blinkered hedonism to him. He just wished he could have discovered its falsity without losing his life in the process.

Eventually Leonard began to feel at peace with the life that he had lived, in the knowledge that he had done what so many people do, namely to take the intensity out of life by pretending that it will last forever. It was the understanding of his own frantic attempts to deny death that made him capable of beginning to value the reality of his now approaching death. As he was struggling with these issues with such urgency, his last few weeks became a most intense experience.

He decided to speak to some of his closest friends and relatives about these issues and he was surprised at the vehemence of their reactions. Though many of them refused to discuss life and death with him in such a direct manner, he also found some intimacy and depth of exchange that he had not known to be possible. It was not gratuitously that Leonard spoke of himself as 'a lucky man', not long before he died. He had seized the opportunity of his terminal illness and made the most of it. Although it was a little late to start living deeply only just before he would die, he discovered that it was certainly not too late. In spite of much physical pain, Leonard died with great dignity. His final weeks made a considerable impact on several people in his near environment. Existential counselling had enabled him to address the issues more forcefully than he might have if he had remained encapsulated in his disgust with his former self. But of course it was Leonard who sought existential counselling and not the other way around.

With James it was the exact opposite. He did not actively seek or want counselling. He just wanted to be cured of an unpleasant symptom. James was also in his mid-forties and he was referred to a practitioner because he suffered recurrent nightmares. These had begun after a near fatal accident, some years previously. He had been treated in a private clinic for his multiple injuries and though he made a total physical recovery after a bit more than a year, the nightmares did not recede.

James by this time was back at work with the same company that was responsible (through negligence) for his accident. He put great emphasis on the company's responsibility in having to restore him to health. They were in fact well insured and no costs had been spared in James's treatment. He had already been through various neurological tests and assessments for his nightmares and it had been decided that his symptoms must be of a psychological nature. James felt greatly offended by this as he took the view that it insinuated that he was not entirely sane. He was himself convinced that his symptom was purely a physiological one and that it had no psychological significance whatsoever. The idea that his nightmare might express his own attitude to life was particularly unsavoury to him. He was quite reluctant even to recount the contents of the nightmare.

James liked to think of his nightmare as the simple repetition of his traumatic experience. In fact it did involve the climbing of a ladder and its collapse just as he reached the top, which was more or less how the accident had happened. But what made the dream terrifying were the people who were sabotaging the ladder while he was climbing up, obviously intent on killing him. There were also a variety of disasters that he had to try to escape from each time he went up the ladder in his dream, which made the sabotaging doubly tragic and frightening.

It seemed that there was great scope for an existential analysis of these dreams, yet James would not even consider the possibility of their wider significance. To him these dreams were a residue of his accident, not an expression of his particular way of dealing with his accident. He wanted treatment, not understanding. It was pointless to attempt to convince him of a view that he would not feel comfortable making his own. When James's viewpoint had been elucidated it became self-evident that the referral had been inappropriate. James did not wish to take stock of his life or reflect on his attitude towards others. He thought that if he began to wonder about his fears of other people undermining and threatening him, he might lose his grip on reality.

It was then decided that James would be best served with a behavioural approach. He was referred on for relaxation therapy and he was treated for acrophobia. While his fear of heights receded, other symptoms were now appearing. These were treated with medication and although the results were still not entirely satisfactory, James was getting the sort of treatment that he wanted. The existential approach would not have been effective or even possible as long as James was in total disagreement with the idea that it might be beneficial for him to examine his way of being in the world. As a coda to James' story it is interesting to note that he did eventually return to see a counsellor after medication had failed to cure his insomnia and remaining lack of confidence (which developed into occasional panic attacks) and that the issue he wanted to work on was his fear of giving up control. It was then possible to work with James, when he had decided that he might indeed be able to understand his own predicament.

The first basic assumption of the existential approach, that life makes sense and that people create the meaning of their world by their own attitude to life, must be in principle acceptable to the prospective client. Only then can the existential method of working help the client to sort out and make sense of her particular way of being. The process of investigation and discovery that is then embarked upon can lead to a reordering of experience and a revelation of new ways of creating meaning. There is clearly a circular argument here, which contends that people can only create or re-create meaning to the extent that they believe in their own ability to do so.

The existential approach in this sense is founded on the notion of self-fulfilling prophecy. However confused and disorganized life may seem to those who believe themselves to be adrift on a sea of contradictions and chaos, it is always possible to find clarity and order for those who believe life to be basically meaningful. The existential position is neither that of belief in chaos nor that of belief in order. It is that of belief in people's ability to create meaning and order, in spite of seeming chaos and absurdity.

This introduces the second fundamental assumption of the existential approach, which is that of the intrinsic flexibility of human nature. However much people are determined by circumstances, they always retain a significant ability to determine how they will respond. Whatever the 'givens' of a person's situation, it is still up to that person how to respond and create something with these givens. It is up to the individual whether she is going to make or break herself given her initial conditions. It is always possible to turn a situation to one's advantage or disadvantage. It is possible to go under in or rise above adversity; it is possible to respond to favourable conditions by growing weak or by moving ahead.

The existential perspective is that it is well-worth considering what one's options are and that insight into the risks and hazards of human living as well as into its promises and possibilities is essential if one is to live well. In this sense existential therapy can be likened to a practical tutorial in the art of living. By helping people to explore the givens of their particular existence and exploit its inherent possibilities while accepting its limitations, their lives can gain a new dimension of meaning.

It is by no means always the people who have suffered most who can benefit from an existential approach. Sometimes adversity or suffering bring people closer to themselves and make them more able to appreciate life's challenges and chances unaided. It is often the person who has taken life for granted as a pleasant experience who is most in need of assistance when things start breaking down. Learning to live includes facing the inevitable pains and afflictions of human existence. Those who are exposed to the full force of misery that living can bring from early on may be better equipped for their trials and tribulations than are those who were initially shielded.

People may have inborn instincts for survival, but this does not include the art of living a deeply meaningful human life. That art has to be learnt and can be learnt through experience only. The experience will be more likely to be fruitful if some guidance from a well-informed fellow human being is available at the right moments. Without this nothing is easier for a person than to become despondent and bitter rather than wise. Exposure to life's limit-situations of suffering, loss, death, pain, isolation, failure, guilt and absurdity can only be overcome if one can find the direction and motivation to travel on, come what may. This resolution must almost certainly be learnt from an experienced elder at a moment of crisis. With their support much can be endured. If elders are not available then resoluteness has to be learnt in another way. Without it no amount of luck or fortune will save one from going under.

Jake was a case in point. He had polio as a child and lost the use of both legs. His family was on the breadline and unable to provide Jake with any of the comforts or compensations for his disability that were available at the time. Many people pitied Jake and his family and they would often predict a miserable future for them. An uncle who was also partially disabled lived with Jake and his family. He spent most of his time with Jake and taught him the art of woodwork as well as some very basic and perhaps even simplistic philosophical principles.

It was commonsense or even banal and clichéd truisms that laid the foundation for Jake's strength of character as he built it up over those difficult years. He used to repeat to himself what his uncle taught him whenever he felt like giving up. The sayings that gave him heart were simple and unpretentious, but nevertheless comforting and encouraging: 'Least said, soonest mended', 'You never know what you can do till you try' and 'Fortune favours the brave' were some of his favourite sayings.

At the same time Jake learnt the lesson that 'an idle brain is the devil's workshop' and he undertook to find out all he could about the considerable manual skills that he was cultivating. At the age of twelve he designed and constructed a vehicle for himself out of scrap-yard materials and his joy in his own inventiveness and growing independence spurred him on to further study. Through independent study he eventually reached the level at which he was able to succeed in training as an engineer and to become professionally involved in vehicle design. In his company he stood out as the most original and cheerful person. People would invariably turn to Jake if they needed some sort of encouragement. Jake had clearly succeeded in turning a difficult situation to his advantage.

Jonathan did the exact opposite. From a situation of ease and opportunity he reduced himself to vegetable status in less than ten years. He drifted from one private school to the next, from one group of 'keen on money' friends to the next, from one party to the next. He was rarely interested in anything for more than a week. His extremely well-off parents provided the money that bought the alcohol and the drugs, which landed him in psychiatric clinics several times. Before long he had taken up breaking down as a career and drifted his way through a dozen different therapeutic approaches.

All was to no avail. Jonathan had long since given up any desire actively to construct a life for himself. He could only lean on others, wait for them to tend to him and wilt if they did not. Psychiatric nurses taking care of him often took a dislike to him for what they perceived as a wasteful attitude. One of them once remarked: 'If I had been given half the chances Jonathan has had, I would have really made it big.' Jonathan had made a real mess of what could have been a life full of opportunities. He did not understand anything about living. The plain fact was that nobody had ever bothered to teach him. He had been largely sheltered from life's real impact and was totally unprepared to deal with the shock of his own down-going. At the same time people around him were assuming that there was no need to teach him, as his social position and his wealth were supposedly protecting him.

Jonathan himself was realizing a self-fulfilling prophecy. He was convinced that his character was basically weak, because his childhood had been too comfortable. He assumed that there was not much point in trying to resist his fate, which would inevitably lead him back to alcohol and drug abuse. He helped his fate along nicely by giving in to all his impulses and by dismissing as a waste of time and energy any inclination to redeem himself. He claimed that it was his privileged position that had destroyed him and that with his kind of passivity and lack of taste for life, he would not even have bothered to get the money to finance his addictions unless it came without effort.

Interestingly Jonathan was able to borrow many a new rationalization for his behaviour from his various therapeutic experiences. Exploration of his past would throw up new proof of his victimization. He had been raised by nannies who did not care for him as a mother would have. His parents were expecting him to do well, but they did not pay any attention to his wishes and needs. Money had replaced personal affection. No one had ever really loved him. He had been pampered to such a degree that only drugs could provide him with a sufficient kick to enjoy himself, since everything else was boring.

While all this was undoubtedly partially true, Jonathan was clearly select-
ing certain aspects in his personal history and ignoring others. The story he
told himself about himself was concretely shaping his destiny and reducing
his chances to exploit the many positive aspects of his background. Against
all odds he was doing extremely poorly in the same way in which Jake, against
all odds, had done particularly well. But what was more, Jonathan was not
aware of his own destructive thinking process; he did not see the role he was
actively playing in his own passivity.

His eyes were opened for the first time when a fellow patient in the clinic
got fed up with him and during the course of a group therapy session began
to tell him outright what so many people had only said behind his back for
years. She told him that she was sick of his excuses and revolted by his self-
satisfied attitude. She said that she knew scores of people whose parents had
treated them far worse than Jonathan's parents had and who had done far
better than him. If he knew so well what was wrong with him, why did he not
go out and do something about it? Why did he not go to work at some private
school to help other rich kids like himself, so that they would not have to
become disgusting parasites like him?

Her sneering attack actually roused Jonathan's anger, which was a rare
event. He tried to enlist the support of his therapist against the offensive,
which went on for several weeks. His therapist was at a loss for the correct
attitude to take. She was both amused and satisfied with this new development which laid bare her own resentments against her client. At the same
time she felt inclined to appease Jonathan and agree with him, especially as he
would cleverly hide behind things she herself had suggested to him in the past
about the roots of his behaviour.

Jonathan's therapist remarked to her supervisor that there was not much
point in upsetting Jonathan. It was clearly impossible to have any positive
influence over him, so she might as well take the soft option with him. The
therapist was shocked to hear herself saying this as she realized suddenly
how much she had been colluding with Jonathan's own perception of himself. She thought him to be entirely weak and incapable of any future
improvement. Nevertheless, upon reflection, it was evident to her that someone who had succeeded in failing so completely in spite of favourable
conditions could not possibly be as intrinsically weak as he appeared to be.
Moreover he must be quite astute to be able to build such a credible picture
of his own incapacity.

When Jonathan was presented with this new perspective on his abilities in
the next session, not only did he agree with it but he seemed grateful for a first
glimpse of hope. In fact it seemed as if he had been waiting for such appreciation of his real character-strength. He elaborated the theme with great
gusto and told the therapist how he had for a long time been fascinated by a
story he had once been told as a boy. The story was about a man who had
made a bet about being able to lose a considerable sum of money by a certain
date. It had been nearly impossible for this man to do so as his money would
keep accumulating more money before he was able to get rid of it. It had

seemed to Jonathan that losing money was more of a challenge for a rich man than earning money. In this light he agreed with his therapist that his own behaviour of failure had in many ways been a greater accomplishment than the easy success that his parents had planned for him.

An entirely new phase started for Jonathan from that moment. He no longer needed to prove his weakness in order to affirm his strength and independence. He could begin to take pride and pleasure in openly admitting his strength and his wit. The foundation was laid for his motivation to get better. For now there was a new challenge for his self-affirmation. Everyone expected him to be doomed to self-destruction. What greater challenge could be found to test his strength and further develop it than having to climb up from the depth of despair and addiction into which he had let himself slide?

Jonathan proved what amazing transformations people can and do undergo once they have found their motivation and faith in themselves. It is often sufficient for people to start viewing their situation from a different perspective. Recognizing the active part they play in maintaining or creating a particular situation for themselves leads to the option of continuing or ceasing to do so.

The important factor as far as therapeutic counselling is concerned is to emphasize how the client is already taking charge or proving his insight or strength. This is much more effective than reproaching the client for what he is not doing or for what he is supposedly doing wrong.

The basic assumption is not that people ought to become more responsible and take charge of their lives, but that they are invariably already doing so in some way. The existential practitioner does not teach people to become self-directive; she simply encourages them to notice how they already are so. She also helps them to reassess the direction in which they are going.

In this process a third basic assumption comes to light. While people are considered to be significantly capable of influencing their own direction in life and the way in which they respond to situations, the latter are to a certain extent given and in this sense they present people with definite limitations. The boundaries of human freedom are set by a universal order, which expresses itself in an absolute manner.

Birth and death are the most obvious of these boundaries. But the time in between those two extremes is also filled with natural limitations. Everybody grows old for instance. Everybody is vulnerable to extremes of temperature or to certain chemical reactions. People are ruled by basic physical and biological principles, which determine what is and what is not possible. People cannot live without taking the laws of gravity into account, for instance, or without attending to their bodily needs.

Anybody who tries to ignore these basic laws ruling life on earth will experience the immediate consequences of such foolhardiness. It is crucial for survival to have a basic understanding of the principles of life. Much of this happens in a purely instinctive way, but some of it needs to be learnt in a social context. On top of that there are the limitations generated by the rules of this very same social context. They are almost as definite and absolute as the natural laws. Once again people need to take these laws into account if they are to find their way around in a relatively safe and effective manner.

Beyond these there are the personal laws and rules of individuals to take into account. People's inner world of feelings can be as limiting to the freedom of action as an external rule or principle. The way in which a person perceives a situation determines her sense of freedom to respond. In some ways personal characteristics obviously do limit people. It is again only by a recognition of these specific personal limitations that one can maximize the profit from those aspects that are strongest.

The same thing is true for the ethical laws and principles that constitute a fourth limitation and boundary to human freedom. People's recognition of their own and other people's values is crucial for the making of any choices. Freedom can only be assumed to the extent that one is aware of the necessary, the impossible and the desirable.

This emphasis on the boundaries of human existence is typical of the existential perspective. It is frequently ignored in the humanistic orientation, which nevertheless prides itself on its existential roots.

The humanistic stance puts the accent on human freedom and choice at the expense of a healthy recognition of its counterpart of necessity and determinism. A decidedly existential approach will always include a thorough consideration of realities, limitations and consequences. A serious analysis of the human condition cannot fail to notice constraints as well as liberties. The humanistic arrogance which believes mankind to be the centre of the universe and which encourages a blind pursuit of individual rights and freedom can only lead to disaster.

If a client is taught self-assertion, for example, this may create rather than solve problems, if she is not at the same time exploring her life's situation so that she can decide what it is she wants to be self-assertive about and if she is not also helped to understand and work with the usual give and take of human relationships.

An existential approach ensures that the client will explore the whole range of available options, including that of becoming even less assertive. It will also encourage the client to wonder about her current ways of assertion, such as passivity or helplessness. Finally and most importantly it will investigate what the client actually feels motivated for. Sometimes people who find it hard to express themselves in a self-assertive manner have simply not yet found anything worth fighting for.

When people do find something that is important enough to live and fight for, the problem is rarely that of becoming more self-assertive. More often than not it is, on the contrary, the ability to consider effects and consequences of one's actions which needs to be further developed at this stage. Once people are motivated their actions sometimes become so enthusiastic and self-assured that the long-term view is obliterated.

Unfortunately some of the prevailing assumptions in counselling circles are based on this type of short-term vision. Clients are sometimes encouraged to put self-development or self-actualization before anything else. In this way an ethic of wishful thinking is embarked upon. People are helped to take their lives in their own hands and to believe that their current lives are based on a number of mistakes, which can be easily eradicated.

In reality life is a little more complex than that, for people are rarely engaged in anything without there being a number of good reasons for it. Only to the extent that a person is aware of the wider existential context of her situation can she begin to move forward with a sense of direction. Picking up notions about what is desirable from the current ideas in circulation can only lead to landing oneself in an impasse if the implications and consequences have not been fully thought through privately. Practitioners have to be particularly careful in monitoring the client's personal investigation of the wider context. It is only too easy to influence a client towards change without previous reflection.

Clients are usually particularly suggestible because they are fed up with their life as it is at present. They are keen to pick up any new and promising rules that the practitioner proposes. Ideas such as personal choice, freedom and self-realization or assertion are picked up rapidly because they appeal to the imagination and create a picture of an ideal world where all one's troubles will be gone. Nothing is gained from teaching the client simplistic new rules which will not keep their promises. The client may jump from the frying pan into the fire by acting rashly in the belief that change for the sake of change will cure her existential pain. Sooner or later she will find that her own actions create new problems which she will still be unable to solve if she does not face the principles of existence.

People will discover sooner or later that freedom is an intangible concept or even a fallacious one if it is not counterbalanced by the notion of obligation or necessity. Self-realization will seem very bleak indeed if it means that everyone else has to be discarded and affection is lost on the way. Change is only exciting until it is found that one has lost all sense of permanence or orientation. Liberating oneself from a stifling life of order may be a great challenge, but its satisfaction and exhilaration may momentarily hide the need for a new order. If this new order is not prepared for and actively created, chaos may ensue. Existential practitioners will stimulate clients to address these kinds of issues for themselves, so that they gain a wider perspective than that of compulsive self-improvement.

Frances's experience illustrates the difference between an existential orientation and other approaches on this point. She was confused and she felt cheated after her life had taken a turn for the worse when she had started to apply certain humanistic ideas. Now her marriage had broken down after two years of drama and suffering and she did not understand what had gone wrong. She wanted to get clarity on what had happened in order to be able to avoid making further mistakes. She felt the need to 'sort out her life', as her attempts at sorting herself out had gone dreadfully awry.

She presented herself as a housewife with two young children. She was in her mid-thirties. She recounted how after a marriage of seven years, she had suddenly begun to feel disenchanted with her husband Steve and bored with her life. After the children were both in school, she had taken up various activities, first simply as a way of amusing herself, then as a way to assess what might appeal to her as a second career.

As part of her educational touring Frances went to a number of personal-growth groups. Eventually she became a permanent participant in an ongoing leaderless support group. She gained tremendous confidence from member-ship in this group. She felt more energetic than she ever had since her teens. Part of this was the fact that she had at last made friends with women who would talk about things other than house and children. In fact many of the people in this group were considerably younger than her and most of them were childless.

At the time it did not occur to Frances that there was this discrepancy between her own experience and that of most of the other women in the group. She was so eager to be part of this new culture that she gradually picked up new standards and rules, which clashed with the standards and rules of her home life. She was blindly soaking up new ideas. In her eagerness to come alive Frances became incapable of any kind of critical awareness or thoughts about the direction in which she was heading. She convinced herself that she had done all the wrong things with her life and that she must have been too frightened to really live until now. She dismissed any hesitations as 'silliness and fear' and condemned herself for having been stuffy, uptight and behind the times.

Encouraged by her group companions Frances rejected the idea that her children were more important than herself and came to the conclusion that she must attend to her own needs first. Her relationship with her husband became easily written off as an old-fashioned and possessive business. She believed that many disturbing feelings that she used to experience, such as jealousy and loneliness and panic about the welfare of the children, were only due to her previous erroneous attitude and position. Everything would be different once she had made the necessary changes.

Frances found herself a lover, a regular baby-sitter and a new life was initiated. She discussed the possibility of having an open marriage with her husband. At first Steve was shocked and hurt. There was much upset and dis-appointment. Frances felt that she must encourage Steve also to experience the liberation of self-fulfilment so as to help him over his reluctance. She introduced him to one of the women from the support group, Ros. Steve's attitude changed abruptly after a few weeks, and before long both of them had busy social lives. In the evenings and at weekends they hardly ever met any more.

The first disenchantment came for Frances when the children's school notified her that her eldest child had missed lessons for nearly two weeks. It dawned on her then that the children were missing out and that they were responding by acting irresponsibly. She was particularly concerned when her child told her angrily that he did not see why he ought to go to school if he did not like it there as his mother kept repeating that people should be free to do what they like. Frances now felt a growing doubt about the rightness of her new lifestyle, but nobody seemed to want seriously to discuss these doubts with her.

In the group there was far more interest in the exhilaration of Ros's intense love affair with Steve than there was for Frances's second thoughts. In fact Frances did not dare contemplate, even by herself, just how wrong she thought all this had been. Trying to discuss these things with her lover led to the end of that affair. Now she needed Steve's shoulder to cry on. But Steve was not available any longer. He was with Ros. This was more than Frances could cope with. She felt jealous, totally isolated and quite confused about the children's role in all of this. Everything that was supposed to have happened had happened and instead of feeling liberated and happy, she experienced greater pain and more of the old feelings than ever before.

When Frances made an attempt at patching up things with Steve and going back to the way life had been before, she realized it was too late. Steve was in the middle of a honeymoon period with Ros and unwilling to give her up. In fact Ros and he were thinking of starting a family together. Steve preferred the idea of making a fresh start with Ros to attempting to repair the damage done to his marriage with Frances. This was the final blow for Frances. She felt abandoned and cheated and really worried about the children's future. This was not how she had imagined that things would end.

A period of utter panic now began. Frances did not know what to think or how to handle the situation. She felt torn between wanting to regain a sense of security for herself and the children and wanting to hold on to her newly discovered freedom. Twice she left home in a desperate attempt to rekindle the spark of enthusiasm for adventure and independence. Twice she came back, with the intense longing for her family to surround her again and for her children to be happy. Now that she had an inkling of what was at stake she could no longer just go off and ignore what was happening to her husband and children. But when she gave up her freedom and came back home, she would feel consumed with jealousy when Steve was not there with her. Then she wanted to go off again and have nothing more to do with caring for other people, but only to think of herself.

Steve was just as confused as she was and he moved back and forth between her and Ros, consumed by feelings of guilt, whatever he did. Eventually the children turned against their father because they perceived him as the one who was destroying their safe home and family life. Frances knew that this was unfair and yet it was comforting to her. She realized that she needed some independent help in sorting things out if she were to stand a chance of finding a constructive solution and together she and Steve turned to a couples counsellor.

The only constructive result of this was that they received an implicit encouragement to separate and reorganize their lives around their new interests and discoveries. This enabled them to start acting rather than just reacting to each other. Steve moved out of the house and they began to deal with the concrete aspects of a divorce. The children took better to the new situation than to the previous confusion as they felt at last sure of where they stood. Frances experienced the whole process as unreal and nightmarish. She felt more and more frustrated in her longing for clarity. She just could not understand how things could have deteriorated so fast. Nobody seemed remotely interested in the rights and wrongs of what was happening. She could not understand why she was left with so much pain, if all they had done was to start living in the way they liked rather than in a dutiful manner.

Frances was referred on for further individual counselling, as it was obvious that she was very unhappy and upset with the situation. What Frances needed to do in these sessions was to clarify and grasp the general issues involved in her personal situation. So far she had assumed that her feelings should be her only guide and that was how she had become lost. She had felt bad and bored as a housewife and so she had looked around for something more stimulating. She had felt good when discovering her own independence and freedom and so she had concluded that this should be her way of life. Frances had decided to dismiss any bad feelings such as jealousy and sadness or boredom as unworthy, rather than understanding their message. Her philosophy of life had been that feeling good must mean that one was good and feeling bad that one was bad. Her intention had been to bring about an ideal situation where things would take care of themselves as she would take care of herself. She had rejected any ideas about bad feelings being necessary as indicators of boundaries. She had refused to consider the effects of her own attitude and actions on other people and thus on her own future. By opting for Utopia she had brought about chaos.

Frances did not need empathy with her feelings of terror and upset at what had happened. She needed to be faced with the logic of the situation and to become aware of the way in which she had underestimated the relentless and ironic justice which had landed her exactly there where she had apparently wanted to be. She was free of the oppressing marriage. She now had to take on an active professional life. She still had her children with her, but her relationship to them had been transformed as well.

It was a great relief to Frances to start facing up to her own responsibility in what had happened. It was reassuring for her to discover that people function according to certain general principles. She had, for instance, so far totally disregarded the fact that Steve had originally been hurt by her proposition of an open marriage. She now began to explore the notion of commitment and began to understand the implications of breaking one. Frances realized that the commonsense notion that it is not possible to 'have your cake and eat it' was based on experience after all. Her original choice of commitment to her husband and children had created a certain sort of life for her. Her subsequent choice of ruthlessly putting her own need for self-development first had then undone the previous situation and brought about new conditions. In both cases she found herself getting more than she bargained for. In both cases she had omitted to consider the implications of her actions before engaging in them. She had ignored the boundaries of her situation and found herself crashing into them unexpectedly.

With hindsight Frances could see how naive she had been. Opting for freedom and self-development was a perfectly attractive choice as long as one was prepared to face the loneliness and isolation that would logically follow from refusing to honour commitments to other people. She had underestimated the way in which she felt bound to her husband and children because she ignored the value they had for her. She had neglected the people she cared for most and it was therefore to be expected that they would turn away from her, disappointed and feeling betrayed.

For the first time Frances could now contemplate Steve's new commitment to Ros as his desperate response to having been let down. She felt genuine regret for having hurt him. Until then she had experienced only bitterness about him hurting her. When she could express this new point of view to Steve, it became possible for the two of them to talk without reproach. They even rebuilt some confidence in one another. Frances felt very heartened when she saw what immediate effect her own willingness to be honest with herself and with Steve had. Clearly the logic worked in both directions.

She now felt ready to look closer at her own ideas about life. She examined the difference between dependence as she had experienced it originally and interdependence which she was now discovering as a possibility. She contrasted this with the rebellious counterdependence that she had fled into at first. Frances understood how her need for autonomy had been pulled out of context by her pretence to the kind of independence that could not co-exist with belonging to a family and being needed. She was now ready to consider the possibility of gaining autonomy in some areas of her life while still being fully committed to her children or perhaps even her husband. She learnt about priorities and having to forgo, or give up, some things no matter what one chooses. She discovered how value is found precisely in the things that one is willing to give up other things for.

Counselling was a time for Frances to start realizing through practical experience what is meant by various commonsense rules that organize human existence. She understood how she had believed she could magically reorganize these rules with impunity. She had believed it was possible to opt for only the bits of life that seemed appealing and leave out the bits that seemed bothersome. She had discovered that the ensuing chaos was not attractive at all and she felt relieved at the existence of some logic in this chaos. Now she could start again and play by the rules this time. She would have neither to content herself with dissatisfaction nor to expect total satisfaction. She could instead learn to live whilst paying attention to both the possibilities and the limitations engendered by her own choices and commitments.

Once Frances felt on safe ground she became more self-assured about what options were open to her and which were desirable. She developed an independence of mind, which no longer needed artificial or frenetic gimmicks to assert itself. She set out on part-time professional training but she also initiated a number of projects at home together with her children. She thus created a new cosiness and aliveness for herself and the children, which attracted many of the children's friends to the house as well. The long-term effect of this was also to make Steve more and more keen to spend time with them rather than with Ros. Frances was quite enchanted by this and felt that she was being appreciated for herself rather than just as a wife. She was delighted to find that she was yet again reaping what she had sowed, only this time it was positive.

The lesson Frances learned was that paying attention to her environment and to the people that she cared about was ultimately more profitable than a blind assertion of her own needs and interests. As she put it: 'When I was trying to have everything for myself, I lost all I had. Now that I make the most of what is there already, it just keeps on growing and improving.'

Frances's discovery had been that of her own and life's limitations and of her ability to work within the boundaries of these given limitations. The assumption of the existential approach is that it is necessary for clients to come to terms with both these aspects of life. Recognizing abilities and inabilities, the possible and the impossible are the only way forward. Many people hesitate to do this and they live a life of self-deception. Frances's original attitude of wishful thinking was a good example of such self-deception. Fortunately life usually ends up confronting such naivety and experience brings home the reality of one's errors, exposing human vulnerability and fallibility.

Though people strive for perfection in themselves and in their lives, they have to realize over and over again that such perfection can be only a remote and never fully achieved goal. In the absence of real perfection many people content themselves with the illusion of perfection. They go to great lengths to forget about the unavoidable realities of their own destructiveness or their inevitable suffering. Death and loss are denied or pushed to the background. While the facts say otherwise people continue to pretend that they are happy or enjoying themselves. If things are not entirely satisfactory today, it is hoped that they will be one day soon. Living can thus be postponed until a later date. At a later date some other dissatisfaction catches up with them and so on until they finally wake up to the fact that life is precisely about coming to terms with such imperfection. Many people never do and to them life is one long sequence of disappointments and disillusionments. Death then becomes a last and total disillusionment, to which they cannot help but give in.

Josie, who was dying of cancer, summed this up quite well, when she said: 'I'd rather be in my position than in yours, for I have got nothing left to lose, so I am not afraid any more. You are still trying to hold on and maintain your illusions about life and yourself. That's why you're frightened'. Mark, who was also near the end of his life, when asked whether he was ready to die, put it this way: 'Quite frankly, I was more afraid to live than I am to die.' Both Josie and Mark thought it would have been easier to live a good life had they been more aware of the significance of death and less set on trying to deny its inevitability. Self-deception with the intention of ignoring weakness, limitation and death is based on a fear of life rather than on a fear of death. Giving in to death is often easier than people expected. The hard thing is to acknowledge its possibility and still keep going.

The challenge of life is therefore assumed to be that of making creative use of the very paradox involved in living. The self-affirmation involved in living life to the full can only come from facing the inevitability of one's death. The courage to be goes hand in hand with the courage not to be. As many people discover, intimate relationships only become possible when one has first accepted one's aloneness. Creating meaning in one's existence begins with the questioning of everything that seems absurd. Freedom is only initiated once boundaries have been explored.

An existential approach to psychotherapy and counselling assumes it to be of importance to gain an understanding of these basic rules of the human condition. Clients are believed capable of enough self- and life-reflection to gain insight into the functioning of their own existence. Practitioners are there to assist them in this process of making sense of their lives. When the implications of their life situation become concretely obvious, clients become capable of actively influencing the situation and of determining their own attitude towards it. At the same time, the wider boundaries are acknowledged and the rules and laws that apply are taken into account. Clients are in this way helped to manage the paradoxes of living in a creative and dynamic fashion. It is obvious that these basic assumptions lead to a type of therapeutic counselling which has a number of precise goals. These are discussed next.

The aim of existential psychotherapy and counselling

The aim of existential counselling and psychotherapy is to clarify, reflect upon and understand life. Problems in living are confronted and life's possibilities and boundaries are explored. The existential approach does not set out to cure people in the tradition of the medical model. Clients are considered to be not ill but sick of life or clumsy at living. When people are confused and lost the last thing they need is to be treated as ill or incompetent. What they need is some assistance in surveying the terrain and in deciding on the right route so that they can again find their way.

Existential counselling or therapy does not set out to change people as in the tradition of behavioural science. It does not assume that people necessarily need to change or that they are willing or able to change. The assistance provided is aimed at finding direction in life by gaining insight into its workings. The process is one of reflection on one's goals and intentions and on one's general attitude towards living. The focus is therefore on life itself, rather than on one's personality. The aim is to assist people in developing and consolidating their personal way of tackling life's challenges.

As a result some clients may conclude that they need to change little or not at all, as life itself has taken on greater significance. Others, conversely, may make considerable changes when they recognize that their current direction in life is not as they would wish. Often clients will relinquish previous symptoms of unhappiness in the process of making these discoveries. Yet work is not directly aimed at this. Assisting people in the process of living with greater expertise and ease is the goal of existential work. Learning to face the inevitable problems, difficulties, upsets, disappointments and crises of existence with confidence is what it is all about. Discovering endless sources of enjoyment and wonder in the process is the usual by-product of this venture.

Living is seen as an art. As with every art, the artist improves only through practice. Insight into the secrets of the art is gained through making mistakes. While many people learn the art of living successfully by their own efforts through the years, many can also benefit from an extra tutorial now and then. The existential therapeutic session is very much like an art tutorial.

The art student turns to the art teacher for guidance in the process of perfecting that which she is already engaged in. The client is equally already engaged in living and turns to the practitioner for assistance in ironing out existing imperfections and confusions. When the art student applies to the teacher for tuition, she is motivated to want to do better at what matters to her. The client who comes to the existential practitioner is in the same way motivated to improve her life.

What both art student and client want above all from the professional to whom they turn is expertise. Sometimes the art student is already quite accomplished, but may need the detachment of the teacher to improve on a number of precise points, such as the management of colour or perspective. The client in therapy in the same way is often quite capable of living decently, but may be experiencing difficulties in handling her emotions or understanding a new situation.

The aim of the art lesson is to acquire mastery over the art of drawing or painting, so as to maximize the artist's proficiency and therefore her enjoyment and satisfaction in the pursuit of the art. The aim of existential therapy and counselling is to gain mastery over the art of living, so that life's challenges can be welcomed and enjoyed instead of feared and avoided. One of the tasks of art lessons is for the student to recognize and further develop her initial talents. One of the tasks of existential work is for the client to recognize her talents in living and to explore ways of further developing these and putting them to positive use. Another task of the art lesson, of course, is to train the student in those aspects of the art that she has difficulty with. The same applies again to existential work.

Yet, above all, it is important to recognize that it is not the technique which makes a good artist. It is the ability to see and express what is seen that matters most. A good grasp of the medium is of secondary importance and never sufficient for the creation of a work of art. In existential work a good grasp of one's personality is similarly important but secondary to a good sense of how to live life and how to understand it. But tackling life's issues must be done in a specific, concrete and individual manner. Generalizations, abstractions and imitations are of little practical value in the long run.

A good artist is formed through practising personal ways of expression, once the basic techniques are mastered and the observation skill is acute enough. Creativity and authenticity are the ultimate goal, not that of being adequate at copying other people's work. Existential counselling and therapy do not teach people to live in set ways. The existential approach does not propose to provide a pre-fabricated framework of meaning for people who are having difficulties in living meaningfully in their own way. Attempting to coach people who feel alienated in particular skills or in ways of expressing themselves may be counterproductive and result in more rather than less alienation.

An example of this is the practice of teaching social skills to people who are shy or withdrawn. It is easy enough to teach them to imitate certain attitudes or sentences and make them perform in superficially more acceptable ways. Underneath this surface of outward compliance the opposite result of increased withdrawal from real human contact may however be achieved. Under a veneer of polite and efficient communication the loneliness and isolation may have increased.

Daniel experienced precisely that. He was an inpatient in a psychiatric hospital and was considered in need of social skills training. While Daniel was indeed very withdrawn and uncommunicative, he had his own good reasons for this and he experienced the social skills workshop as interfering with his own way of being. After attendance at another of these workshops Daniel confided to his therapist how demeaning the process appeared to him. 'It is like trying on clothes that don't fit me – they don't suit me – they're not comfortable. I'll wear them if I have to. You know that I don't want more trouble. Still, I don't like it. Never have and never will.'

For Daniel every form of therapy and counselling involving pressure on him to conform to a predetermined standard was a waste of time. He was very sensitive to any hint of the therapist's implicit disapproval of his way of being. Although he suffered from his isolated position in life, he was not ready or willing to give in to the 'normal' way of being and to compromise his integrity. He would go along with things to an extent, because he knew that if he totally resisted therapeutic work, he would end up with more electric shock treatment. Yet, with every new concession to the 'normal' world he felt even more isolated in his private world and more convinced of his intrinsic difference.

The aim of existential work with someone like Daniel is to acknowledge the validity of his sense of specialness, to investigate with him what the specialness is about and rather than fighting it discover the hidden strength and potential in it. It is a useless and counterproductive exercise to try to cure people of what they essentially experience as their greatest strength and talent. They are usually willing to suffer immeasurable pain and torture if that is the price to pay for holding on to what they value. Well-adjusted normality is certainly no attractive alternative option to them.

As Daniel put it: 'They are the ones who are crazy, with their rat-race and their icy frozen normality. I don't want their alienation. I much prefer mine. They can lock me up, but my thoughts are my own. Their thoughts are determined by the mass media. They are so blinkered that they cannot even see that I don't want their way.' Daniel rejected therapy as long as he thought that the practitioner was trying to make him conform and prove him wrong. Only when it became apparent to him that his view of himself and the world would be respected and would remain intact did he begin to open up. When he realized that his therapist was not trying to change him, he gradually ventured to consider more constructive ways of exploiting his particular way of experiencing the world.

People like Daniel often withdraw further and further into isolation because they despair of finding anyone whom they can trust to respect their ideas. Yet because their criteria of what good living means are so personal and exacting they may find it hard to live up to their own standards. Sticking to one's own truth only brings peace and certainty if one has great strength and stamina and there is some external recognition that one's views are valid. You are far more likely to end up going mad when everybody consistently indicates that you are wrong. Withdrawal can be a last attempt to preserve a centre of selfhood, but without meaningful exchange with others, the source of inspiration may soon dry up or go wild.

What is needed, then, is the discovery of a way to express the inner truth artfully and constructively, rather than clumsily and destructively or not at all. The original artist needs a teacher who can stimulate and channel her originality, not one who attempts to stunt its growth or make it conform. The aim of existential work is to assist people in developing their talents in their own personal way, helping them in being true to what they value.

The first step in this process is to uncover the abilities that are already there, although they may be hidden deep down. Although these may have been turned to negative or destructive use, the person rarely entirely doubts her own basic talent. Daniel for instance had never doubted his own great sensitivity, his special ability for intense experience and his powerful sense of integrity and honesty. As already mentioned, he valued these talents greatly, even though nobody else seemed to. His vital self-affirmation, even at times of extreme crisis and isolation, was maintained by his pride in these qualities and by his consideration of himself as a martyr for the sake of the truth. He would sooner have given up all his worldly goods and material ease, he would sooner have gone on without any friendship, respect or esteem from others, than compromise what he valued so dearly. As the circumstances of his life did not make it very easy or likely for him to exploit his special qualities, he had had to resort to his own romantic imagery about himself in order to remain faithful to his principles. In this manner he had before long created a world of his own in which he trusted no one else.

When all his efforts to find ways of connecting his inner world with his everyday life had failed, Daniel began to use his sensitivity and specialness in a negative way. He became expert at picking up every hint of dishonesty in the people around him and he construed this as a sign of their inferiority and their malevolence. He soon came to believe that some of them were in fact plotting against him because they were scared of his insights into their dishonesty. He started writing letters to people accusing them of these things, in many cases hitting sensitive nerves because his accusations had a core of truth to them. He was soon hospitalized for the first time and treated for paranoia.

After an initial period of suffering, Daniel came to the conclusion that a career as a psychiatric patient, however limiting and demeaning, offered more scope for being true to himself than his previous lifestyle. In the hospital there were people more like himself. Some people actually seemed capable of understanding what he meant. He struck up several friendships with other patients and even with some of the staff. There was time to be spent on oneself rather than having to slave away at mindless tasks for people he despised. Now that he knew there was a way of being just himself, he was certainly not going to let anyone shrink his head back to the size of normal people.

Working existentially with Daniel meant first of all resisting the temptation to try to change him, influence him, condemn him, fight him or prove him wrong. It meant going over to his side in order to find out in what ways he was actually right. Only by co-operating with him did it become possible to start understanding what truth lay at the foundation of his current attitude. His desire to be free for integrity, honesty, sensitivity and intensity was absolute. Those four qualities were the cornerstones of his philosophy of life. Paradoxically this desire had led him in the opposite direction.

Daniel had opted out of the direct affirmation of his values by settling for the security of a career in hospital. He was going along with an appearance of co-operative therapeutic effort in order to stay out of 'trouble' (ECT), while dismissing the very idea of therapy wholeheartedly in private. He was therefore being fundamentally dishonest. The intensity of his experience was greatly diminished by anti-psychotic drugs. He was only using his sensitivity as a means of recognizing threats, never as a means of creative understanding. In short, he was in no way enhancing his own values. Daniel's condition might have given him the necessary breathing space while saving him from utter isolation, but it had now turned into a most undesirable and counterproductive way of life. He was squandering his abilities and the qualities that he really prized. It was high time to consider how he could turn them to good use instead.

By viewing his mental illness as a way of life rather than a condition, Daniel was able to start conceiving of more constructive ways of living, through which he might develop rather than suffer from his talents. His motivation to stand by what he valued was very strong. The realization of his own self-deception was sobering enough for him to stop thinking badly about other people. If he had made the mistake of dishonesty then it was no longer such a crime for others to do the same. It became imperative, however, that he should redeem himself and fight his way out of this impasse. He wanted to find a way of living in accordance with his principles and he applied himself to finding this way with much eagerness and devotion.

Daniel's courage, combined with some luck and fortunate meetings of the right people at the right times, enabled him to establish himself professionally in a new field. The milieu there was much more to his liking and more congenial to his aspirations. He could now apply the same perceptive honesty with total intensity and put it to creative rather than destructive use. His sensitivity became the formula of success in his new profession and within a few years he had built himself quite a reputation. People might still think him slightly crazy, but this had now become a recommendation rather than a diagnosis. In fact Daniel was able to use his psychiatric past as a veritable source of inspiration in his new line of work.

Daniel's success was without a doubt more to do with his own vigour and determination than with the existential sessions as such. Nevertheless, Daniel had needed the catalytic experience of the sessions to gain the necessary insight into his own talents and abilities and to become aware of his own misuse of these. The crux had been for him to learn to be consistent with his own values. He needed to be encouraged to tap the source of his motivation and strength so that he could find a direction in life that satisfied his own search for meaning and truth.

The existential approach encourages people to live life well by their own standards. It also aims at encouraging the clear understanding required to discover what those standards and ideals are. Moreover, it provides a framework for monitoring the consistency of those standards and ideals. It facilitates their practical application in line with the person's abilities and talents and it examines their logical implications and consequences. The existential approach centres on an exploration of someone's particular way of seeing life, the world and herself. The goal is to help her to establish what it is that matters to her, so that she can begin to feel more in tune with herself and therefore more real and alive. Before the person can rearrange her lifestyle in accordance with her priorities she has to examine her own preconceptions and assumptions which stand in the way of her personal development. Much of what has always been taken for granted is therefore re-examined in the light of a search for truth about life. Taking a sober look at the basic structure and dynamics of existence itself shifts the focus away from individual pathology. This has a liberating effect and with this regained freedom the personal will to do better at living emerges.

The goal of existential work is to enable clients to enter a new phase of development of their talent for life. Existential therapy or counselling can be likened to a training in the art of living. It involves learning to see the world and human existence anew, with interest and imagination rather than with boredom and bigotry. In reconsidering what was previously thought of as already known certain fresh discoveries are made. The sense that many more secrets are buried in the very heart of existence brings hope and undreamt of joy in living. New meanings and possibilities are revealed and with them the source of personal motivation and courage.

A person's experience of life can in this way change dramatically without the need for any specific external changes. This was the case for Lydia, who came for therapy when she felt that her life had become like a stagnant pool. She was sure that life was an essentially drab experience, which inevitably lost all interest as soon as you were over thirty and settled down into a routine. She was convinced that the problem for her was that she had a depressive character. Lydia wondered whether the practitioner would be able to help her to change her character. She did not think this would be possible as she had a particularly deterministic view of human nature. She was rather shocked when the practitioner indicated that change in her character and her situation might be unnecessary as well as impossible. She had felt sure that a therapist would press her to change and she had been prepared to prove to her therapist that she would be unable to do it.

Now that the pressure to perform in a particular way was taken off her, Lydia could take her time to examine her own assumptions about change being a necessity and a threat. It turned out that she had judged her life to be stagnant only because she felt that she ought to be doing more. Exploring her own sense of what it was that she imagined as desirable change was to her like opening a door which she always thought she could not open. Lydia discovered that what she had always wanted to do was to enjoy deeply the life that she was already living. The only thing that was keeping her from doing so was her own notion that that would not be sufficient. The reason why she thought it insufficient was that she perceived enjoyment and change as contradictory concepts. She felt that in contenting herself with what she had already she would be in danger of missing out on life. When it was brought to her attention that she was at the moment missing out on life by her frantic self-depreciation and discontent with what she had, she experienced a great sense of relief.

It was a true liberation for Lydia to stop feeling that what she had was not good enough. All along she had simply wished that she could hold on to what her life consisted of as there was nothing in the world that she valued more. It was a revelation for her to discover that even in holding on to things exactly as they were there could still be change and movement. Life as a process of transformation was a new and reassuring concept. It occurred to her that she had previously always felt obliged to make change come about actively. Refusing to keep on changing had therefore conjured up the image of stagnation. Feeling assured that she need not worry about change and that life itself would bring the necessary transformations gave her a much needed sense of peace. She could now stop worrying and start to enjoy what she had. Life suddenly seemed far from dull to her.

Lydia never made any dramatic changes in her life, but she stopped telling herself that she ought to; she chose to develop her talent for cosiness instead. Taking care of her house, her garden and her family now became her unashamed addiction and devotion. She felt a certain pride in opting for what she wanted and leaving previous notions about achievements in other areas to others. To her life now seemed full of promise without her having changed either her situation or her character. She found that what she had thought of as a depressive trait turned out to be a longing for stability and security. Rather than changing herself she learnt to stop going against her inclinations.

Lydia's experience might have sounded more impressive if she had decided to make dramatic changes in her life or if she had undertaken some big and successful project. The success of existential work cannot, however, be measured by such external and superficial criteria. The aim is to help people to recognize their own standards and values, not to make them conform to some preset notions. For Lydia the recipe for success was living according to her own principle of contentment with a quiet process of slow transformation. Prodding her along to perform in more ambitious ways would have left her feeling more inadequate and depressed than ever.

Supporting clients in finding the direction of their own destiny is not an easy thing to do. It is much easier to have a conformist picture of what human achievement is about and to coach every client in this direction. An existential approach is therefore doomed to be unfashionable as it aims to help people recognize their personal vocations rather than fit in with current trends. Sensitivity to the client's particular interests in life also requires the practitioner to be detached enough from her own views of what is desirable not to impose these on the client.

This kind of authenticity is the ultimate goal of existential work: inciting people to express their own view of themselves and the world, whilst recognizing both their possibilities and limitations. The process involves an exploration, questioning and clarification of people's sense of their own talents, abilities and destiny in life. It also refers these back to the general laws and principles that rule life and living. Finding personal courage, direction and meaning in managing the paradox of affirming oneself individually while recognizing and accepting the universal is the final goal.

Encouraging clients to set their own standards and live according to their own value system, whilst monitoring their reflectiveness and consistency, is clearly no light task. Let us next consider what is required of an existential practitioner in facilitating this process.

The attitude of the existential practitioner

Existential therapy or counselling is a philosophical investigation rather than a medical or a psychological one. The practitioner therefore functions as a mentor in the art of living. The accomplished existential practitioner is more like a sage than a brilliant technician or a cunning strategist. Working existentially means choosing to focus on the client's mode of being. In doing so techniques and strategies are discarded in favour of reflection. Participating with clients in an existential exploration means thinking through with her all the issues that matter to her.

The existential practitioner has to be deeply interested in piecing the puzzle of life together. No one can work from an existential perspective without a commitment to reaching an ever-greater understanding of human existence. The existential practitioner values truth above all. But the truth that she aspires to is a living truth, not a dogma or an abstraction. Her curiosity about the human condition is primarily directed at an exploration of the way in which people create and destroy truth in their everyday existence.

It is the particular way of being of the client that is under scrutiny, in all its ramifications, in all its implications, in all its depth. The practitioner's presence and participation in the session is therefore quite intense. During the fifty minutes of the session the practitioner encounters the raw reality of the client with all the lucidity and wisdom that she is capable of. This concentrated effort can obviously only be maintained as long as the boundaries of the sessions are clearly determined. The practitioner functions as a fellow-investigator, maintains the focus on the investigation into the client's living style and enables her to broaden her perspective and increase her sense of mastery over her own destiny.

To accomplish this the existential practitioner needs to maintain the necessary distance from the client and preserve her inner integrity. She must be able to be with another person, while remaining true to herself. Rather than absorbing herself in the process of listening and empathic responding, she makes sure that she remains composed and collected. Only in so far as the existential practitioner is firmly at one with herself will she be capable of hearing the meaning of the client's words, spoken or unspoken. It is not merely a matter of being there for the client and listening. It is far more a matter of hearing and grasping what the client herself is not yet able to understand or even express clearly. The practitioner has to initiate the process of making the implicit explicit.

It is not support and acceptance that the existential practitioner provides, but the encouragement to think through the unthinkable. When the client gasps and sighs because a problem seems insurmountable, the practitioner needs good heart and resolution in the calm conviction that this obstacle too can be tackled and overcome. In the background of the interaction there will undoubtedly be a strong bond of compassion with the client's fundamental humanity. But in the last analysis it is the determination to face up to the trials and tribulations of life that dominates the session rather than an emotional appreciation of the difficulties involved.

Existential practitioners must be mature and experienced enough to have seen so much of life and human nature that they are not easily shocked or taken aback. They will be familiar enough with self-examination to recognize their own struggles in every client's mistakes and misfortunes. Yet they will not need to secure a superior position for themselves by pretending to commiserate or congratulate. They will only resonate with the client's experience when the tragic or uplifting aspects of a situation genuinely move them. The practitioner should always vigorously remind clients of the ways in which they are themselves influencing their fate.

Existential counselling and therapy are clearly not a substitute for human friendship. They are closer to a pastoral or mentoring relationship, where the practitioner offers a reminder of common sense, personal integrity and universal wisdom. One of the dangers here is that of presumption or pedantry. Practitioners can easily fall into the trap of a 'holier than thou' attitude, even or particularly when it is disguised as humanitarian concern and caring. The only way to guard against this is for the practitioner to be ready and able to question her own ideas, insights and points of view along with those of the client. She must remain ruthlessly honest about her own limitations. If she takes the client as seriously as every client deserves to be taken then she will not fall into complacency. Every client will in some ways challenge the practitioner's previous assumptions and stretch her experience. The practitioner must be open to an incessant dynamic interchange and capable of accommodating new views and recognizing her own errors.

Humility is the essential characteristic of the true philosopher. Socrates's definition of the wise man as 'he who knows that he does not know' provides a suitable standard for the basic attitude of the existential practitioner. Through this fundamental scepticism a practitioner can remain open in the search for truth. As soon as she begins to think that she has figured the client out or starts to admire her own cleverness she will know that she is on the wrong track. By reminding herself of the value of a naive and unbiased approach she can protect herself against becoming pompous and stop herself preaching at the client.

With this attitude of continuous learning, the deepest gratification that the practitioner will gain from her work is that of an increasing understanding of human contradictions. Doing a decent job of helping the client to address the pertinent issues in a meaningful manner is another important gratification. The fee received for professional expertise is the final gratification. Apart from these three ways in which the practitioner gains from the work, she is entirely at the client's service.

Some other important attributes are prerequisites for the right attitude towards guiding the client's life and self-examination. Existential practitioners are likely to have a broad perspective on the human condition and on human nature. Their stance crosses cultural, class and national boundaries. They do not copy the ideology of any one approach or conviction, nor do they attempt to convert the client. They develop a personal style, freeing themselves as much as possible from any therapeutic, political or cultural cliché which may tempt them. The practitioner's message to their clients is to think for themselves.

Thinking for himself was precisely what Gabriel found hard to do. He was referred to counselling after he had been absent from his college for a number of weeks because of his sense of not being able to cope with the classroom situation. Gabriel was a young African who had been in Britain for only a couple of months and who was having grave doubts about having accepted a scholarship for study overseas. In his home country he had always been in a very privileged position. He was the eldest son of a prominent member of his society, and was used to being treated with great respect, as he was also used to respecting and venerating his elders.

The term *culture shock* was too mild to express the extent of Gabriel's disarray at the situation he encountered in Britain. Although he considered himself very broadminded he had been amazed at various attitudes he met in his fellow students. It was perhaps exactly because he was so broadminded that these attitudes had had such an impact on him. Although there were two other Africans in his year group, they had kept pretty much to themselves, while Gabriel had been immediately invited into an established group of young British men.

Gabriel felt completely confused about the contradictions between the values and expectations of his new friends and those of his childhood and his parents and relations. The former seemed to assume that he as a black man had to engage in a fight for the liberation of his people. The latter had always made him appreciate his privilege in being such a prominent member of a commonwealth society. It seemed to him that the world had suddenly been turned upside down. Everything that he used to consider an honour and strength was referred to as a disgrace and threat.

His first reaction had been one of disbelief. Then he had wanted to turn away from his new companions and remain with the people from his own country. But Gabriel felt that his scholarship was awarded to him so that he would become thoroughly acquainted with Western thinking and he had decided to immerse himself more deeply with the people who never ceased to surprise him. To remain in contact with his homeland and culture he had begun to prolong the daily rituals of cleansing himself of the influence of his new environment. The rituals involved the use of water and one day he unintentionally provoked a minor flood in the residential hall of the college.

When Gabriel was asked to account for his responsibility in the flooding he denied his role entirely. As several people knew that he had been having extensive sessions in the bathroom for weeks, he was forcefully accused and challenged about his deceit in the matter. The incident turned into a proper crisis when his friends told him privately to own up if he wanted to remain their friend at all. Now Gabriel began to explain to people that his ancestors had made the flood happen as they disapproved of his new way of life. As he stuck to this version of events with great conviction it was only a matter of time before he was referred to a counsellor. It was clear that most people considered that Gabriel was not entirely sane and from that moment his isolation in the college grew daily.

At first Gabriel considered the counsellor as some kind of spiritual authority, as a judge to whom he had to explain and justify himself. He was fully convinced that his ancestors had indeed intervened to remind him of the sinfulness of wanting to desert his own culture by mixing too closely with his new friends. If this had occurred while he still was in Africa amongst his own people there would not have been a problem. Then his father might simply have ordered him to give up this friendship and be true to his own values. He would have obeyed and he would have been at peace with the situation.

In the present case things were quite different though. His father had indeed wanted him to find out about British culture, so that all this was a necessary experience. At the same time Gabriel himself enjoyed being close to his friends and he did not want to give up being liked by them. Yet he could not assimilate their ideas about himself and the world. It just did not make sense. In particular he could not understand why they insisted that he should take the blame for the flooding incident, which to him did not seem like his responsibility. The very notion of personal answerability seemed alien to him. He could not dissociate the idea of guilt from that of responsibility.

To Gabriel the power of individuals was much more relative than it is in Western thinking. For him it mattered far more that he should act in accordance with the rules of the group he belonged to than to have a sense of his personal independence of thought. The problem to him was not one of insanity or not owning up to something he had done. The problem was that nobody could guide him in what was right and wrong. The problem was not medical but cultural. He was caught between two contradictory value systems. If he could just stick with one of the two and reject the other then he would be safe again. But Gabriel had gone too far into trying to allow both systems to have a simultaneous impact on him. He was confused and he could not understand what was right and what was wrong. Then when he needed guidance in making up his mind about this ethical problem, there was no one to turn to.

It took quite a while for Gabriel to get used to the idea that the counsellor was not going to tell him how he must solve his problems. This was very much what he wanted. He was used to referring to an authority whenever a new situation needed dealing with. The authority of the counsellor was telling him that he must make up his own mind about what was right for him and so he did. Once he had caught on to the idea of counselling as an opportunity to explore all his available options and to think through the consequences of each, he regained some inner composure. If the counsellor had judged his sanity by Western standards he would almost certainly have been dismissed as beyond reason. If the counsellor had offered him nothing but an expectation of him taking responsibility for his own counselling sessions, these would certainly have floundered.

What was needed was in the first place that the counsellor grasped Gabriel's isolation and the essential cultural miscommunication that had been taking place. Gabriel had not had a fair chance of fully presenting the situation from his own perspective. In the second place he lacked the plain and simple comprehension of what people were trying to get him to do. An explanation of Western notions of personal responsibility and honour went a long way towards easing the situation for him. He had felt accused, when he was only asked not to deny his part in an event. He had felt offended in his honour when people rejected his mention of his ancestors as the origin of all this. Western dismissal of magical thinking had to him seemed like a personal affront. While he needed to be understood from his perspective he also needed to be told about the perspective that he misunderstood himself.

When the two ways of thinking were more and more clearly juxtaposed, Gabriel could make much more sense of events and also of his own confusion. It started to dawn on him then that there was indeed some choice in the matter and that he could make up his own mind about the aspects of each culture that he liked or disliked. In the event his choice was to return to his home country at the first opportunity, as he had come to the conclusion that he valued his own traditions above all. Even though he was most eager to go back home, his study trip abroad had taught him much in terms of his understanding of human nature and Western society. In turn his critical appraisal of his British friends' assumptions had a considerable impact on their views. What could have ended in catastrophe had turned out to be a constructive experience emphasizing the importance of an active enquiry into other people's perceptions and values before judging them by one's own standards.

The broad perspective of the existential approach makes it particularly relevant to working with cross-cultural issues. Its philosophical underpinnings make it stand out as a method for working in crisis situations. The overall attitude of existential practitioners is one of confidence, courage and vitality. Their interventions denote their acceptance of life as essentially demanding and challenging but always potentially rewarding.

If the client feels overwhelmed by life, as she is often likely to feel, the practitioner does not dismiss or discount the logic of her weariness. The practitioner does not counter or challenge the client, but neither does she agree or condone. She simply assists the client in the examination of her attitude in all its implications and she will therefore often, together with the client, come to the conclusion that it is no wonder that the client feels as she does. At the same time the practitioner will help the client to translate that feeling into a concrete understanding of what is wrong with or missing from the situation. Her attitude will invariably indicate that a greater insight into what is expressed by the client will help her find ways of altering her experience of the situation. The practitioner guides the client in the direction of such increased insight by dialectic questioning in the spirit of a philosophical investigation.

Susan came to therapy after having attempted suicide. She was greatly relieved to find that her therapist did not treat her as if she needed to be handled with kid gloves. She needed to be taken entirely seriously and have an opportunity to examine her preoccupations in a disciplined rather than in a complacent manner. Susan was seventeen years old and she found living a rough and unrewarding business. She had taken an overdose of sleeping tablets that she had spotted in the family medicine cabinet. Although she had never been in any grave danger of dying, her intention had definitely been to put an end to her life.

Susan's truth at the moment she tried to kill herself was that life was not worth living. It was just one problem after another. Things never worked out the way you hoped they would. People never understood you and most likely they would ridicule you if you ever let them know that you needed their approval. The situation was hopeless and the only sensible thing seemed to be to have the courage to end it all.

As is often the case, to Susan her suicide attempt had a heroic and brave connotation rather than a cowardly one. Because she valued her action so much she felt offended in her pride by all those around her who discounted the importance of her overdose. She disliked those who felt sorry for her as if her attempt was the symptom of an illness and she detested those who lectured and reproached her for being silly. There was nothing to be gained from trying to pacify her or confront her. The only thing that could be of benefit to her was to help her face her own reality.

Existential work with Susan meant confirming those aspects of her out-look on life that were based on her discovery of hard realism while helping her to reach a more constructive conclusion in her thinking about those facts. It was no good pretending that life could be easy and that people would end up understanding her. Her recognition of life as basically rough and of people as basically unfair was one of her greatest discoveries and personal realities. She needed to get some credit for daring to look at life in such a way. Moreover, she needed to be reminded that if she had had the courage to brave death, all on her own, then surely she would have the courage to brave life as well. At least she had no illusions left, so she would now be able to move forward without the paralysis of constant disappointments.

An existential attitude always involves squarely facing up to what seems neg-ative and difficult in order to discover the positive implications of it. For Susan finding that someone could understand her point of view and value it while pointing out its potential strength was extremely gratifying. Reconsidering her suicide from this new perspective, she decided it had been a waking up experi-ence like nothing else. Going this far had enabled her to see how serious she was about not wanting to put up with certain things. It had also given her an absolute sense of herself as a separate person: she really could choose to end it all if she really wanted to. Life and death were a matter between her and her-self. Never before had she fully realized that. In a way she had gained the right to live for herself, now that she had dared to take the right of dying for herself.

All this was very hopeful, even though the practical circumstances of her life remained a mess. What became the most potent force for Susan in tack-ling this mess was her knowledge of her own capacity for courage. In many of the difficult situations that she was exposed to in the next few months she sur-faced through simply repeating to herself that she was brave enough to die and had nothing to fear. Because she had been prepared to die, she now felt entitled to her own opinions about those things that she found hard to toler-ate. So, instead of letting her disagreements with other people eat away at her whilst remaining silent, she learnt to speak her mind.

Susan learnt gradually, through making many mistakes, what things she valued and which people it was worth making an effort for. Each time that she added a small piece of new information about what she did find worthwhile to her understanding of herself, she engaged further with life. A year and a half after her suicide attempt, death no longer seemed like an attractive option at all.

The existential attitude can be likened to that of the Buddhist or the stoic. Life is considered a constant challenge, which can be faced more effectively with equanimity and determination than with escapism and self-deception. Life may be tough, but that is what makes it interesting. For those who give it their best, living can be an enriching and rewarding experience. Existential therapy is in the final analysis a process of exploration of the value and meaning that an individual can find in her life. The attitude of the existential practitioner is therefore one of encouraging her client to consider what she is most serious about, so that she can decide on the general direction she wants to take. In the next chapters I describe this process in more detail.

Chapter summary

1   All approaches to counselling and psychotherapy have basic assumptions and clients can only benefit if they are in fundamental agreement with the basic assumptions of the approach.
2   The existential approach focuses on clarifying a person's views on life and living.
3   Its basic assumption is that it is possible to make sense of life and that people need a consistent framework of reference.
4   Clients need to be fully engaged with the work and be willing to face themselves honestly.
5   People are able to create meaning and order in spite of apparent chaos and absurdity.
6   It is possible either to go under in adversity or rise above it.
7   People are already taking responsibility for the way in which they direct their lives, even though they may not be doing so deliberately. They are still voting with their feet.
8   The boundaries of living are set by a universal order. We are all bound by:

- Natural laws, such as the law of gravity and the laws of life and death.
- Social laws, established by culture and human relationships.
- The law of our internal feelings and the reality of our inner strength and weakness.
- The ethical law that governs our beliefs and values.

9   It is possible to learn to live more effectively when we know the rules of living.
10 Life is regulated by both constraints and liberties: people can be helped to explore and understand these.
11 It is essential for a person to find something that is worth living and fighting, or even dying for.
12 Helping people to understand their situation and find a meaningful way forward is more important than showing them empathy.
13 It is crucial to oversee the possible consequences of actions, priorities and values and determine what is important enough to give other things up for.
14 Perfection cannot be achieved, though it might be a valid goal, and therefore living should not be postponed till a later date when things might be better.
15 Self-deception is often based on a fear of life rather than on a fear of death.
16 Life is an art and we get better at it through practice and by making mistakes.
17 Existential therapists should have considerable expertise at living and at helping others to explore their own talents and abilities, turning them to optimal use.
18 Tackling life's issues is best done in a specific, concrete and individual manner.
19 Existential therapy values truth above all, that is to say, living truth as individuals discover it in their everyday existence.
20 We need a naïve and unbiased approach, with curiosity and wonder for the client's unique experience and with humility in the face of new discoveries.
21 Life is a constant challenge that can be faced most effectively with equanimity and determination.

2

Establishing Contact

Starting point: anxiety

When a client arrives for her first therapeutic session one of her major concerns is whether the process will work for her. Entering into a therapeutic
relationship is as great a challenge as entering into any relationship that one
expects to be significant. In turning to a professional, the client exposes herself all the more as she is applying for assistance in conducting her own life,
thus admitting a lack of ability to manage by herself and entering the relationship in a position of extreme vulnerability. This is likely to add
considerably to her state of anxiety.

The therapist needs to be aware of this fact and sensitive to the ways in
which the particular client attempts to alleviate her anxiety. The therapist also
needs to provide some evidence of her ability to encompass this and further
anxiety. She can do this by clearly introducing and establishing the working
model for the sessions. It helps enormously to set out the parameters of the
therapeutic work in writing and send this to the client before the first meeting.
It generally makes good sense then to have a preliminary session, in which
client and therapist can both assess whether they want to work together.
After this therapist and client should be in a position to make a firm decision
about the desirability of engaging in a therapeutic contract. The frequency,
duration, length and cost has to be clearly agreed. I have elaborated on these
structural issues in detail in my book *Everyday Mysteries* (van Deurzen,
1997).

In the initial session the therapist can explain her way of working and the
client can ask any questions about this. It is important to clarify the
therapist's role as mentor and her commitment to discovering with the client
what are the latter's difficulties in living. The therapist will probably describe
the process as an opportunity for the client to take stock of her talents and
abilities as well as of her limitations. She will emphasize how their combined
efforts will be focused on the client's search for new direction. She may char-
acterize her own role as that of throwing new light on issues that are confused
for the client, putting problems in a new perspective when the client is stuck
and encouraging her to exercise her strength and finding constructive and creative ways of proceeding onwards. She will also mention how her role
excludes attempting to change or cure the client and how her expertise on

human living will not make life any easier, although it may make it easier to live. She may finally want to point out that her role does not designate her as a substitute father, mother, brother, sister, friend, spouse or lover, but as a companion and guide in the discovery of the client's own way into the future.

Thus from the outset the therapeutic relationship will be strictly defined as a professional one, where the practitioner is the expert, consulted and employed by the client. The fee is paid in return for a service of disciplined and methodical exploration of the client's way of life and living ability. It does not buy the client any sympathy or empathy or other forms of emotional involvement, but it does entitle her to be understood and be taught to understand herself. If these terms are acceptable to the client the session can proceed to the initial exploration of the client's world.

It will soon be evident how the anxiety around the beginning therapeutic relationship is a reflection of anxiety around other aspects of the client's engagement with life. The way in which different people deal with the anxiety generated by the subject of their vulnerability and difficulties in living is generally a good indication of the way in which they handle the anxiety generated by life. Thus the client who talks a lot, clearly having prepared extensively for the session, attempting to appear in charge and well organized, is likely to go about the business of living in this same frantic manner. The client who sits back and waits for the practitioner to take the initiative is likely to practise a similar form of apathy in life. There are many different ways in which people can cope with their anxiety, but underneath the coping surface most people experience anxiety as a constantly returning threat.

The existential literature has paid considerable attention to the fundamental role of anxiety (Kierkegaard, 1844; Heidegger, 1927; Sartre, 1943; May, 1950). In this tradition anxiety is seen as an inevitable part of human living. What is referred to is not fear. It is not even the fear of fear, as some people like to describe anxiety. Existential anxiety or *Angst* is that basic unease or malaise which people experience as soon as they are aware of themselves. It is the sensation that accompanies self-consciousness and awareness of one's vulnerability when confronted with the possibility of one's death. It is therefore the *sine qua non* of facing life and finding oneself.

Plunging oneself deeply into existence in a mindless way can only temporarily eliminate anxiety. By living as if one were like an object, solid and predetermined, existential anxiety can be postponed until the time when this pseudo certainty is proved false. As soon as awareness of the fundamental lack of substance and security of the human condition is reached one is again exposed to the bare reality of existence, which evokes anxiety.

Some people succeed in living in an anxiety-free state, mechanically moving along with the ever-returning duties of daily life. They pretend to themselves that life is just this way and that they themselves are made the way they are, without there being anything that they can do about it. When there are no options, there is no anxiety. As soon as people are aware of the basic choices that life involves them in they are condemned to the experience of anxiety.

Anxiety is therefore indicative of the level of awareness in a person. In the final analysis this awareness is essentially that of a realization of the basic freedom that human beings possess. People, unlike objects or animals, can make conscious decisions about their life. They may be greatly influenced by circumstances and environment, but they always maintain a fundamental ability to affect things in some way. Even the prisoner or the slave has a choice over how to respond to the situation. When all other options are barred people still remain in charge of their destiny by their capacity for deciding to take their own life. Suicide in this sense can be seen as the final affirmation of human freedom.

To be or not to be is undoubtedly the most fundamental human question and asking oneself this question means to plunge oneself into the experience of anxiety. For those people who attempt to eliminate the awareness of this fundamental choice, life brings acute anxiety whenever their basic security is threatened. For those people who choose to live in awareness of their fundamental ability to decide, a daily struggle with anxiety ensues. They are acutely aware that life is based in death and that they will only live as long as they continue to create and protect their own existence. When life is not taken for granted existential anxiety is experienced.

An existential approach does not attempt to eliminate anxiety but rather encourages people to face it. Curing people of their capacity for anxiety would mean curing them of life itself. The task is not to suppress, disguise or deny anxiety, but to understand its meaning and gain the strength to live with it constructively. The courage to live can only be found if the possibility of death is faced resolutely. Existential therapy sets itself the task to help people to find this courage. It therefore starts by encouraging them to unearth all their anxieties and face life squarely. Anxiety provides all the potential energy required for facing up to one's responsibilities.

Cecilia wanted to run away from the experience of anxiety. When she came to her first counselling session she said that she wished that she could find a way of soothing the sudden attacks of anxiety that were disturbing an otherwise perfect life. Out of the blue she would suddenly feel so anxious that she had to stop whatever she was doing and go to bed. But even in bed she was not safe, for she often, on the edge of sleep, would get a sudden sensation of tripping and falling. Her body would then jerk as if she were trying to regain her balance and her hands and feet would flail out wildly, searching for solidity in the void around her.

Cecilia's external circumstances seemed particularly stable and secure. She was married to a man of considerable wealth and influence, eighteen years her senior. She was extremely well provided for and she in turn provided Michael with an ideal wife and impeccable domestic surroundings. Her only complaint was her anxiety attacks, which sometimes suddenly rendered her incapable of attending to her duties as mistress of the house. She would at these times take to her bed and read book after book, mostly romantic novels in which she found again the peace that had so suddenly deserted her usually calm personal life.

She did not understand why this should occur and she had feared that it was some symptom of epilepsy, especially as her recurring dream sensation always ended in this jerking movement of panicky groping for support. After she had been reassured about the state of her brain in a thorough neurological check-up, she decided there must be something she was doing wrong and she was determined to find a remedy. She had hypnotherapy for several years during which time her symptoms receded but she became depressed. By now she had been prescribed a number of drugs, all of which she had tried, then discarded without telling anyone about it. She came for counselling as a secret last attempt to discover what was bothering her. The psychiatrist who was treating her had invited her to enter into his clinic, but she considered that if she had to go into a clinic she would have failed as Michael's wife. Thus this last resort request for counselling.

In the counselling sessions it was soon established that the idea of having failed as Michael's wife did not make her particularly anxious. There was a strange attraction to the idea that she might end up as mad Cecilia. After having been a good wife for so many years, she would unfortunately have become incapable of carrying on with her duties for reasons quite beyond her control. On the downside there was, however, an unpleasant taste for Cecilia to the idea of giving up control as mistress of the house and mistress of herself. She felt as if she would have lost a battle.

When she tried to describe what this battle was about she started to feel anxious; here was a welcome change back to the original complaint replacing the depression, which had followed it. The anxiety, she now remembered, had started bothering her in this extreme form when she first began to think rather smugly that she had acquired a life of ease, comfort and security. She thought it was maddening to realize that the moment you think you have got things under control, something like this should happen to spoil it all. She considered this to be most unfair, as she had not asked for much. Although Michael provided material ease, she had never wanted anything more from him. She had never been in love with him. She had given up her wish to continue her career as an airhostess, because of Michael. She had even given up her hope of having children of her own, as Michael already had three by his first wife and did not want any more. She did not complain about any of this; she knew what she was getting into when she married him. All her sacrifice was justified by the seemingly perfect life that had ensued. What was not all right was that this life had not brought her the peace of mind she had intended to obtain with it. She had imagined that by giving up all the things that could make life interesting and rewarding she deserved also to be safe from the upsets and threats that she feared would have come with a life full of things that mattered.

When she started to understand her anxiety as a message to herself about the impossibility of hiding away from life, as a reminder of her own vitality and vulnerability, she immediately understood her depression as the logical consequence of ignoring that message. She constantly tried to cover up her unease with the situation and efface her anxiety with pills or therapy or even simply by the routine of her everyday life. But each time she did that she also killed some of her own vitality, her own ability to take up the challenge of life, her hope of becoming more as she wished to be, her hope of being herself.

Cecilia's depression was the result of her opting out of life. The next step on that road would have led her into a gradual withdrawal from normal life altogether, a withdrawal into a psychiatric clinic. Indeed, the clinic, to Cecilia, meant the end of the line. There she would give up all hope of a normal life and admit defeat. Interestingly, she found that prospect strangely attractive, yet also alarming in its absoluteness of renunciation. She likened it to entering a convent. She expected that there she would find peace at last. She would give up her material ease, her aspiration to being happy and with it her sanity as well. What else was there, what more could she be expected to pay for being safe?

She became very worked up and excited when considering the possibility of her bargain with fate finally succeeding. It was quite clearly a mad kind of bargaining and she saw this herself. She sobered up as soon as she was reminded of the cost to herself of having acquired semi-safety, in her marriage to Michael. If giving up love, career and children had not been a guarantee of her security, why should giving up her freedom, dignity and sanity make her fare any better? Had she not paid too high a price already for something that might perhaps not even exist? Did she really think that turning herself into the heroine of a romantic novel who marries her sugar daddy would render life sweet ever after? Did she seriously consider it possible that she would make life more easy and safe by hiding in a psychiatric clinic, where all around her she would be confronted with human suffering and confusion? Was it possible that by trying to escape once again she might bring more insecurity, more anxiety, more depression onto herself rather than less?

All these questions led her in the same direction. She must finally make up her mind about what she wanted: life or death. If she wanted a total guarantee against misfortune, against suffering and insecurity, the only possible option left after the clinic would be death, and even that would be no certain guarantee of peace for she believed in the possibility of the existence of an after-life where she would have to continue what she had not yet dealt with on earth. She was therefore faced with the only remaining feasible option, which she had for so long tried to postpone or ignore: living life in a less perfect and less secure way.

When she began to explore the implications of such an option, she started to realize that this might in fact open up a whole new perspective, a whole new range of possibilities. Imagining making a new start and aiming for life rather than for security brought the excitement of re-opening avenues that she had purposefully closed to herself previously. To think that it might not be too late to start going towards that which could give her hope rather than despair was like breathing fresh air. Of course, in comparison with the sacrifices that she had already made or had been prepared to make, the sacrifice she felt she would now have to make seemed fairly insignificant. Indeed, she knew that she would have to swallow her pride in relation to friends and family and admit that she might have done things wrong all along. She also realized that the consequence of reasserting her own life might be to alienate her from Michael. This in turn might lead to having to sacrifice her material ease. She soon realized that if she was only with Michael in order to be protected by him it was not a relationship worth much, whereas if Michael could only love her if she remained oppressed, then his love for her was equally weak.

It did not take her long to make the necessary decision, once she saw her situation in this light, because she had all along known in herself that it was wrong. She had felt ill at ease with her life for so long and her anxiety attacks were always there to remind her of this. She was not afraid to face the anxiety that came as a result of her new decision. Once the choice was clear she experienced intense relief. Preparing for her renewed single life gave her more than enough to be busy with, thus dissolving any remaining feelings of depression. Although things were very tough at first, she gained a sense of certainty about the rightness of her decision, once her new life started taking shape. This gave her strength and a sense of security greater than any gained from her previous way of life.

For Cecilia it was only when she gave up her desperate attempt to eliminate anxiety from her life that she gained courage. Only when she started welcoming the anxiety and the challenge of existence, did she gradually become able to live fully and did she begin to explore her possibilities and opportunities. This first change, which seemed rather dramatic, came about very fast, because she was on the verge of making this kind of decision anyway and because she was ready for the insights that prompted it. It took a long time afterwards for her to come to terms with the full implications of her decision when she realized that there was little real love between Michael and her.

When things did not go smoothly or when she felt lonely, Cecilia would start hankering after another escape into marriage or madness. She would start reading more romantic novels and constructing romantic notions about herself and a life where worries would be a thing of the past. There were times when she fled into flirtations with other wealthy men in the hope of attracting a new partner who might flatter and cosset her. Fully accepting life as a basically dangerous enterprise and welcoming anxiety as a valuable experience was excruciatingly hard for Cecilia. She needed monitoring for a long time before she started to pick up her own escapist strategies in the small decisions of everyday life.

In this Cecilia was very much like most people. Human beings can spend tremendous energy on trying to remedy what cannot be remedied, and in attempting to establish security where danger will unavoidably reappear. The way in which we often attempt to organize life into a safe experience is by pretending that life is concrete, safe and solid. We act as if reality is tangible and controllable. We behave as if people are substantial, stable and unchanging. If this were true there would be no place for anxiety and there would be very little room for life itself. Things would be highly predictable and reliable, people would function in totally normative and well-adjusted ways. There would be no question of choice or decision-making since decisions would automatically follow from their premises. Situations would never hold any surprises and could therefore be perfectly regulated.

While people constantly attempt to create such a world, our efforts are inevitably undone by fate and by the unpredictable laws of nature which are at work all around and inside us. As long as these laws are at work there will be no total control and therefore no immortality and no total certainty and no escape from anxiety. It follows from this that those people who try hardest to deny the realities of life will also be those who will be most forcefully reminded of their own limitations. Those who run from their inner anxieties will experience the stalled anxiety even more acutely later.

An excellent illustration of this is the experience of withdrawal symptoms after drug use. Temporary artificial inner peace is purchased at the cost of increased anxiety afterwards. This is true for alcohol, nicotine and any other drugs. It is now a well-known fact that people trying to stop taking sleeping tablets frequently experience the rebound of dream activity, which is suppressed while on the drugs. This can result in nightmares so frightening and intense that sleeping is experienced as a threat and only acceptable with renewed recourse to tablets. This is precisely the reason that people are generally advised to come off drugs slowly and that they are warned about the need for support in handling their increased anxiety and irritability. Life in this sense is absolutely merciless: it will persecute those who attempt to play by their own rules until they too submit and bear their fate with courage rather than trying to escape.

The existential practitioner does not, therefore, try to make life seem better than it is. She does not try to soothe anxiety, for she is convinced of people's basic capacity to face whatever comes to them, and she helps them to find the courage to bear their anxiety, however intense. The existential practitioner does not pretend that problems will ever be completely solved. She will realize that it does not make sense to suggest that life can even be safe. She will help the client to recognize her basic vulnerability and limitations. The practitioner's task is to encourage the client to wake up from her self-deception. If there is any reassuring to be done it will be about the client's ability to stand reality in all its complexity and with all its challenges, never about the presumed difficulty of the situation.

In this respect, as in many others, existential therapy is a truly educational project. An effective parent does not try to belittle the occasion that the child is anxious about, she does not say 'Oh, that is nothing, your first day at school is not frightening, don't be so silly, pull yourself together.' She says: 'Of course you are afraid, this is a big new experience, anyone would be anxious going to school for the first time. It means you are getting ready to start something important.'

Child and client alike might find solace in the notion that good actors, however experienced they are, feel anxious before an important performance. Actors frequently report how this is a valuable and essential part of preparing for their performance, which is diminished if it is approached without this build-up of anxiety and its concomitant increase of available energy and concentration. Client and child alike may find heart in the knowledge that brave acts are seldom committed without anxiety and that bravery without anxiety can easily turn into mere recklessness or foolhardiness. This demonstrates the role of anxiety as the instigator of reflection on the situation one is in and its use in mustering all one's inner strength and abilities to tackle the situation most effectively. An attitude of passivity and self-deception in the pursuit of comfort will inevitably lead back to the experience of anxiety. Facing this anxiety and opting for an active and authentic way of life brings rapidly increasing strength and confidence and leads to an overall experience of vitality.

While most people are inclined to opt for passivity and comfort, once they get going on tackling life actively they often experience a surprising and gratifying sense of potency, adventure and excitement. It is rather like wanting to stay in bed in the morning, yet finding it even harder to get to bed in the evening for not wanting to abandon the interesting activities one has become absorbed in.

The practitioner keeps this general principle of human inertia in mind and she pinpoints the various ways in which the client evades her anxiety and attempts to opt out of life. Encouraging her to face the anxiety once it is uncovered is the next step. Assisting her in understanding the significance of her anxiety is the third step. Exploring constructive and creative ways of rising to the challenge pointed at by the anxiety is the last step. This process will go on as long as the counselling continues as new occasions for anxiety will never cease to arise. When the client becomes expert at unravelling her own self-deception without too much assistance from the practitioner the end of the sessions is in sight.

In the existential counselling process it soon comes to light that anxiety is not always present in undisguised form. It takes on various guises as people attempt to cover it up and get rid of it. The client who appears to have a problem with anger, may in fact be experiencing anger with people or situations that provoke anxiety in her because they remind her of her basic insecurity. She may learn various tricks to handle her anger, but none will really make a difference to her basic experience unless she is willing to face the anxiety that she is trying to cover up. When she does acknowledge that she is not facing the basic insecurity and vulnerability it becomes possible to remedy her situation by building inner strength rather than hiding behind an external and artificial bulwark.

The client who is depressed may in a similar manner have come to feel depleted of her inner strength through having given up the fight with life. She may have gone for the cowardly option of avoidance of what made her anxious and has therefore deprived herself of her own vitality. Cecilia's experience was an illustration of this. Only when she could begin to face her inner anxiety about life not being capable of providing guaranteed safety, was she ready to leave her depression behind.

Even neurotic anxiety in this sense can be a cover-up for the more essential deep anxiety. For Cecilia bouts of sudden anxiety attacks, which seemed like an illness, were only a reminder of her avoidance of the everyday struggle with life's basic anxiety. She had succeeded in pretending to herself that she had obtained security, but she had not succeeded in fooling her own conscience. It did not require much jolting of her memory for her to start feeling guilty about all the things that she was not attending to. Cecilia's existential guilt about having given up so many things of value in return for safety was another expression of her basic anxiety evasion.

Existential guilt is experienced by many people who feel that they have opted out of the basic anxiety of living by doing something which gives temporary relief but which they feel is wrong in essence. It can also be felt as boredom, if nothing wrong but nothing right either has yet been done about tackling life's challenges. An intense sense of meaninglessness can follow such a withdrawal from life.

So it appears that there are two basic strategies for escaping from the existential anxiety generated by the recognition of the basic insecurity of the human condition. The first is to decline to live altogether. This can be done by committing suicide, or it can be done by gradual disengagement. When people become aware of the great effort and risk that active human living involves they sometimes decide that such an existence is not worth the bother. This usually only occurs if they have not much hope that there is anything to be gained from the effort and the risk. Gradual disengagement and withdrawal can lead to drug addiction, alcoholism or other forms of hiding away. Eventually this strategy leads to isolation and dissolution. People on this path are eventually plunged into the depth of despair that brings madness and destruction of life.

The role of existential counselling or therapy in this case is to help people come to terms with the risks and anxieties involved in active living, rather than going under in the despair ensuing from passive withdrawal. Tough logic can do far more for people in this position than understanding and holding of hands. Once their options are clearly perceived, tackling life with all its unfairness and all its threats is invariably preferred over escapism, which can only bring doom and despair.

The second strategy in attempting to escape from anxiety is that of accepting life as if there was no choice in the matter. Existential anxiety is generated through awareness of human ability to participate actively in existence. Choice and responsibility are the origin of all trouble, so it is possible temporarily to eliminate anxiety by pretending that choice and responsibility do not exist. This is the option of self-deception, or bad faith (Sartre, 1943).

People can live as if their lives are entirely determined by fate and they dismiss their own responsibility. They imagine themselves to be safe because they are Mr or Mrs Smith and safely ensconced in their neighbourhood and their family or because they are a cab driver or a postmaster, a personal assistant or a dentist. Their lives are organized around a multitude of habits and regular patterns, which they have come to consider as intrinsic to life itself. Though they crave a taste of freedom now and then, their lives would be endangered by the very thought of turning their backs on the old 'nine to five' and stepping out of the groove once and for all. Their cautious excursions into freedom, called holidays and leisure time, are usually equally well organized and shaped by the expectations of the self-image they have created for themselves. These are sensible people, living sensible lives, protecting themselves from the dangers of real life by hiding in a bubble of security. They realize that opting for freedom means opting for anxiety and so they opt for duty instead.

This strategy works because culture is a product of this attitude and provides a network of shared illusions and realities supporting the individual willing to play the game. It fails as soon as an individual loses her safe place and discovers the ultimate inability of the system to protect her from her own emptiness, its inability to protect her from life and from death. This happens sooner or later in most people's lives. Existence is rarely so well organized that it can overcome life's inevitable obstacles without failure. The death of a loved one, the loss of a job or of the esteem one had started to take for granted can all cause the bursting of the protective bubble.

When this happens panic often sets in as there seems to be nothing left to live for. The illusion of security is suddenly gone and with it the strength has gone out of one's self, which feels deflated and depressed. People compare themselves to an empty shell or report that they do not feel like themselves any more. They find it nearly impossible to get used to the experience of emptiness that they had so successfully avoided before. Sometimes the system provides them with new opportunities for safety. But often people face life's inevitable crises without being able to fall back onto already prepared solutions. When people are then faced with the fact that they can no longer maintain the illusion of security they fall ill or they look for help in some other way. They may even turn to the 'opting out of life' strategy previously described. In other words, the strategy of pretending that one is secure and that one has no choice in life is not necessarily any better than the strategy of disengagement.

The following chapters look in more detail at the ways in which the existential practitioner can help people to deal with their anxiety. But first we must consider what possible alternative can be found at the end of such an enterprise. It is all very well to be able to recognize how and where people go wrong, but it only becomes useful in so far as they can be helped along in the right direction. It is therefore crucial to have a clear idea about what authentic living consists of before attempting to encourage people to undo the ties of their usual ways of life. These may seem false and full of superficial solutions but they may still be a preferable reality to the gloom of diving into the pure vacuum of deep anxiety. If authentic facing up to anxiety is to become a feasible and attractive option it is essential that one has a clear and realistic representation of what it involves.

Towards authentic living

The client's position can be compared to that of someone asking for directions in the street. Although she is preoccupied with the sense of being lost, confused and stuck, she is primarily interested in finding the right direction so that she can start proceeding that way and remedy her upset by doing so. After having unsuccessfully wandered about trying to find her way, she has perhaps approached some passers-by and asked them for help, but they have made her even more confused by giving contradictory or vague instructions. She has therefore decided to get the assistance of a professional, who she expects will not only know the way but will be capable of giving the most clear and efficient instructions on how to get to her destination.

Some clients have very precise ideas about the direction in which they want to go. They might come to the practitioner saying: 'I just want to be able to keep my marriage together' or 'All I want is to enjoy myself more and sleep better at night' or 'I need your help to break free from my parents and build a life of my own.' They often do not understand why they keep losing track of the way but at least they have an idea of where they are heading.

Many other clients arrive at the first session without the slightest notion of what they are looking for. All they know is that they are lost, uneasy, confused and that they want to put an end to that state of affairs, but they have little or no idea about where they want to go. They might say: 'You tell me what to do, you are the expert,' and it is often tempting for the practitioner to oblige and start making suggestions about possible ways to proceed.

Many practitioners are of course trained in person-centred or psychodynamic methods and will in principle abstain from giving any direct advice. All the same, they may be tempted to make implicit suggestions by reflecting back the feelings of anxiety in such a way that they are conveying the message that the client will be all right once she starts to acknowledge her own feelings. Or they might make interpretations that reveal particular judgements about where the client is in the wrong. Working existentially means remembering that no one can stop feeling lost or confused and get on her way until she has decided where it is she wants to go. The existential practitioner will not prescribe a direction but will press the client in making up her mind about her destination.

It is only when clients gain clarity about their goals that the motivation to proceed will be activated. No artificial goals will do: clients must gain insight into their own intentions. It is the practitioner's role to ensure that the client is reaching into herself and that she is searching for her own inclinations and purpose. Nobody else's purpose will do. Only in as much as one is in tune with one's original intention (Sartre, 1943) can one find full motivation for the project one embarks upon. This is what authentic living is all about: becoming increasingly capable of following the direction that one's conscience indicates as the right direction and thus becoming the author of one's own destiny. Quite simply, being authentic means being true to oneself.

Clearly to be true to oneself is just as essential for those clients who are lost without a sense of direction as for those clients who believe that they know where they want to go. Examining your own motivations and intentions until you become sufficiently certain that the direction that you choose is indeed the one you want is an ongoing process.

A client who starts out in the belief that, for example, she just wants her marriage patched up, may discover that she also wants a worthwhile intimate relationship with her husband. A bit further on in the counselling she may recognize that she actually wants to increase her ability to be intimate and genuine with all the people that matter in her life. As long as she pursues the patching up of the marriage, she may think that some of her motivation for this is exclusively based on the fear of what people will say if she gets a divorce. She may imagine that she does it basically to please her mother, who always told her that she ought to be able to keep her husband satisfied no matter what. This means that she is unsure about her direction, because it seems as if other people have told her to go that way. She does not consider that she herself wants to pursue this direction as it is not satisfactory and as it was not her own choice to start with. However, she will soon discover that abandoning the idea of patching up her marriage and getting a divorce may be just as unsatisfactory, if she is only doing it because some people have suggested this as an alternative goal.

She will eventually discover that going this way or that way, simply because people persuade her to try it, does not lead her very far, but makes her go round in circles and get dizzy and confused. It is only if she becomes capable of examining and understanding her own deeper motivation for wanting to patch up her marriage that she can learn about the ultimate goal that she is pursuing in this desire to stay with her husband. If she comes to the realization that it actually is important to her to be able to be intimate with her husband and that she genuinely values being able to be close and genuine with her parents as well, she will tap into a far greater motivation to work hard at her marriage.

It is now no longer a matter of doing the right things to make her life look acceptable and liveable. She is no longer content with an appearance of married life. It now actually becomes crucial that there is a genuine and substantial relationship between herself and her husband. She no longer sees that as resting on the elimination of certain externally irritating factors, such as his smoking in bed, or blowing his nose on the sheets. She sees it now as having to come about through her own effort to relate to her husband differently because she wants to get to know him rather than primarily reform him. This authentic motivation to relate intimately will spread to her relationship with her parents and colleagues at work as well. It may in itself be a sufficient purpose in life.

Learning to be close to other people, learning to know them and understand them, learning to bridge the gaps and irritations, becomes a challenge in its own right. It may even become the most valuable aspect of her life bringing its rewards as soon as she gets down to it seriously and learns its craft through lots of practice.

Authentic living brings with it motivation and enthusiasm to do well what is worth doing. This experience of increasing vitality and enjoyment in living is the hallmark of authentic life. Living authentically provides one with a deep sense of one's inner reality. Where this is lacking the person is almost certainly immersed in inauthentic living.

Inauthentic living is characterized by a sense of imposed duty or the experience of discontentment with one's fate. The client who arrives for counselling or therapy complaining of a sense of alienation from her everyday life, perhaps even from herself, is almost certainly living this kind of second-hand life. Living this way means that people do what they imagine is expected of them. But in so doing they are rarely deeply affected and are therefore less and less motivated to continue doing what feels more and more like an obligation. In extreme cases clients may describe this experience as one of not being in charge of themselves, as if they have lost all authority and cannot even claim their own experience as real any more. It is to them as if they were living somebody else's life or as if someone else were doing their living in their place.

Catherine was referred for counselling by her general practitioner after she had seen him several times for what he had diagnosed as post-partum depression. She complained of not seeing any point in continuing to change nappies and feed her baby because in a few hours' time she would have to do it again. She felt as if she was only coping with this pointless and boring life because she had gone, as she put it, onto her 'automatic pilot'. It was as if the real Cathy had renounced all interest in life and she was now being taken over by this stranger, some other Catherine who was an excellent nurse to her five-month-old baby, but who felt unreal and crushed.

Her family (particularly her husband and her mother) thought that she ought to take some time away from the baby and they had arranged everything for her to stay with her sister in Ireland for a few weeks, while mother would take care of the baby. Catherine was afraid that this would make her feel worse rather than better, as it would increase her sense of not being properly involved with her baby. She had expressed fears to her doctor about her husband and mother teaming up on her and wanting to harm her and the baby. She had sounded sufficiently distressed for the doctor to conclude that she was imagining things and that she was about to lose control. He prescribed tranquillizers, which she refused after realizing how they made her feel even less real, less herself and less in charge. She verbally attacked her doctor for having attempted to make her conform to what her husband and mother expected from her. This confirmed the doctor's suspicion that there was something seriously wrong with her. Counselling was considered a last option before psychiatric treatment. It was hoped that she could be convinced of the need for a break and that she would accept some treatment. Catherine was well aware of this and started the sessions with mixed feelings and on her guard.

Catherine's relief at finding an opportunity to explore her fears and sense of unreality was almost tangible. As soon as she felt assured that she would not be told to 'sort herself out' or 'get herself together' her attitude changed and she stopped expressing fears about people persecuting her.

She now started really to consider her situation and she was gradually able to make some sense of her experience. It transpired that she had been very disappointed with motherhood. Before the birth of her baby she had worked in a bank and although she used to quite enjoy this, she had never really felt as if she belonged in that world and she had often experienced a sense of unreality about her everyday life. Marrying John had also seemed like something she ought to get round to, after a long engagement of four years. They got on well together but then they were both easy people to get on with. There was never anything really bad, but never anything outstandingly good either. She felt as if she was just doing what she was supposed to be doing, work and marriage, good relations with both families, few parties and outings. She felt as if she was waiting for life to begin.

Then she became pregnant and decided that this was it. She knew that she wanted to stop working and devote herself to her baby. She felt very alive and excited and she read lots of books about childbirth and knitted dozens of baby garments. Although she wanted to give birth to the baby naturally she ended up with an emergency Caesarean section. Although she tried to breast-feed the baby, this became so problematic that she found herself back in the mediocre world of just coping and doing her duty in a detached sort of way. Only now it felt as if there was no more hope left; what should have been her saving grace turned out just as poorly as the rest. It would go on like this for-ever. What was the point? She felt hopeless.

Clearly, in spite of her hopelessness, Catherine resisted everybody's attempts to make her give in to her 'illness' and give up her efforts to cope. She felt more alive at the times when she was fighting them in this way. It was terrible to feel so alone but she knew she had to resist their view of the situ-ation all the way. Understanding why this was so crucial to her and how fighting for this gave her a feeling of dignity and strength was the most important task in the counselling sessions.

In exploring her will to stand by her decision to take care of her own baby no matter how badly she felt, Catherine discovered that far from having lost her illusions about mothering she now more than ever believed it to be of great importance for her to be a devoted mother. She was disappointed by how difficult it all was and by how little bliss she had encountered on the way to motherhood, because she had previously imagined it all to be rather rosy and uplifting and joyful. It definitely was not the easy way out of the drudg-ery of everyday life she had believed it to be. It had on the contrary brought her face to face with the inevitability of the ordinary and rather tedious aspects of living.

Though she had been tempted to flee and hide away from this discovery she was not willing to pay the price of abandoning her baby. She was not going to lose the opportunity for showing her resilience and her ability to make the best out of motherhood even though it turned out to be a less easy option than she had originally thought. No one, not even the best intentioned doctor in the world, not even her husband or her mother, was going to take her last chance away. She could still be a good mother.

Catherine now discovered that being a good mother did not just mean attending to the baby's needs. She had done that adequately most of the time. It did not even necessarily mean giving birth naturally or breastfeeding. 'Caesar and bottle' were fine in the end, even though she would have preferred it differently. No, being a good mother to Catherine meant being close to her baby and enjoying the specialness of this intimacy, inventing little games and cuddles, learning to understand this small human being and wonder at his progress. It was that in the end which she had not got round to. She had been too preoccupied with her own disillusionment and with her physical discomfort to take time for what mattered most. It was the sense of missing out on this most precious aspect of mothering that had made everything seem worthless. She had been so busy coping and convincing the doctors, nurses and midwives that she could manage, that her own desire to be with her baby had got lost. Only when people started suggesting that she was not doing well and that she ought to take a break from the baby had she been reminded of her real desire for her baby.

The more Catherine reminded herself of this original desire the closer she came to her baby. Instead of letting other people feed the baby she insisted on attending to Jamie herself and learnt much about his character by becoming so involved. She discovered that now that she was claiming him all for herself she could love him much more, which in turn made him more gratifying to be with. She coped a lot less well with the housework, which used to be her priority, but took the time to roll around on the floor with Jamie to find out about all his tickle-spots. Before long Catherine went to visit her sister in Ireland, but she took Jamie with her. On her return she seemed like an ordinary, tired but satisfied mother. The depression was a thing of the past.

Catherine thought that two crucial things had been needed before she could find her own reality. First of all she had to accept the fact that her illusions had been lost and that she had done less well than she had imagined she would. Second, she had to recover her original desire and motivation to do what she set out to do in the first place: learning to be a full and real human being in mothering a child. To others it had seemed as if she were suffering from depression because she was overwhelmed with the task of motherhood and perhaps regretting her old working life at the bank. In fact she was depressed because she was not yet closely enough involved in motherhood and afraid that she would fail to do well in the one thing that mattered greatly to her.

As long as Catherine went along with other people's views on what might be wrong with her, she felt terrible and unreal. Of course this was nothing new, as she had been habituated to feeling unreal and dull and not in control of her own destiny. She was used to living life in a second-hand way. Motherhood was a chance for her to become real and to take charge of her own life. That is precisely why it mattered so much when things seemed to disintegrate. That is why she became so desperate when everyone seemed to imply that there was nothing to do but to abandon the idea of motherhood as a vocation.

As it turned out in Catherine's life this experience was the challenge that shook her awake and made her realize what she wanted out of life. This was not to be relieved of baby care or allowed back to her old job, but to learn to commit herself fully to what she sensed was her vocation. She wanted to learn to be good at mothering Jamie, even though this was exhausting and sometimes disappointing. In committing herself to this task with inner conviction, rather than out of an empty sense of duty, she discovered the intensity of life when it is lived first-hand and that was enough to encourage her in overcoming the unavoidable new obstacles on her way ahead.

Catherine's experience was a splendid illustration of Jaspers's definition of authentic living as 'becoming oneself while suffering defeat' (Jaspers, 1931). It is often mistakenly assumed that authentic living consists of doing as one pleases, being able to choose freely and pursue the inclination of the moment. Spontaneity may be a consequence of authentic living, but it is not its origin.

Authentic living is about following one's own personal direction, while taking the limitations of the situation and of oneself into account. It never means taking the path of least resistance. It always means going in the direction that one's conscience dictates and gaining the strength to persist, no matter what, from the sense of reality and aliveness that comes with being in tune with one's own purpose and intentions. This process always includes the experience of defeat and the recognition of limitations. This is what differentiates authentic living from ambition and arrogant striving.

Authenticity literally signifies genuineness or authorship; it indicates a concern with ownership. If something is authentic it is something of one's own, it is, literally translated from Greek, self-prepared, self-made. In fact the Greek word *authentes,* the one who is authentic, more generally indicates the person who rules or who is master and from there even more specifically the one who murders or commits suicide. Thus being in charge of self is seen to extend to mastery over others and to the ability to take life as well as create it.

In English the concept of authenticity clearly does not have these strong connotations. All the same, authentic living implies the same resolute choice about what is one's own and what is not. It requires the person to affirm and stand by all that she recognizes as belonging to her and to reject and relinquish what she does not recognize as hers. Authentic living is about being able to make clear and well-informed choices in accordance with the values one recognizes as worth committing oneself to. Instead of following the lead of the public or the crowd (Kierkegaard, 1846a) or living immersed in the 'They' (Heidegger, 1927), drifting along with what is 'done' or 'not done', the authentic person follows her own guiding principles. She models her life after her own views of what is right and wrong, going in the direction of her own project and original intention, being loyal to self before anything else. To be authentic one has to have been confronted with one's limitations, possible failure and death, as well as with one's possibilities.

Being loyal and true to oneself and one's principles is easier said than done. Catherine's family and doctor thought that they were encouraging her to be true to her need for peace by telling her to take a break from exhausting baby care. She herself had doubts about this but was not sure what it was she wanted. At one point she expressed this in the following terms: 'Maybe I do need to take a break from Jamie, maybe I owe it to myself, maybe I am not taking care of myself properly, maybe they are right, but still I don't seem to want to do it, the thought of it just makes me more sad.' Catherine did not feel any pull in the direction that seemed sensible to others. Though she was not explicitly aware of what she wanted, she was sufficiently in tune with her own deep intentions to be able to tell quite clearly what she did *not* want.

She was like the traveller lost on the way, exhausted and distressed with the search for direction and the sheer effort of survival in difficult conditions. The people around her, with good intentions and noticing her distress, advised her to stop searching and go hide in some friendly hotel. She experienced disgust at the thought of giving up her search now that she had got so close to her destination. Yet she was too tired to think clearly and she gradually became convinced by other people's concern for her that her quest was doomed to failure. She was afraid that no one could set her in the right direction now that she was lost and she did not have the energy to keep staggering from one road to the next, always finding them blocked or not leading anywhere.

All she needed to do was to remind herself of her destination and rekindle her motivation to carry on. For this she needed to remember her desire to be close to her baby. She needed to go back to her original intention in a more realistic way. The practitioner's work was to help her in this process of recollecting her original orientation and direction. Then it was necessary to assist her in situating her current position on the map of her existence and help her to gain some insight into the peculiarities of the road ahead. It was additionally of importance to help her gain confidence in her ability to accept the challenges facing her and to support her in her determination to surmount the inevitable obstacles on her path.

As was to be expected Catherine moved from depression to anxiety while she was gaining these insights. Her anxiety was particularly centred on her ability to question other people's views of her illness. She was used to falling in with the opinion of people whom she considered greater authorities on these issues than herself. Now she started to believe that she might be right after all in wanting to continue taking care of her baby even though everybody she respected was advising her against it. This induced high levels of anxiety in her. Far from indicating her self-doubt her anxiety was a manifestation of her growing ability to decide for herself what she must do and how she must do it. When she realized this herself her anxiety became to her a sign of anticipation. It was a reminder of the need for her to be prepared for difficulties in going ahead in the direction that she opted for, rather than expecting everything to go smoothly and her dreams magically to become reality. Anxiety was a sign of her engagement with life and it expressed her readiness for its inevitable crises.

Catherine learnt her lesson quickly because her inner awareness of what she really wanted was quite strong in spite of her hesitations to make this explicit in external reality. She was able to implement her new realizations almost instantaneously because she had a considerable body of experience to draw from. She had taken care of younger siblings in her childhood and she actually knew how to enjoy babies and young children. She only needed to remind herself of that knowledge and build some confidence in her ability to combine her old dreamlike enjoyment of playing with babies with her new-found adult responsibilities.

Although Catherine had worried a great deal about how to convince those around her of the rightness of her views, once she had convinced herself, those around her almost immediately fell into agreement. It is often like that: those people who are sure about the direction they want to go in encounter few people who want to hinder their movement forward. In the same way those who are hesitant meet many people who try to stop them or convince them to change direction and take the road that they are on themselves. Thus those who follow their own destiny in a self-assured and resolute manner can become leaders, as the word *authenticity* suggests. Those who live non-authentically, unaware of their own sense of direction, will tend to be followers, until perhaps they feel that they are being misled by those they follow.

Of course, there is no guarantee that authentic decisions about your direction in life will automatically lead you in the right direction. People make mistakes even when they are fully aware of their responsibility and ability to make their own choices. Authenticity is not a sufficient virtue in itself and it is certainly no guarantee of truth. There are abundant examples of people who have been able to discover their inner authority successfully and who live energetically and enthusiastically by their own rules, firmly set in a direction which will lead them and their followers to certain destruction. Authenticity in isolation can be synonymous with madness. The moment one becomes capable of living authentically one needs to find new criteria for deciding on right and wrong. While the old rules have become outdated with the rejection of external authority, one's inner authority requires a compass to travel by if it is to stay on the right tack.

So while the first step in existential therapy is always to help the client rediscover her original intention and her own direction, it is necessary to encourage her to check this intention and that direction in terms of their ultimate rightness. Guidelines are required to monitor one's orientation.

Finding guidelines

When the client is starting to follow her original intention and when she begins to organize her life around her own views on right and wrong, she needs clear criteria to test the truth of her position. Humanistic approaches perceive human beings as basically positive creatures who develop constructively, given the right conditions. The existential position is that people may evolve in any direction, good or bad, and that only reflection on what constitutes good and bad makes it possible to exercise one's choice in the matter.

The humanistic practitioner might simply seek to encourage the client in the exploration of her potential. She will feel confident that increased awareness of the internal process will be a gain and will lead to growth and positive change. The existential practitioner is less certain of human goodness and she will take into account people's weaknesses as well as their strengths. Cultivation of intense emotional release for the sake of catharsis is not an aim of the existential approach. Neither is the frantic reorganization of an individual's living conditions. The existential practitioner will be wary of the client's sudden bursts of self-righteous decision-making, which may be regretted later.

The aim instead is to encourage the client to orientate herself by the compass of her own conscience. The practitioner helps the client to develop a reflective rather than an impulsive and action-oriented attitude. Clients are bound to end up making some new decisions about their actual living conditions sooner or later. Excessive haste in wanting to make considerable shifts in her life however usually indicates that the client is still deceiving herself on her ability to transform life into a kind of paradise.

Orientating oneself by one's conscience always requires the ability to situate one's perspective within the wider framework of universal guidelines. Without this one's personal view is quickly reduced to a blinkered and often self-indulgent attempt to flee from external authority to the safe haven of one's own rules. In this case the outcome will almost certainly be self-destructive and it will probably lead to greater confusion rather than to greater clarity in the end.

So the first criterion of living wisely is to be able to find one's direction after gaining a wider perspective. Whilst external authority and established order are questioned in principle, they are not simply done away with and replaced by chaos. They are examined for their ultimate significance in the larger universal order and only abandoned in so far as internal authority has discovered a more encompassing guiding principle.

Take, for instance, a client who starts out complaining about the constraints imposed by her family life. She feels that she has to carry too many burdens and is rewarded only with a feeling of being taken for granted. She may be ready to file for divorce because her feelings of extreme dissatisfaction tell her that she cannot bear this any longer. Nothing would be easier and more self-congratulatory than to support this woman's intense disgust with her seemingly untenable situation. One could implicitly encourage her to go ahead with divorce proceedings simply by consistent (and probably quite genuine) empathy. It would be easy to condone her newfound would-be authenticity and her desire for freedom by praising her for self-assertive behaviour even if it were ultimately quite destructive. Indeed, the client's discovery of her own ability to make choices rather than silently suffer and her discovery of the ability to express her feelings might seem like sufficiently valuable gains in themselves.

However, detaching oneself from the situation rather than evaluating it from the client's position clearly reveals how one-sided and erroneous such an approach would be. Experienced counsellors or therapists will know that much can be learnt in difficult situations and that encouraging clients to jump ship too quickly may lead to much regret later.

Existential counselling and therapy are not about providing comfortable flights from reality, but about reminding people of the implications of their situation and of the need to face their own limitations as well as their own strengths. The measure of this task must necessarily be that of the limits of the human condition.

If the existential practitioner wants to approach clients from a perspective of insight into the unavoidable aspects of existence a number of issues stand out as crucial. These are the boundaries of human existence and they can provide guidelines for living. While no one can claim to understand the workings of the universe perfectly, the accumulated insights that people have formulated through the centuries can supply one with a useful map.

What stands out as a basic principle is that human existence is a struggle between opposites. There are two sides to every experience. Each argument has a counter-argument. Positive aspects turn out to have negative counterparts and vice versa. People always find themselves somewhere on a continuum between life and death, good and bad, positive and negative, active and passive, happiness and sadness, closeness and distance.

Most people seem to strive to secure a safe, stable position for themselves somewhere along the continuum of opposites. They think of themselves as embodying only some of the universal aspects of human existence and reject the others. They may, for instance, consider themselves basically healthy, intelligent and honest and ignore their own vulnerability, capacity for error and propensity for untruthfulness.

Sylvia, for instance, used to think of herself as particularly non-violent and peace-loving. She was a committed vegetarian and a great and active supporter of various causes. She turned for help after yet another boyfriend had deserted her – which had made her start to wonder what was going wrong. Sylvia's boyfriend – like his predecessors – had said that he was leaving her because of her 'fanatical' commitments which left no room for him. At first she tried to attribute the problem to her difficulty in finding men who would be able to match her own good qualities. She claimed that it was her pacifism that got to them, especially as she was not prepared to back down from her position just to please them. She thought that this was something that men just could not put up with in a woman.

It was obvious that Sylvia was not aware of the contradictions in her attitude and that she was insensitive to the aggressive undertones in her own non-violence. Only through starting to appreciate the uncompromising orientation of her stance could she begin to articulate her problems. She soon realized that she was inclined to affirm her principles strongly. She refused to do anything to pacify those who disagreed with her, but could not recognize her lack of gentleness and understanding. Sylvia needed to realize that aggression and violence can serve a function and that she herself, although she thought that she had thrown them out and replaced them with peacefulness, was in fact using aggression and violence in disguised ways.

Sylvia discovered how her condemnation of these qualities and attitudes had made her a prisoner of a one-sided type of behaviour, which in practice had proved to be non-viable. She had ended up contradicting her own principles without even being able to notice it.

When she let herself express her violence not just in violent disagreement with her boyfriends, but also in areas where she had previously tried to maintain her role of peace-lover, she gradually became able to manage a more flexible attitude. This made it possible for her to get on with one of the boyfriends well enough to envisage a long-term relationship. He did not seem so unsympathetic now that she could recognize aggressive aspects of herself. She had become more even, she said, much less extreme and therefore easier to live with.

Though Sylvia was now able to get along better with her boyfriend, this was not the result of her having compromised her ideals in any way. What she did instead was to look at the consequences of her ideals and discover more realistic ways to express them. This then enabled her to understand her own limitations better and to live in a more complete way. Once she relinquished her rigid self-image it felt like a relief. She said it was no loss but all gain. At last she could understand other people's aggressive behaviour, which she previously rejected out of hand. She could also see the contradictions in her own attitude, when she fought for peace and forcibly resisted appeasement.

Recognizing one's limitations in this sense is like acknowledging that one has been trying to paint with only half the colours in the spectrum. The initial recognition may be painful, but it is well worth the fuller perspective that is gained. Within the boundaries of the human condition people are in fact capable of much greater diversity then they usually give themselves credit for.

Practitioners often encourage their clients to start recognizing parts of themselves that they had not previously known were there. This certainly goes in the direction of a fuller awareness of different aspects of personality and character, but it does not go far enough. The existential approach replaces a view of the individual as an amalgam of bits and pieces with the image of the person as a sensitive instrument, which can tune into a broad band of waves. In principle each individual has the ability to tune into the whole range of human qualities, attitudes and experiences, although many limit themselves to a narrow band.

From an existential point of view, then, the exploration of the whole range of experience and a familiarity with the laws of harmony, which organize it, are the background against which the client will be encouraged to expand her repertoire. Whilst recognizing opposites, the aim is never to shift one's position from one to the other permanently. The assumption is not that one or the other will prove to be the ultimate truth or provide the key to happiness. On the contrary, the existential practitioner believes that recognition of the value of the entire range is essential, so that experience can be modulated and harmony generated. In other words, recognizing opposites is not about choosing one or the other, nor is it necessarily about striking a happy medium: it is about making movement possible between the two poles and having as wide a range as possible available to one.

In counselling Sylvia the goal was not to encourage her to choose between being more consistent with her pacifism, or give it up, nor was it to lead her to abandon it for a more aggressive mode of living. The aim was to enable her to recognize the presence of both extreme tendencies in her own way of being and to stop pretending otherwise. The supposition behind this was that like any other person Sylvia was capable of the whole spectrum of experience and therefore must have been suppressing part of her repertoire in seeing herself as all one way and not the other. The idea was that she would gain greater freedom and greater reality in herself and with others by recognizing her full abilities rather than by restricting herself. Sylvia's experience confirmed this hypothesis.

It is important to remember that the object of coming to terms with polarities is not compromise. The existential ideal is not to come to the sort of integration where starkness of experience is lost in bland medium-term unification. The object is to expand a restricted repertoire and thus become able to accommodate greater contrast in self and others. The existential goal is to master the use of colour rather than settle for dull grey. What is achieved is symphony of variety rather than banal harping on a single tone. Any point of view that cannot take its opposite into account must be partial. Versatility and diversity are marks of a genuine striving towards wholeness.

Of course, nature is the model, the inspiration for this dialectical view of life. Nature's never-ending movement from light to dark and dark to light, from hot to cold and cold to hot, its diurnal rhythms, its seasons and weather changes, is the prototype of existence. The world is transformed from the starkness of winter through the greenness of spring to the lushness of summer and through the gold of autumn back to the starkness of winter. Seasons and climate are the most obvious reminders of the cyclic and transient nature of existence. Although it is tempting to moan and groan about these things, no one would actually welcome the notion of a static world without changes in weather or season.

In the same way, attempting to make people conform to pre-set patterns of behaviour and feeling is often considered an attractive option but is ultimately a non-viable and deadening solution. Instead, the identification of the outer limits of human experience will give access to those areas that each individual is not yet covering. It will provide a map against which individual position, velocity and trajectory can be plotted and projected.

The most significant poles on the map of existence are life and death, being and not being, presence and absence. Virtually all polarities can be understood in connection with the primordial opposition between life and death. Life is meant to include everything encompassed by being in the world.

Thus, life is synonymous with people's finite existence, including the reality of their birth and death, the confrontation with pain and suffering, the need to labour and struggle for survival, fallibility, isolation and ultimate dependency on fate. Death, or nothingness, indicates the perspective of the infinite, the beyond. It signifies transcendence, the dimension in the far background of human existence. This dimension includes the wider structure surrounding human life: the cycles of nature, space and time, and experiences of awe and wonder.

All other polarities can easily be understood as variations on the basic themes of these two great opposites. When alternation between the two poles has become obstructed, a natural oscillation needs to be re-established. This can be done so much more easily once the basic principle and function have been understood.

Some of the basic polarities which frequently impede people are active–passive, past–future, affirmation–negation, inclusion–exclusion, control–surrender, good–bad, doubt–faith, giving–receiving. None of these opposites have to be contradictory: they form two sides of the same coin. The tension between them is the very substance of life. Energy flows from the positive pole to the negative one and power is generated. Creative living is about allowing the current between poles.

All too often people have opted for one side of a polarity, believing the truth to be simple and partial rather than complex and paradoxical. They short-circuit themselves this way and burn up all of their energy in a hopeless attempt to maintain a lopsided position. Others recognize the polarities but are frightened of their implications. They try to manage contradictions by effacing them; synthesizing and compromising until all potency is drained from life.

Some brief illustrations will clarify and amplify these theoretical guidelines in their application to counselling and psychotherapy. They demonstrate the importance of the search for the missing element. The questions that the practitioner must constantly keep at the back of her mind are: how is this person trying to bend the rules; how is she blinding herself to part of her experience and attempting to erase elementary principles? What part of the truth is missing? In what ways is she not fully coming to terms with the tensions, paradoxes and contradictions of life?

When Ed came for counselling he felt that his girlfriend, Mandy, was letting him down. He said that he did not know how to make her love him. This was a good illustration of Ed's worldview, which was focused on the task of remaining in control. He was aware of his domineering attitude of which he was, in fact, quite proud as it had taken him a number of years to develop this degree of self-confidence, which he saw as making it possible for him to affirm his position with women. He was therefore rather disappointed that his hard-won confidence and ability to take charge of the situation did not guarantee Mandy's fidelity.

They had had an intense love affair. He had told her that he wanted to marry her. Almost from that point onwards she had started making overt passes at his friends, even though she had agreed that they were to be married eventually. The more he told her to stop flirting, the further she pushed her provocation. He now knew that she had slept with at least two of his friends and he could not take it any longer. He broke off the relationship with Mandy telling her that she was a slut and no longer welcome in the local pub where he had first introduced her to his friends. He was heartbroken and humiliated to find that Mandy refused to give up her new friends. He now faced a dilemma. He could either suffer being constantly reminded of his defeat and continue to associate with his friends, even though they were clearly sleeping with Mandy, or abandon his social network. He would then have to give up the security and familiarity of this particular local pub, his friends and his girlfriend with whom he remained desperately in love.

Ed decided after only two counselling sessions that there was another solution to his dilemma and that he knew how to handle the situation. He tried to get his friends to be loyal to him and stop seeing Mandy. This did not work out, as they did not believe her to be very important to him. He tried to force Mandy to swear an oath of faithfulness to him and proposed marriage to her a second time. It was all to no avail. She laughed at him, then ran away sobbing. Ed could not understand what was going on and came to the third session with his mind made up about which course of action to take next. He was convinced that he needed to take things back into his own hands. He had let everybody make a fool of him. He would show them. He was going to start a new life. He had already found a new room to stay in, in a different neighbourhood served by a different local pub. He was going to find a different job too, where he would make new friends. He was done with his old life.

What Ed was unable to grasp was the one-sidedness of his approach to the world and the people around him. All of his attempts to put things right consisted of reinforcing the same mistake. He was caught in a vicious circle. The more he attempted to assert himself and control his world and the more his fellow human beings consequently revolted against him, the more he then felt compelled to exert even greater pressure and further entrench himself in trying to control his environment.

Although Ed regarded moving away as an example of giving in and admitting defeat, he came to realize that his avoidance of the troubling situation was designed to avoid having to own up to the mistakes he was making. It also stopped him having to consider other people's perspectives. He just wanted to build a new world, hopefully this time all in his own image.

There was a missing dimension to Ed's experience: surrender, need, yielding and vulnerability. In his vision of the world only he could be master, stay on top, make sure that others would not let him down by staying in control of the situation. Through his approach to life and other people he created a climate of reluctance and rebellion in those around him, for they often felt disregarded and disrespected by him.

When Ed started to see how his whole world was built around his need for self-preservation through control he initially reacted by becoming obsessed with his own guilt and badness for having behaved in such a way. He felt ashamed when he thought of how Mandy might have felt every bit as desperate as he. It distressed him to begin considering whether perhaps she had simply not known any better way to tell him that he was disrespectful to her than by being disrespectful to him by sleeping with his friends. He remembered her tears when she had left him and started wondering whether after all he might have been the one doing the lion's share of the hurting.

Ed was learning to turn his world upside-down. What had been good was now bad, and what had been bad was now good. This was not going to be any more accurate or useful than his previous way of looking at things. He needed to see the sense in both sides, the value in his ability to stand up for himself and be in control as well as in his ability to shift his position when wanting to be close to another human being.

All this time Ed had had very little contact with his friends and none with Mandy. Though he was keen to understand what he had done wrong he could not face putting his findings into practice. It now became apparent that Ed had great difficulty expressing what he had come to see as the vulnerable side of his nature. He was tortured by the still desperate intensity of his love and longing for Mandy, without being able to translate his concern into new words and actions. All that he could bring himself to do in the counselling sessions was to punch his knees with his fists and call her a bitch for making him want her so badly.

And that was just it. In his world there was only room for control and therefore he could only conceive of Mandy as wanting to control him by making him want her. Because of his very partial approach he lived in a world of fear and retaliation. Starting to imagine that Mandy cared about him and actually suffered rather than that she was just attacking him was the key to uncovering his own suffering. It took a long time before he could muster the courage to go and tell Mandy about it. This hinged on his growing understanding of the importance of retaining the gains of his already-acquired ability for self-assertion, courage and control while balancing it with the new insight into his vulnerability and need.

It took months of slow practise with minor occurrences in his everyday life before Ed grew confident enough to be courageously yielding. Even then all he managed to say to Mandy was that he could not put up with the situation any longer and that he wanted her to understand that he had had to leave because he could not stand seeing her do what she did. Eventually he added that it had caused him too much pain. When Mandy reproachfully replied, 'So why didn't you just say so?', he started wondering why indeed he had not.

Thinking about this Ed realized that at the time he could not have said that because he did not actually feel hurt, but simply out of control. Now that he did recognize his pain Mandy responded to him very generously, which amazed and delighted him. He discovered that a certain way of being and relating to others creates a world inside you and around you, which then, in turn, re-creates more of the same in response.

It is not just that we imagine other people to have the qualities that we have. By our way of relating and being who we are, we bring these qualities to the fore in other people. Projection and projective identification, as the principles are usually called, are based on a wider and more basic principle: kinship. Kinship is the fact that human beings, in all their individual variety, are basically engaged in the same tasks of living and that they do this equipped with the same basic kit. In principle, human beings are all capable of the entire spectrum of experience, even though each has developed certain aspects more than others.

New facets are constantly discovered and may be brought out by new relationships. No facet is intrinsically better than any other. Each is part of a more encompassing totality. Each can be used positively or negatively, and each has a counterpart, which can also be used positively or negatively.

Ed was well able to be in control of his life in the positive sense. He was even able to make some quick and efficient major changes in his life in response to adversity. He was not aware, however, of the negative consequences of being totally and always in control. This was because he was also unaware of the positive implications of yielding and surrendering – the opposite of control. He could see only the negative side of the latter and therefore systematically tried to avoid it.

Elizabeth's story is another illustration of the advantages to be reaped in using universal criteria to assess personal values and to test their absolute validity and completeness. Elizabeth, herself a counsellor, was strongly committed to the principle of accepting other people's imperfections. She had cultivated an ability to understand and empathize with other people to such an extent that she found it very difficult to form a judgement about the rightness or wrongness of anyone's position.

Elizabeth worked in a youth centre; she had done so for years. She had known and worked with hundreds of people from many different backgrounds and found that her capacity for questioning her own prejudices had grown to such proportions that she was now unable to make any decisions involving discipline. She was too worried about making the wrong decision and harming someone in the process. This had become a real problem, which interfered seriously with her managerial responsibilities at the youth centre. Work in the centre had become paralysed. Elizabeth felt caught in a double bind; she wanted to remain true to her principle but realized that doing so consistently got her stuck. She complained of not being able to win. This was the clue that set the search in the right direction.

It soon became apparent that her loving and all-embracing approach was based on the desire to win. Winning meant being liked in return and having lots of friends and being esteemed by clients and colleagues alike. She believed that if she could be very understanding and full of goodwill towards others they would then return this to her and everything would be all right.

She was afraid that disapproval of others implied shortsightedness on her part and that it would reduce her to being rigid and moralistic. This was why she hesitated to express her disagreement with certain practices in the centre even though she felt deep down that they were wrong. She was terrified of standing in judgement.

While she had been very popular in her job for years and had a reputation for being liberal and democratic in her leadership, she had recently picked up rumours of criticism and she was very disconcerted about this. She felt weak and exposed. She knew that the teenagers would continue to like her but she feared that her colleagues despised her for not being more firm.

Elizabeth recognized then that her principle of understanding and liking everybody, no matter what they did, was an expression of something that she wanted for herself. She could not feel at ease unless everybody understood and liked her. Because of this she was exaggeratedly self-conscious of her attitudes and behaviour, as she wanted to avoid at all costs offending anyone's opinion lest she might forfeit their approval of her.

Elizabeth operated from the principle of total inclusion. She was able to include almost everyone and everything in her liking and esteem and she had been pretty effective at getting other people to include her in their liking and esteem. What she did not see were the negative implications of this all-inclusive attitude. She was paying the price of her inclusiveness by ending up with softness and woolliness as a result of a lack of sharpness and discrimination between right and wrong.

What brought this home to her was to realize that while she believed in including everything, she was in fact excluding the possibility of being exclusive. The notion of exclusiveness captured her imagination and conjured up all kind of things that were entirely taboo for her, such as exclusive dresses and exclusive hotels, things out of the ordinary, things only people with exclusive tastes could afford. Talking about these secret longings brought her to life for the first time in the session.

Being exclusive, Elizabeth thought, would also lead to making bold statements about oneself and the world. This was another terrifying but attractive prospect. People who did this would make themselves enemies rather than friends, she thought. With reflection she amended this to 'enemies as well as friends'. She realized indeed that such people would probably win respect from many people and that they would certainly be very definite in their dealings with the world. 'If I dared to have my own exclusive views on sex, abortion and violence at the centre,' Elizabeth said, 'it would become a simple business to make new policy decisions and end the paralysis.' Once she had reached the stage of conceiving of the advantages of a more exclusive position, which she had previously simply dismissed, she could start to discover its value as a counterbalance to her usual inclusive attitude.

Realizing that exclusiveness was not necessarily a bad thing made her recover her liberty to take the plunge into making bold statements and taking firm decisions. Relearning to balance permissiveness and firmness was a revelation for Elizabeth. She did not find it hard to be exclusive because she had had plenty of practise at being exclusively inclusive. A small insight into her own limitations made a big difference in her everyday life. The therapist was able to help Elizabeth gain this insight by checking Elizabeth's attitude to life for partiality and by helping her to face the paradox that she had been trying to evade. This was feasible only because the practitioner assumed all along that Elizabeth, like everybody else, would be capable of both attitudes and that it would be to her advantage to discover that for herself.

Clients can only be counselled from anxiety to authenticity if they take this universal principle of complementarity of opposites thoroughly into account. Once they face their basic anxiety and look for ways to live according to their own values, referring to this principle of paradox can widen the scope of their outlook. A simple rule of thumb in pinpointing this is that people are usually right in what they affirm but wrong in what they deny. The things that a person believes in are bound to be at least a partial truth. The denying of some other things is usually the indication of a limitation and a blind spot as it implies a turning away from some other aspect of the truth.

At times it is appropriate to pick and choose and thus eliminate some of the whole picture for the sake of focus and sharpness. In the long run a return to the full picture in all its aspects is the only way in which contrast and aliveness can be maintained. Systematic long-term exclusion of certain aspects is therefore usually an indication of some fundamental error in the person's attitude to life. The existential approach is here in tune with common sense.

Common sense makes people intuit the unlikelihood of anyone ever being all good and perfect or completely in the right. People may admire another person's strength and virtue, but they will invariably long for the moment of this person's weakness and error. It is a relief when people turn out to be ordinary and capable of mistakes. The people who stand out ultimately are not those who create a temporary image of total control or sublime perfection, but those who are able to take their own weakness in their stride and rise above the difficulties that life poses them over and over again.

The existential practitioner will help the client to face her paradoxes, conflicts and contradictions, rather than aiming for one-sided accomplishments. Sessions will therefore be evaluated by the consideration of the extent to which the truth of the client has been pinpointed and contrasted with its missing elements. The final goal is not to produce the perfect human being, but one capable of negotiating contradictions in a personal, constructive and creative manner.

While paradox pervades the whole of human existence, it can be more easily pinpointed if different levels of experience and possible conflict are recognized. In Chapter 3, I present a framework that can provide a map for the location of particular areas of experience. In this way clients' problems in dealing with their inner contradictions can be made more specific. It can also make it easier to ensure that the principles that are recognized as guidelines for living get generalized to all levels of experience.

Chapter summary

1 Anxiety is the starting point of all counselling and psychotherapy.

2 Existential anxiety is that basic unease which we experience as soon as we become self-conscious and aware of our vulnerability and possible death.

3 Anxiety is an inevitable experience if we are to face the bare reality of existence. It can be temporarily silenced when we engage ourselves mechanically in life without asking questions. As soon as we are aware of our choices and possibilities anxiety becomes active again.

4 Anxiety indicates the level of awareness in a person. It is a measure of the extent to which we face up to the basic question of whether we will be or not be.

5 The existential approach does not seek to eliminate but rather to free anxiety: the courage to live is based on an ability to confront death. Creative use of anxiety then becomes possible.

6 People try to make it seem as if life can be safe, solid and secure. They have to learn to tolerate anxiety and uncertainty if they are to rise to the challenge of their own choices and responsibility.

7 Existential guilt is often a sign that people have failed to rise to the challenge of their anxiety and have tried to evade it by hiding away and not doing what they know is possible for them to do.

8 Not living to one's full capacity is one of the tragedies of human existence that can easily be remedied.

9 Dutiful living can be as much of an avoidance of life as opting out of it altogether by suicide or isolation and withdrawal.

10 Authentic living requires us to have clarity of our goals and intentions as well as a realistic assessment of our talents and abilities.

11 Authenticity cannot be attained unless we have a full awareness of the human condition and its inevitable struggles, limitations and impossibilities.

12 No one else's purpose will do. We have to find our own meaning of life and follow our own sense of direction. We have to be the author of our own destiny.

13 Authentic living brings motivation and enthusiasm to do well and with commitment what is worth doing.

14 Living authentically is difficult and can never be achieved fully, but aiming for it leads to increased vitality and enjoyment.

15 Inauthentic living is dutiful or haphazard and filled with discontents. It is based on alienation from life and estrangement from oneself.

16 Authentic living is not about pleasing oneself or being spontaneous and unrestrained. It is rather about genuinely making the most of life within the constrictions that we encounter.

17 Authentic living always takes the experience of personal defeat and fallibility as well as the limitations of human existence into account.

18 Clients are encouraged to find their own direction by the compass of their conscience.

19 The test of whether they are being truthful is whether or not they are taking contradictions and paradoxes of life into account.

20 To be ordinary and yet productive and creative to the best of one's abilities, whilst negotiating adversity constructively, is an objective worth working towards.

3

Clarification of Personal Worldview

The physical world

When examining the client's experience of the world it is useful to have a frame of reference to enable you to have enough distance from the client's experience to make sure that all different aspects of the client's reality are explored. The existential approach encourages a very personal approach to working with the client's predicaments and such a close resonance with clients needs to be safeguarded by a secure framework of reference.

Instead of using a diagnostic framework, which categorizes and labels personal characteristics, the existential approach proposes a framework that describes the basic dimensions of human existence. The idea is to provide a map of human existence on which an individual's position and trajectory can be plotted and understood. This allows the therapist to facilitate her clients' journey through life and encourage their expansion into new territory rather than restricting and limiting them by assigning them certain qualities and characteristics, which confine them to a set position.

Traditionally the existential dimensions have been described as being three-fold to include a physical, a social and a personal dimension, usually referred to with their German names of *Umwelt, Mitwelt* and *Eigenwelt* (Binswanger, 1946; Boss, 1963). Authors such as Buber (1923), Jaspers (1931, 1951) and Tillich (1952) imply a fourth, spiritual dimension, or *Uberwelt*, and this needs to be included and made explicit (van Deurzen-Smith, 1984). Translations of the German terms have varied with authors and with differences in understanding of the underlying concepts.

The *Umwelt* describes the natural world with its physical, biological dimension where the person is likely to behave in an instinctual manner. The *Mitwelt* describes the public world with its social dimension of human relationships and interactions where the person is likely to behave in a learnt, cultured manner. The *Eigenwelt* describes the private world with its psychological dimension of intimate and personal experience where the person is likely to have a sense of identity and ownership. The *Überwelt* describes the ideal world with its spiritual dimension of beliefs and aspirations where the person is likely to refer to values beyond herself and make sense of her existence.

Of the four dimensions, the natural world is the most fundamental. Clearly human existence is always anchored in an actual physical presence in a material world.

While it is tempting to assume that this physical world is entirely factual, even on this level of experience there are obvious individual variations of experience of those 'given' factors. One person will relate to her environment differently from another, according to her needs and to her perception of the pertinent features for her own survival (Von Uexküll, 1921). Subjective reality can thus be extremely diverse, even at this most basic and apparently concrete level of experience.

The implications of this observation are significant for the understanding of a client's personal experience of the natural world. Whilst people are, in Heidegger's terms, thrown into a factual physical environment (Heidegger, 1927), which puts certain constraints and limitations on them, their individual reactions to the given situation can vary considerably. Attitudes to the actuality of the natural boundaries are subjective even though the boundaries themselves are absolute. Inhabiting the natural world requires the observation of certain rules and laws, but the home one builds in it can constitute an experience of an utterly individual interpretation of that given world.

Exploring clients' relationships to the structure of their natural world is a crucial step in the full understanding of their way of being in the world. Various aspects of the natural world need to be taken into account. The dimension includes attention to bodily awareness of the whole range of physical sensations, both from internal and external sources. Body image, ability to stave off illness, fitness or weakness, attitude towards food, sex and procreation are all part of the particular natural world of the client. Notice needs to be taken of the client's ease or unease with the given climatic conditions, weather conditions and the concrete surroundings. Disturbances and preferences with any of these are seldom irrelevant.

Whereas the practitioner does not specifically question the client on any of these issues, whenever the client brings up one of these topics further exploration and clarification needs to be stimulated. It will often turn out that apparently unimportant topics brought up by the client in fact contain valuable information about her world and her reality.

Consider the following dialogue, for instance:

> *Client:* Yesterday was one of those days again, just as I went out to post a letter it started raining really hard, I had to dive back into the house so the letter got posted after it should have been.
> *Counsellor:* You hate getting wet, do you?
> *Client:* [*somewhat surprised*] I don't usually, I love the rain, it makes my hair curl. I think I didn't really want to post that letter.

After this the client goes on to develop the letter issue and its significance. The counsellor does not show particular approval or disapproval, nor does she focus on the avoidance issue or make any suggestion about other possible behaviour or about possible motivation for actual behaviour. All she does do is to indicate consistently where the client might turn her attention for examination of her own attitude and worldview. Simply by doing this the climate for further exploration is created. Not agreement, not challenge, but invitation to further exploration and clarification are the therapist's objective when worldviews are being examined. This creates an atmosphere of openness and wonder at new discoveries as the client's world starts to unfold in front of her. It gives her confidence to tackle any problems.

Gradually a clear picture will emerge depicting the client's natural worldview. Of course this will not happen in isolation but alongside the emergence of pictures of the other dimensions of the client's world. It will now become apparent whether the client has particular difficulties in managing her natural existence or whether she feels securely based in the physical world.

An obstruction in this area usually has far-reaching consequences for the other dimensions of existence. The natural world is the foundation of a person's being and a basic harmony on this level is a requirement for smooth functioning on other levels.

One can, for example, imagine a client who complains about her inability to establish a satisfactory love relationship, but who turns out to want that relationship only as a confirmation of her physical attractiveness. When it is found that she basically doubts her physical security the work will be directed towards her relationship with her body, before tackling the more complex issue of relating to another human being.

An ability to tune into the natural dimension of existence, with faith in the ultimate rightness of natural laws and a talent for creatively playing into these laws, generates enjoyment as well as it secures survival. People often cultivate such an ability in their hobbies, sport or leisure. Fishing, gardening, horse riding, sailing, rock climbing or playing golf are all examples of people's ability to play into their natural world and experience the thrill of being in tune with the environment and their body.

Because most leisure skills are such good examples of positive living in the natural world, it is often worthwhile using the metaphor of a person's preferred sport or leisure occupation to illustrate the more complicated struggles with life on other dimensions in a simple and concretely helpful and evocative manner.

Colin, who had tremendous difficulties in getting on with his teenage sons and who felt close to despair about ever improving his relationship with them, was also an avid sailor in his spare time. He became able to start making personal sense of his difficulties at home when he began to consider them in comparison with his expertise in sailing. He initiated this comparison indirectly by one day referring to his boys as gale-force winds who would soon devastate all he was trying to accomplish. Although he was at his wit's end in dealing with the boys, when asked how he would sail against gale-force winds, his imagination and resourcefulness were lively.

First he said he would not, which was a revelation in itself, as he had never considered not responding to his sons' provocations. Then he started describing occasions where he had had to face gale-force winds and the applications of this experience to his everyday difficulties were manifold.

The most fruitful element in this exploration was Colin's recognition of the fact that one would never go straight against the wind, one would have a flexible attitude and veer whenever necessary. In his relationship with his boys he would never veer, because he was afraid that they would not respect him if he were weak. With the sailing comparison it became suddenly obvious to him that, far from appearing weak, he would in fact be far stronger and more in charge of the situation by being capable of veering.

Moreover Colin was reminded of the importance of knowing the force of the wind and the currents in the water, which brought home his lack of knowledge about his sons' motivations for their destructive behaviour. He became appalled at the naivety of his approach with his boys. It had never before occurred to him that it would be possible to learn about the forces involved in relationships in the same way as one could learn about the force of the elements.

As soon as he had new hope for his improvement as a father, the idea of the possibility of enjoying his sons arose in his mind. Colin was particularly struck by the notion that it can sometimes be fun to drift with the wind, to change one's original plans and to steer in the direction the wind dictates, gaining great and exhilarating speeds.

At first his boys, who were not used to a playful father, resisted his attempts to join rather than fight them. Colin had to muster all his know-how as a sailor in order to steer clear of the rocks and icebergs they seemed to put in his way. It was only because he believed himself capable of tackling the gale-force wind of his sons' behaviour that he kept trying rather than giving up with irritation as he had been inclined to do in the past.

When Colin eventually sat down with his elder boy, determined to follow his lead rather than thwart him, he discovered the unknown pleasure of growing affection between the two of them. His son came sailing with him for the first time in five years. Though his relationship with the younger son remained strained for much longer, the improvement with the elder transformed the atmosphere in the house and, more importantly, opened up new prospects for Colin as a person.

Colin's basic ease and expertise in the natural world stood him in good stead when tackling problems in a domain where he was uneasy and relatively inexperienced. For other people difficulties are, on the contrary, focused on the very basic relationship to the natural world. Sometimes it may be that they lack confidence in their own body, sometimes that they lack trust in their physical environment. Almost always this kind of difficulty finds expression in bodily symptoms.

The respective experiences of Sophie and Michelle illustrate the two ends of the spectrum of natural world unease. Sophie had a relatively well-established trust in the external world, but a very poor sense of her own body. Michelle, on the other hand, had a relative confidence in her own body but an almost total mistrust of her physical environment. Interestingly, Sophie was grossly overweight (nearly twice what would have been considered a weight appropriate to her height) and Michelle was very thin (so thin that she looked transparent, with her bones showing through her skin). Neither of them had physiological problems other than those caused by their weight problem. Both came to counselling because of their dissatisfaction with their bodies. They did not know one another, but they contributed to each other's improvement unknowingly because their experience was so similar and yet in some ways so diametrically opposed that in clarifying one end of the spectrum light was often thrown on the other end.

In each case it was clear that the bodily manifestation of unease was a consequence of a more fundamental discordance with the natural world. For Sophie there was on the surface only one problem in life: her discontent with her body, which she referred to as a blob or a dead-weight. If only she could lose half her weight she would be fine and dandy, she said. For Michelle the problem was similar, she just wished she would stop throwing up food so that she could start to look like a normal human being. Everything would be all right as soon as her body would conform to her expectations.

In fact, the dissatisfaction with their bodies was in each case an expression of a much more radical difficulty in relating their own physical being to a material and substantial surrounding. Each of them tended to suspect their problems to be of an interpersonal nature. Both at some stage referred to fashion and pressure on women to conform to an ideal and unrealistic image of the female. Both also attempted to blame their difficulties on specific influential relationships in their lives. In the end, however, both only progressed by tackling the issues as primarily nature-related.

Sophie's story was very different from Michelle's. Sophie was in her middle thirties with a husband and three children. She did not work outside the home; in fact she hardly left it at all. She was ashamed of herself and thought it wiser to hide until she could lose weight. Of course the more she stayed in, the more she ate.

Michelle was in her early twenties, unmarried and unemployed. She had worked as a shop assistant several times but was unable to keep to the exhausting schedule. She would sometimes faint after standing for a long time. She would end up missing too many workdays and then get fired from the job. When on the dole she would sometimes spend days in bed without eating, surviving just on milk, which was the only sustenance her body would accept.

Both Sophie and Michelle had a loving family and relations who were willing to support them in their efforts to get back to a normal shape. Both despaired of the impact this sympathetic encouragement could have on their relentlessly failing efforts.

Sophie and Michelle had this in common: they lived their lives in alienation from the natural world, spending most of their time indoors and out of touch with their own bodies. Neither of them had an active sexual life. Sophie had sworn she would never allow her husband to get her pregnant again after the birth of her youngest child (now seven). Two years previously she had been sterilized for medical reasons, but that had not made any difference to the established situation of abstinence between her and her husband.

Michelle had great and intense horror of the very idea of sex after having been sexually assaulted when she was sixteen. She had in fact quite tender feelings about her own body, which she liked looking at in the mirror, but did not imagine how it could ever become strong enough to survive happily under the strain of life in the external world.

Sophie and Michelle each had a secret longing for the kind of security that would allow them to develop a vigorous and lively bodily existence rather than the fear and disgust with their natural world with which they currently lived.

For Sophie the image of bodily happiness was that of Lady Godiva: riding naked on a white horse with long hair flowing in the wind. In this fantasy it was the aspect of mastery over the environment, the speeding along with confidence, which appealed to her most. The nakedness symbolized pride in one's own body when the body was capable of such masterful mobility. She could in fact have comparative ease with a heavy Lady Godiva; she need not be slim, as long as she was strong and confident and dignified. The long hair was important. Sophie usually cut her own hair out of sheer frustration with her appearance, thus making sure she looked worse, with hair cut to shreds and out of shape.

In answer to the question of how she could make Lady Godiva come to life for herself, Sophie decided to take horse-riding lessons. She phoned several riding schools and sank back into despair on realizing that none of them had horses large enough to carry her. This made her aware of her weight in a more real way than ever before. For the first time it actually prevented her from doing something she felt motivated to do.

But this was not enough to make her diet; on the contrary, it made her despair about her own ability ever to make peace with the natural world. The effort was too big, too intense. She felt sure that if she had been able to experience the sense of freedom of galloping in the wind she would then have started losing weight, simply from using up more energy, from sheer enjoyment and thus not having to seek pleasure in food.

Now that Sophie was convincing herself that she would be all right if she could create this new experience of herself, it became easy to help her focus on finding alternatives to riding a horse. She attempted running and swimming, but felt discouraged and embarrassed when she realized how little stamina she had.

Then Sophie hit upon a brilliant idea. If horses were not strong enough to carry her, why not turn to a steel horse. She decided to learn to ride a motorbike and did so, although she had not even known how to drive a car previously. She enjoyed the challenge of this more than she had enjoyed horse riding as an adolescent and she became quite fanatical about it. She proved herself correct in her assumptions when she lost three stone (19 kg) without dieting during the year of her motorbiking apprenticeship. Even though this still left her overweight, she was not preoccupied with her weight, as all her attention was focused on what was turning into an absorbing hobby. She became fascinated with the mechanics of motorbikes as well as with riding them and she spent much time at a local garage.

Sophie's story was considerably more complex than this and her difficulties in living were not solved simply by tackling her attitude to her own body and the physical dimension of her world. She did, however, fare remarkably well through paying attention to her own lack of physical confidence and activity and then re-establishing this after pinpointing the direction in which she felt motivated to go.

Michelle likewise acted on her own insight into her lack of natural world confidence. For her the image of natural happiness was that of the ark of Noah, where all the animals lived side by side in peace. She imagined herself living on the ark and getting suckled by some of the mother animals whenever she was hungry. The idea of being close to animals appealed to her enormously. She often referred to the Disney film *Jungle Book* and wished that like Mowgli she could have been raised by wolves. While all this had significant implications for her experience of the social world and her relationships with various important others in her life, for the purpose of this account the focus will be exclusively on her relation to the physical dimension.

While Michelle became aware of her own desire for harmony with the natural world, specifically in the shape of closeness to animals, she also became acutely conscious of how she had consistently deprived herself of any such contacts. She had been forcing herself to try to come to terms with the harsh world of everyday life without letting herself breathe and enjoy the safety and comfort of the kind of physical world where she would feel at ease.

The idea of rearranging her life in such a way as to try to introduce positive elements into it, rather than trying to fight her symptoms, took root in her with enthusiasm. She started looking for a different type of job and after several disappointing experiences in applying for veterinary assistant jobs and pet shop positions, she decided to write to a number of kennels. She was taken on as helper in kennels a long way from her home. She earned very little money and worked hard, cleaning, feeding and walking dogs and enjoying every minute of it.

Michelle's problems were far from solved by this change, but the physical symptoms diminished. She developed a more healthy physical condition and stopped feeling distaste for and rejecting food. She was unable to pursue counselling on a regular basis in her new location and became excruciatingly aware of her isolation from other people. For Michelle, attention to the lack of natural-world relationships led to her perception of a lack in other areas as well. When she had built up enough confidence in the world outside through her close contact with animals and with concrete hard work on the most basic physical level, she felt ready to start tackling other issues.

So, while making adjustments to life on the natural dimension does not make everything all right (as indeed nothing will), it will often be a first step in the direction of a fuller appreciation of life in its various aspects. An ability to be in tune with the natural world, both in your own body and outside in your relations with the biological and physical environment, is a *sine qua non* of further development. When the ability to move between the various polarities in this sphere is established, this becomes a major strength to draw on.

The basic polarities on this dimension are those of surrender to the laws of the natural world or control over them. The aim in one's dealings with the physical dimension is therefore to develop a flexibility in one's interactions with the concrete and material demands of existence. It is about balancing activity and passivity and being prepared to face life and death, health and illness, security and insecurity. An aim of attempting to attain a situation of total material security must necessarily be illusory as it takes only one side of the polarity into account. By the same token, an aim of total control or mastery over the natural world is one-sided. Sophie found a way forward in recognizing her own desire for mobility, thus counteracting her previous attempt to fill herself with reassuring sustenance and hide away in the safety of her home. Michelle, on the other hand, benefited from the recognition of the need for her to discover ways in which she could find a safe environment to nestle in until she had gained enough resilience to move forward.

A balance needs to be struck between the security of the fireside and the challenge of new adventures. To use another natural metaphor, living can be likened to gardening, which requires insight into the necessity of a mixture of active controlling of the environment at times of seeding, weeding and pruning and passive receptivity during times of growth. At harvest time the intermediate position of active receptivity is then finally reached, completing the whole range of creative use of nature's cycles.

The social world

The second dimension of human existence is that of people's relations to others. Intimate relationships do not entirely fall into this category since they extend into the third, personal, world dimension. The relationships of the social world are primarily those of ordinary everyday encounters with others in a public capacity. The public world is the arena for all aspects of social interaction, which are an inevitable part of human existence.

In the same way in which human living is always situated against the background of the natural world, so the social world stands out as a second fundamental context. People's experience is embedded in a social, political and cultural environment, which determines actions, feelings and thoughts to a considerable extent. Whilst biological factors will always remain the most primary determinants, interpersonal factors must not be underestimated.

The role of the counsellor or therapist while focusing on the social dimension of the client's experience is similar to the one she plays when working on the physical dimension. She encourages clarification of the client's current attitudes towards the 'givens' of her world and stimulates insight into a wider perspective. The social realm of experience includes people's relationship to their race, their social class or other reference group, their country, language and cultural history, their family and work environment and their general attitude towards authority and the law.

Some of the crucial polarities that require attention are those of dominance and submission, acceptance and rejection, love and hate, sameness and difference. As with the other dimensions the aim is not to hold a systematic investigation of all of these elements, but to be alert to any consistent imbalance and elicit clients' reflection in areas where their perception is distorted or unclear.

Many clients have difficulties with their social world and many of the existing approaches to counselling and therapy focus on this aspect almost exclusively. The existential approach disagrees with the assumptions of the humanistic approach which dictates that human relationships ought to be modelled on total acceptance of and empathy for the other person, as this represents only one side of the inevitable polarity. This polarity is one of love and hate, appreciation and resentment, like and dislike. It can only be managed successfully if one is willing to face the paradox of human relationships. This paradox, as described by Sartre (1943), must be fully embraced or a situation of false caring or indifference will ensue. It consists of people's desire to dominate others, while being exposed to the attempts of others to dominate them in turn. This interplay of struggle for dominance and submission can be observed in animals as well, but the human capacity for reflective awareness of the process complicates matters considerably.

People are not content to dominate in a social situation. They want the others who submit to them to do this out of their own free choice, in an acknowledgement of their absolute superiority. Overwhelming people by brute force is seldom seen as an assertion of actual human power, whereas the subtleties of the strategic social game of aiming at winning people over to agree with one's point of view are often celebrated qualities.

Politics, legal matters and the media are all clearly and unashamedly based on this power game. But all human interaction on the public level follows the same basic rules, albeit perhaps in a less ostentatious manner.

The power conflict can be solved in four ways. The first three are based on the assumption that competition between people is inevitable. In accepting competition as one's model one can first of all attempt to gain mastery over others. One can secondly submit to others and devote oneself to them and make oneself indispensable to them in this way. One can thirdly withdraw from contact with others entirely and thus avoid the conflict and competition, at least momentarily. The fourth possibility is that of co-operation, which is a model that requires one to think of oneself as not in competition but in alliance with others. On the whole, co-operation can only succeed if the parties have the same interests and purpose. It will inevitably lead to competition with other groups that have opposing interests.

People often get stuck in one mode of functioning with others, abandoning their ability to reflect on the situation and omitting their choice in the matter. Thus people can end up feeling a victim of their own devotion to others or, on the contrary, become so preoccupied with their own interest that they wind up in an isolated position, cut off from any real exchange of contact, communication or affection.

Modern or postmodern Western culture encourages an almost aggressive individualism, which dictates the necessity of standing up for one's rights and protecting oneself against the continuous threat of other people invading one's territory. At the same time the still prevalent Judeo-Christian values require this individualism to be dressed up as humanitarian and unselfish co-operation.

Many clients get lost in this cultural dilemma. In working with them it is important to avoid colluding or encouraging despair by blaming the difficulties on culture or society. Instead, clients should be helped to recognize how the cultural dilemma is only an expression of a more fundamental paradox of human living: the tension between egoism and altruism. Neither can stand on its own, neither is all positive or negative. Both are essential ingredients of the dynamic process of the adjustment between self and others. In other cultures the same kind of conflicts arise, although perhaps for slightly different reasons and in different ways.

Adolescents are particularly likely to have difficulties in this area. Their disappointment with what society has to offer is often clustered around issues of exploitation or disregard of personal value. They struggle to find a place in a world that may seem hermetically sealed or too competitive for them to stand a chance to find a role in it.

Alex's struggle was in many ways exemplary of this teenage predicament. The intensity of her experience of the dilemma nearly cost her her sanity, as her youthful idealism prevented her from compromising and got her caught up in a double-bind situation.

Alex was the youngest daughter in a close-knit middle-class family. She had been consistently helpful at home and good at school until she was about thirteen. Her parents were progressive educators who had encouraged her to branch out from home from an early age. Alex had been involved in many hobbies and extracurricular activities. She had always had some close friends and had been liked by most people for her gentle and sensitive nature.

The moment Alex went into secondary education things started to become problematic. Most of her friends had gone on to private schools, whereas she had gone to the local comprehensive. While Alex realized this was the only option, because of her parents' financial constraints, she resented the fact that they had not even encouraged her to work for a scholarship, as they were strongly committed to state education.

She was able to make new friends at school, but none of these friendships were as close as the ones she had left behind. Perhaps more importantly, she felt alienated from her parents with whom she had always been very intimate. It seemed to her that they had found their principles more important than her own future. She felt especially disappointed with her mother who, she felt, was more concerned with the opinion of dad's colleagues than with her daughter's. Alex's elder sister had recently given up doing A-levels and was given a job in a children's home through a contact of one of dad's colleagues. Alex again felt that her parents had sold out her sister's future, preferring to see her work rather than letting her study. She also missed her sister.

Against this background of isolation and disillusionment Alex went through a number of upsetting experiences in school, involving theft, drugs and peer pressure on her to keep what she knew to herself. Alex was scared and did not know who to turn to: no one seemed trustworthy or interested any longer. Her former girlfriend, who was now at public school, did not take her worries seriously at all when she tried confiding in her. She felt sure that her mother would not want to know or would not believe her, might even blame her for having been involved in the situation. The other kids in school seemed to think her an oddball for having such high moral principles. She felt utterly alone.

For over two years Alex tried to live as if everything was all right and normal. In fact she was withdrawing from relating to other people, and as time went by increasingly became persuaded that the world was wicked. She kept a diary in which she tried to lay down rules that would preserve her own goodness and felt more and more afraid that she would become wicked like everyone else.

New events in her family confirmed her belief that her parents had once been good but now were growing as wicked as the world around them. She would have to try to remain good herself, resisting all temptations to take the easy way out and fall as others had done before her. It became harder and harder to keep going on with her life normally as she became more and more aware of the evil that people were up to around her. She felt that she must be the only one who was trying to resist. The classroom situation was particularly painful. Teachers seemed out to expose pupils for not doing their work properly or for not understanding the material adequately. Pupils were involved in almost continuous deceit, not working and not caring about their work, yet trying to pass for clever or assiduous in the teacher's eyes. Amongst themselves they would despise and expose those who did try to work and they would bully everyone into behaving in vile ways.

Alex felt under unbearable pressure, trying to maintain her integrity, yet going along with current trends. She despised herself for compromising as this only proved her growing wickedness. She was only trying to protect herself in going along with them, she was only being egotistical and so she must be like the rest of them. They too were all egoism with no regard for other people. She must try harder to be altruistic and not be so protective of her own interest. She must not be afraid any longer of being exposed for being different.

As soon as Alex had reached this conclusion her attitude at school and at home changed. She openly declared herself a sayer of truth. She stopped wearing make-up, she stopped smoking, she stopped pretending to be interested in her schoolwork. From now on she was going to be on the side of truth and altruism. At first her attitude was merely noticed as an expression of a purist or idealistic stance. Teachers were soon disconcerted at her open refusal to produce homework, but she became suddenly very popular with her schoolmates.

Alex observed these reactions to her changed behaviour with interest and she was astounded at the misunderstanding it demonstrated. Teachers were afraid of her non-performance rather than interested in the reasons for her refusal to play the school game any longer. The other children were excited by her daring to be different but only in so far as she was opposing the teachers. When she came to school dressed in a dustbin-liner one day instead of wearing her uniform, they made fun of her and cast her out. She was suspended and her parents were informed.

Now things really started deteriorating as Alex became more and more anxious about everyone trying to put a stop to her new form of honesty. Her parents were apologetic to the Head in her presence and she felt they were on his side rather than hers. They wanted to talk things over with her and bring her to reason. She vowed that all their efforts would be in vain. She had gone too far to toe the line again now. She felt she had a mission. She must tell the world what was wrong with it. If she did not do it no one would. Everyone else seemed content to keep wearing blinkers.

A few days after the row over the dustbin-liner there was to be a public performance of the school's orchestra and choir. In the middle of the evening Alex suddenly ran up onto the stage and stripped naked in front of everyone while making a speech about the need for honesty, purity and altruism. The music teacher managed to whisk her off the stage but this act of forceful intervention unchained all of Alex's violent despair. She fought like a wild animal and was only calmed down by an injection that the local doctor gave her half an hour later.

After this Alex spent ten days in a psychiatric ward and was seen as an outpatient for months afterwards. One of the things Alex kept referring to in counselling sessions was her disillusionment with other people's attitudes. It took weeks or even months before she could formulate specifically and concretely what she reproached them for. She would make general statements such as 'They're all in it, they're all playing a game, it looks good on the outside but wait till you see the inside.'

When she finally believed that the counsellor was taking her seriously and was genuinely interested in her worries, she very slowly started to put some detail into her allegations. First of all some factual information came to light which put Alex's paranoia in a new context. One of the few teachers she really liked and esteemed for his familiar way with pupils had been involved in drug dealing to some of her classmates. Making matters worse he had been covering up for one of the pupils who stole to get the money to pay for the drugs. From the way other kids who had known of these goings on had responded to her wanting to expose the teacher, Alex had concluded that she must have been naive about people up to this point. The morals she had thought to be binding apparently were not so in practice.

Her mother's behaviour had confirmed this suspicion. While she had received most of her ideals about human relationships from her mother, she had recently found out that her mother was having an affair with one of her father's colleagues. This made her feel cheated and bereft, even more so because Jane, her sister, had been extremely casual about it when she had tried discussing it with her. Jane told her in so many words that this was only to be expected for dad had had an affair with a female colleague for years and it was about time that mum fended for herself. She had added that Alex better realize that there was not going to be any point in hoping to do A-levels or study, because mum and dad wanted to be rid of them as soon as possible to start living their own separate lives.

Simply saying all these things to someone who would listen was clearly a relief to Alex, but it was not enough. Her view of the public world of human relationships was very negative and disturbed. She had had a rosy and unrealistic picture for years and had now fallen to the other extreme of having a sombre and unrealistic picture after having woken up from the dreamy world of her protected early childhood. Her crusade for honesty and altruism had been a last attempt to rebuild her childhood world and protect the illusions about the existence of a world where people were all good and frank with one another and where motivations of human interaction were mainly pure and aimed at understanding and helping others.

Although Alex had started to trust her counsellor, this trust was to a large extent based on her perception of the counsellor as a reminder of the positive image of human relationships. The counsellor's attitude of understanding reassurance, which had undoubtedly been essential to Alex talking to her at all, in some ways contradicted Alex's realizations about the world and in this sense the counsellor's attitude disturbed her.

One session, out of the blue, Alex attacked her counsellor verbally in the most violent way. She told her that she was a fake and a whore, cashing in on other people's problems, behaving as if she was an angel and in the mean time smirking inwardly about her own deceit. An egoist dressed up as an altruist, out to save the world out of self-interest.

The counsellor felt shocked at such intense disapproval of her efforts to help. She complained bitterly about Alex's lack of recognition of her real wish to help her and she told Alex how offended she was at the suggestion of her being mercenary when she was doing her job mostly out of humanitarian considerations.

Discussion with the counsellor in supervision put both her own reaction and Alex's outburst into a new perspective, which made progress possible. When the counsellor was asked what was so terrible about being told that she had egoistic motives for her desire to help other people, she realized that the intensity of her response and rebuttal to Alex was an expression of the same difficulty that Alex was struggling with. Their social worldview was based on the same erroneous assumption: it is bad to be egoistic and good to be altruistic.

Both the counsellor and Alex viewed themselves as being outstanding human beings who could be all good and devoted to others' well-being. This similarity in their outlook had made it possible for them to trust and appreciate one another. But now, Alex had been reminded of the unreality of her expectation that others would be good and totally devoted to her. She had seen the counsellor arrive in a new car and she had seen her flirting with one of the other staff at the clinic. This had reminded her of disappointments about her teacher's behaviour and about her mother's loyalty.

In supervision the counsellor was encouraged to think about the effect that different attitudes to Alex's aggression might have. She came to the conclusion that there were basically three alternatives. She might first of all try to convince Alex that the world of human relationships really could be as ideal as she wished to believe. She could do this by devoting herself even more to the client than she had done before and by being available for Alex at any time, building up an intimate personal relationship. She imagined that Alex would like this very much at first, but that inevitably a time would come when she would have to disappoint her expectations and that Alex would probably not take that lightly as she would have been allowed to build up an illusory and magical world which would suddenly come to an end.

Second, she might dismiss Alex's behaviour as an expression of her mentally disturbed condition and treat her accordingly as a mad person, giving up counselling sessions and leaving treatment to the psychiatrist. The counsellor realized just how attractive this option was. The inclination was in this direction and everybody else seemed to hold this view anyway. The only thing holding her back from giving up on Alex was her own wish to be able to think of herself as doing everything possible to help this girl. This conflict in the counsellor demonstrated the tug of war between egoism and altruism. Reflecting on this brought her face-to-face with the contradiction in her own attitude. At the same time as she tried to maintain a picture of herself and Alex as ideal people attempting to be other-centred, she was driven by a need for gratification from the other's appreciation of her efforts and acknowledgement of her goodness. This was clearly, as Alex had pointed out so expressively, a manifestation of intense self-centredness.

The counsellor started to protest her innocence until she was asked what was so terrible about an egocentric motivation. What made it necessary to reject any hint of selfishness, what was wrong with self-protection? Was it not precisely because of a lack of egocentricity that Alex was unable to protect herself against others' abuse and why she was going under? What Alex needed most was confirmation of the right to be selfish, confirmation of the positive aspect of egocentricity.

It was considering these questions that led the counsellor to stop feeling threatened by Alex's attack and made her consider a possible third alternative. It was possible to view Alex's outburst as clamouring for a more real relationship with her counsellor; one based on insight into the limitations of people's ability to be there for others without thinking of themselves. If the counsellor could admit her own limitations to herself and, what is more, if she could see the good side of her limitations, then she would be able to help Alex do the same.

When the counsellor started reviewing the dreaded session in a much more relaxed, humorous way, she was able to smile about Alex's caricature of herself. In the following session Alex appeared repentant of her previous outburst, making an effort to re-enlist the counsellor's full support. Drawing on the understanding of her own motivation to make up and pursue the previous idyllic but fake counselling relationship, the counsellor resisted her own temptation to go along with Alex's repentance. The following dialogue took place:

> *Counsellor:* You seem to want to forget what you said on Tuesday.
> *Alex:* I didn't mean it.
> *Counsellor:* You didn't mean to attack me?
> *Alex:* I didn't mean to hurt you.
> *Counsellor:* You didn't want to hurt me but some of the things you said were important.
> *Alex:* [*sounding surprised*] Yes. [*Pause*] They were. [*Thirty seconds silence, then*] Aren't you angry?
> *Counsellor:* No. Not any more.
> *Alex:* I said some horrible things. It wasn't really me you know. It just takes over sometimes. I really can't help it.
> *Counsellor:* I'm glad you can't help it, because you would stop yourself from saying things like that if you could, wouldn't you?
> *Alex:* I don't like it. It's horrible.
> *Counsellor:* It's horrible to realize that you want to say nasty things to people?
> *Alex:* It's horrible to think them.
> *Counsellor:* Why is that so horrible?
> *Alex:* I don't know [*thinking*]. Because I can't help it, it just happens. I want it to be all good and then something happens to spoil it all and I start having these horrible thoughts about people.
> *Counsellor:* Like with me last Tuesday. You suddenly realized I'm here with you doing my job, not just because I like you. [*Alex sighs; ten seconds silence.*]
> *Counsellor:* You wanted to think I was all there for you but you just had to see that that wasn't possible and that there was a limit to what I can give you.
> *Alex:* [*hardly audible and choked*] Yeah. [*Pause, then, still tearfully*] I don't want things to be this way.
> *Counsellor:* Which way?
> *Alex:* Cold and nasty. People using one another.
> *Counsellor:* You mean I'm using you to earn a living and you're using me to get some clarity in your confusion?
> *Alex:* Mmm [*nods emphatically*].
> *Counsellor:* Is that cold and nasty? Is that wrong? [*This is spoken very softly*]
> *Alex:* I don't know now. [*Hides face in hands. She weeps inaudibly for nearly two minutes, rubbing tears off her cheeks violently. Then in a half-suppressed sob*] I wanted to believe in love.
> *Counsellor:* But what kind of love?

Alex now proceeded to describe the way she imagined ideal human relationships. The counsellor encouraged her to be more and more specific about the implications of her views and finally succeeded in helping Alex to acknowledge the pitfalls and weaknesses of such a one-sided position.

Many sessions were spent on the further elaboration of alternative views. Although Alex kept harking back to her idealized notions of a loving and altruistic world, the counsellor would consistently remind Alex of the negative implications of such an unrealistic fantasy and confront her with the negative aspects of altruistic behaviour. One of the most enlightening insights was the realization that Alex's mother had probably withheld information about Alex's father's and her own affairs out of altruistic love, so preoccupied with her daughter's well-being that she was unaware of the harm she was doing her.

Then it also started to dawn on Alex that her parents' protective attitude during her early childhood, during which time they had prevented her from being exposed to the harsher realities of the world, had also been a result of genuine loving intentions. Protecting her had had certain positive effects, but it had also had negative consequences in the form of Alex's sense of feeling lost in the jungle of the 'real world' of her comprehensive school.

The counsellor was now able to use a comparison with her own original temptation to protect Alex from the realization that the counselling relationship was a professional one. She pointed out to Alex that sooner or later she must come to terms with the reality of egocentricity and the necessity for people to protect their self-interest. Alex recognized the advantage of having been made aware of the limitations of the counselling relationship and thus started to develop a sense of the possible positive aspects of self-centredness.

Now that her outlook was broadening Alex started to distinguish between honest egoism and blind altruism. The first was her brand name for the recognition of one's own needs and boundaries and the pluck openly to state these and protect them. This replaced her previous obsession with altruism and pure honesty and incorporated most of the elements of those things that she valued but in a way that respected the demands and givens of 'the real world'. The second seemed to cover much of what she had previously thought of as wickedness. The major change involved her appreciation and acceptance of human weakness and misunderstanding, which she used to disregard entirely. It also involved her recognition of the possibility of good intentions being at the origin of much pain and disappointment.

Alex's problems were a lot more complex than this account but her conflicting views of the public world of human relationships were undoubtedly the most disturbing element for her. Some of these new insights gave her a key to a more liveable approach.

Many young people contend with similar issues. Whilst not all of them come as close to the edge of insanity, many try to escape from the contradictions of which they feel unable to make sense in any other way. Drug or alcohol abuse, crime, violence and compulsive sex are all different ways of reacting to the lack of clarity in the public world of human relationships.

Alex's breakdown was intense and she could easily have stayed locked into her unreal world. The psychiatric system was ready to treat her for schizophrenia, with good intentions but exposing her to the risk of a lifelong career as a mental patient, further undermining her already skimpy belief in her own ability to cope with the harshness of living.

While people like Ronald Laing and Thomas Szasz clearly describe this destructive process (Laing, 1960, 1961; Szasz, 1961), little so far has been said about the way in which the constructive or reconstructive process of unification of the self in relation to others can be helped along.

In sketching such a process the consideration of all the dimensions of existence is important. Looking at Alex's experience, what comes to the fore is that she had a very unrealistic social world relation, but a well-established natural world relation, which was a direct result of her parents' efforts to expose her to many extracurricular activities (including mountain-climbing and swimming). The skill and enjoyment that she was capable of in the natural world were a constant background of hope and support for her in her struggles.

But, perhaps most importantly, Alex was blessed with intelligence and this made her capable of a basic frankness with herself; she had a lively inner world, a constant closeness to herself, which shielded her from falling into the depths of despair. In her worst moments, even if her thinking was sometimes illogical and unrealistic, there was this belief in her own solidity, which made her want to go out and change the world rather than give up completely and destroy herself.

A person's confusion in the social world will be considerably increased if it is unmitigated by this reference to an inner world. It is one's relationship to the private dimension of a personal world that needs to be examined next.

The personal world

The third dimension of the client's world that needs to come under scrutiny is that of her relationship to herself. This private world is the land of intimacy. It includes intimacy with self as well as intimacy with others. The personal world is the home world: the place where you feel at ease with yourself, because you are surrounded by familiarity and kinship. This private world is the world of the I and the We. It encompasses everything that is felt to be part of oneself.

The inner world includes feelings, thoughts, character traits, ideas, aspirations, objects and people, in as much as these are identified as your own. Although modern society encourages individualism to the extent of an outgoing and self-confident, natural and public-world relationship, it does not favour the development of a rich inward life. People's private worlds are often surprisingly arid and empty. Many clients come to counselling or psychotherapy in the hope of finding themselves in the process. Many others are not even aware of their inner void and deprivation.

When clients start out talking about themselves, trying most accurately to describe and express who they are, it soon becomes evident where they situate themselves. Some will devote great attention and detail to descriptions of their natural world, by emphasizing physical ailments for instance. Others will go on at great length over their various roles, describing frustrations in their relationships with others, thus demonstrating a primary concern with the social world. Those who are pressingly preoccupied with their personal world may emphasize the particular strengths and weaknesses of their character and personality, which they feel to be of importance. When working with couples their preoccupation with private-world issues may be indicated by a mutual attention to faults and peculiarities.

As with the other dimensions, the object of exploring the personal-world relation is for the client to get a fuller grasp of her experience and to become able to embrace the paradoxes that she may previously have tried to side-step or evade.

What first needs to be established are those aspects of the client's private world which she considers to be her assets. How does this individual experience her special character and personality, how does she relate inwardly to herself? What does she think of as her special private universe, or how has she compromised such a haven of privacy? The guiding question is: where in herself is this client at home, if anywhere? Then the exploration proceeds in the direction of possibly revealing new and hidden aspects of these qualities. Quite often the exploration starts with an expression of negative qualities and the challenge is then to unearth the hidden potential in what is apparently negative.

Raymond's self-exploration is a good illustration of this process. He was a forty-two-year-old history teacher, who was, as he put it, unmarried, childless, relationship-less and in search of something to sweeten the taste of life. Raymond had attended various humanistic workshops, gaining much enjoyment from new discoveries about himself and others. He had eventually joined an ongoing group, which defined itself as a person-centred encounter group.

In this group Raymond was soon confronted with an almost unanimous and vociferous disapproval of what he himself saw as one of his main characteristics. The other group members told him he was too analytical, too rationalistic and intellectual, in short that he was 'all in his head'. Now, on the one hand, this criticism coincided with his own disgust with his current lifestyle, which he found far too dry and tedious. On the other hand, he resented the attack on a quality that he greatly prized in himself. Finally he decided, and not without misgivings, that he must take their opinion as an indication that the time had come for him to make some changes. If so many people disapproved of his rationality, there must be some sense in blaming his dissatisfaction with his teaching life on this character fault.

Even though he still felt hurt and misunderstood by the other group members, he applied for a leave of absence from his job. He then set out on a journey to India with one of the people who had criticized him most severely and who had persuaded him to let go of his old ways and discover his feelings.

The trip was a total failure. Raymond did not get along with his travel partner after a honeymoon period of a few days. Though he enjoyed the exposure to a different culture, he asked himself often what it all was supposed to prove. He found that he did not want to give up his rationality, that oozing feelings confused him and that an intelligent approach to overcoming difficulties on his journey was far more effective than the self-indulgent sentiments with which his travel partner responded.

He returned to England much sooner than planned and was inclined to pick up his job immediately, but finally decided that he would allow himself some time to think things over. This is when he contacted a therapist.

It was soon evident that Raymond was still preoccupied with the negative reception of his rationality. He was quite sure that the sentimental approach was not his cup of tea and that encounter groups were therefore not the best place to understand himself, since he would not wish to give in to the group pressure to conform to certain norms of behaviour. He was nevertheless terrified that they were right and he was wrong and that he therefore would be forever condemned to a life of staleness and boredom.

Exploring his inner world on his own terms rather than measuring it for size in order to conform was what Raymond wanted to do. He found that the intellectual focus of his personality could stretch far beyond mere rationalism. Apart from intelligence and resourcefulness, it also provided him with quick insights into the salient aspects of a situation or event. This was what made him a good historian. It also made him capable of appreciating the humorous side of tragic situations. He was most appreciative of witty comedy and an admirer of Woody Allen and 'Monty Python'.

What became clear to Raymond when he was elaborating his own views on his rationality was that he had so far really not reaped the benefits of his brainy mentality. He had allowed the whole world to dictate to him certain conditions, which systematically reduced his strengths to weaknesses and made him a slave to either the pursuit of a tedious career or to vain attempts at adopting a lifestyle totally out of tune with his basic talents.

His private world had thus been invaded by the influence of public opinion, depriving him of the satisfactions that he knew himself capable of when allowing the pursuit of the pleasures of his brainy inclination. Talking about these pleasures and this familiar witty appraisal of the world, brought him back to an appreciation of his personal universe.

Now it suddenly seemed absurd to Raymond that he had become bogged down in a boring routine. He remembered his joy at discovering all the different facets of history during his student days and wondered why the teaching of the subject that fascinated him had to be such a dull profession. He surprised himself by hitting on a brilliant notion one day, when he was deploring the fact that school teaching and wit seemed absolute polar opposites. The idea struck him that bringing those opposites together would be just the sort of thing that would challenge him.

There was no stopping Raymond once this idea had entered his head. He redesigned his teaching as a course on humour throughout history. He had his pupils do projects on historical jokes and he had them write and research witty anecdotes about whatever period was on the syllabus. He was extremely gratified to find many pupils responding most actively to this new approach. His vanity was flattered when one of his classes voted him most popular teacher.

Raymond now started writing academic papers about his findings as well as about his own witty observations of historical events. He had devised creative ways of exploiting his inner world of thought. In doing so he learnt to draw on both sides of the existing inner paradox of being both serious and sensitive to humour and wit. He stopped feeling guilty about what he was and trying to comply with other people's suggestion that he needed to let himself be more sentimental and less rational. In following a path into his personal world, he found ways of replenishing himself rather than continuing to deplete himself in an attempt to ignore his inner world and adjust to external routines and demands.

Raymond was dissatisfied with his lifestyle, but change for the sake of change would not do. As he put it, it just was not him, it did not feel right and therefore he felt unmotivated to put much energy into even trying to be all feeling-oriented or live a life of escapism. He wanted to be rational and face reality, even duty, but he had to discover ways of doing this in a creative and stimulating manner.

As soon as Raymond began to be aware of his inner strength, a new motivation started flowing, fuelling his inventiveness and ability to appreciate and enjoy himself by doing well what he was most capable of doing. No one needed to make any suggestions or prod him into action. He had rediscovered a secure base in himself and from there could experiment and explore with confidence. This contrasted starkly with the lack of self-confidence and motivation that he had experienced whilst trying to conform to the norms of his reference group.

Being at home in oneself and with oneself is exceedingly important for satisfactory relationships in the public world, but it is essential if one wants to establish a close and intimate relationship in the private sphere.

Genuine closeness and intimacy with another human being are difficult to acquire. To merge into one being and think in terms of 'us' rather than 'you and me' is these days not only rare, it is also taboo. There seems to be an unspoken rule in modern society that designates close relationships as dangerous and regressive.

From an observation of disturbed and deteriorating marital relationships, it has been concluded that all couples who get too close to one another are in danger of suffocating each other and that therefore moderation in love is as important as passion in sex. While this observation most certainly applies to relationships in the public world it disregards those on the private dimension.

On the public level, as we have seen, there are three main options for relating to others: dominance over, submission to or withdrawal from the relationship. Even in relationships that are apparently built on the principle of co-operation, the underlying motivating force is still that of hoped-for dominance. This makes the co-operative phase of the relationship likely to end at any time where one of the partners sees their way to dominance.

If a relationship is formalized, the formal structure may maintain each of the partners within the prescribed boundaries of their roles. Without such formalization the relationship is bound to become the battling ground for the struggle for dominance. Currently in Western society the boundaries of relationships are rarely so formalized that they cannot be questioned, thus divorce, strikes, political unrest and various other forms of the challenge of authority can be observed to be on the increase. When public relationships are informal people need to become capable of complementing them with strong private relationships if they are not to flounder in chaos and alienation.

In private-world relations people do not seek to be better than another, because they are identified with the other. It would make no sense to fight that which is experienced as essentially part of oneself. Of course most external relationships (even marital ones) are almost exclusively in the public dimension. This explains why too much closeness in most of these relationships must entail a danger of becoming enslaved to another.

In fact, as Binswanger suggests (Binswanger, 1944), even people's relationship to themselves can be structured in the plural mode of the public world. They then experience no unity within themselves but are divided against themselves, struggling with conflicting elements, seeking dominance over themselves rather than finding the inner source of dynamic paradox.

It is important to make the distinction between public- and private-world relations rather than between external and internal ones or ones with others and ones with self. Both relationships with others and those with oneself can take place in the public dimension of competition or in the private dimension of kinship and affinity.

While all relationships with other people have a public dimension, only a few relationships with others ever take on a private and personal dimension. This happens as soon as the other is accepted and recognized as akin to oneself, in the most intense meaning of the word, and adopted as an integral extension of one's selfhood.

Clearly it is only possible to establish such relationships with others if there is a clear sense of 'self-ness' first. Even then it cannot be taken for granted that the private relation to the other will always remain personal; it will fall back into the domain of public relationships as soon as the active merging into a unit fails. This will happen as soon as the two individuals stop experiencing themselves as fully relating to themselves and stop feeling at home with their inner world.

Paul and Pamela had first-hand experience of the tragedy of a lack of private-world relation to themselves and one another. Each had some experience of building up a personal world and a private relationship to themselves before they met. Paul had been used to getting up very early in the morning, to walk in the countryside and spot birds. It used to give him a feeling of comfort and ease and closeness with himself. He gave up doing this within a year of his marriage to Pamela, who disliked the countryside and hated it when Paul got out of bed early.

Pamela herself used to spend her evenings taking baths and doing her hair and face, adoring this solitary grooming as a way of getting ready to confront the demands of the social world. It was the time of the day she used to prefer, because it allowed her to enjoy herself on her own. However, she ceased her grooming activities when it became obvious that Paul hated waiting for her and when there was no time to waste in getting ready, since nearly every evening was spent going out with Paul.

Paul and Pamela loved one another very much, they enjoyed being together and their marriage was a happy one for over seven years. They each had a busy professional life and decided that there would be no time for them to have children. They were involved in many activities and their evenings and weekends were booked for months ahead.

On the outside everything seemed perfectly normal and they continued to see their marriage as a basically happy one. Then, within one week, Paul's father died of a heart attack and their closest friends' marriage came to an abrupt end because of an infidelity. Suddenly they were at loose ends. Paul did not know how to cope with his father's death at all and his friend was not available to support him, because he had run off with his new girlfriend. Pamela, who should have stood by him, was totally absorbed in her friend's distress over her husband's leaving and less interested in Paul's pain over the loss of his father than suddenly suspicious of his fidelity to her.

On his own most of the time all at once, because Pamela spent evening after evening with the lonely friend, Paul felt as if he was waking up from a superficial and transitory state of blissful ignorance. It seemed to him as if the marriage had been like some sort of business transaction, which had now reached its expiry date. It was as if he had never even known Pamela, as if she were a total stranger. He thus no longer felt bound by their mutual arrangements and started getting up early to go walking in the countryside to see the sun rise and watch birds. It gave him the peace he longed for in coming to terms with his father's death. Pamela now had evidence for what she had suspected: Paul was being unfaithful to her and would undoubtedly want to leave her in the same way as her friend's husband had.

At first the two of them rowed over their mutual misperceptions. Paul reproached Pamela for not caring one toss about his father's death and letting him down in the most difficult situation he had ever found himself in. Pamela reproached Paul for not wanting her by his side any more as he clearly had more important things to do. She felt that Paul was entirely preoccupied with his own grief, without paying any attention to the pain she herself was experiencing from identifying with their friends' miserable divorce proceedings.

Paul by this time was rediscovering the pleasure of his own company on his morning outings and felt annoyed at the way in which Pamela tried to force him back into the old pattern of their shared life. He knew already that what he had given up for the sham of married life was too important to lose again. He thought that his father had given him back to himself by dying so suddenly and exposing the weakness of his bond with his wife, reminding him of the world of birds and the morning life: the universe where he felt at home and at one with himself. His father had taught him about this when he was five or six years' old and he had renounced it for the love of Pamela, which now turned out to have not been worth the sacrifice. He was most offended at the suggestion of his infidelity and despised Pamela all the more as she clearly preferred seeing him through the eyes of her friend rather than her own.

Pamela was at first quite excited about the shared experience of estranged husbands. She found a sort of perverse enjoyment in talking with her friend Anne, about the unfairness of her husband's treatment of her and making comparisons with Paul's obsession with his father's death and his increasing absences from home. In this she found the kind of closeness to another human being that she had not had with Paul. She started to realize that what she had thought to be an ideal marriage had in fact been a shallow imitation of the real thing.

While Paul and Pamela continued to live together for another year, during this time they had row after row and Paul turned more and more to his own company, as Pamela's relationship with Anne became her source of intimacy. The situation went on like this until Anne's husband returned home and made it abundantly clear to Pamela that she should stay in her own home with Paul rather than plotting with Anne against him. Pamela, who was impressed with Anne's attempts to fix things up with her husband, decided to make a go of it as well. She tried to persuade Paul to patch things up between them. Paul refused and told her he was not interested in compromising his re-found world for a woman who had no sense of inner dignity and no appreciation for anything but appearances and women's gossip.

Pamela felt devastated. Suddenly she was left with nothing in her life to hold on to. Anne had been trying to persuade her to withdraw from the fashion business that they ran together, because her husband wanted to reinvest the money elsewhere for Anne and him to make a new start at something as a couple rather than separately. Paul would not support her in trying to keep the business, even all by herself, because he did not believe her capable of managing it on her own.

Now it was her turn to discover that she needed to rely on her inner resources to cope with life, but she felt there was nothing solid to rely on. After having begged Paul one morning not to go out but stay with her because she needed him and his leaving anyway after telling her to learn to be happy in her own company, she had an accident in the bath. She washed her hair and then took the hair-dryer with her in the bath to do her hair while still soaking; she nearly electrocuted herself and was found unconscious with her head hanging over the rim of the bath by Paul when he returned home.

Though her physical condition gave no cause for concern, it was obvious that she had come within an inch of dying. The hospital treated the situation as attempted suicide and referred her to a psychiatrist, who in turn referred both Paul and Pamela to a relationship counsellor. Paul and Pamela now started on a year of counselling, which brought them face to face with the way in which they had looked to one another to fill the emptiness of their inner worlds. During this year they discovered how they had given up their private world in order to relate exclusively to one another and to the social world around them. The fact that they each could recognize this superficial arrangement as an interference with their intimacy and their personal enjoyment brought them back in some agreement.

They were encouraged to spend a lot of time giving an individual account of what these last seven years had been like for them and on explaining to the other partner how they had experienced the marriage as not providing enough room for their internal life. Like most couples, they found it hard to listen to each other and were inclined to start defending their own position whenever the other said something that seemed like an attack on their good intentions.

The counsellor then proposed individual counselling sessions with each of the partners once a week, while the other partner was present as an observer, with a time for some feedback and processing afterwards. This way the emphasis was on the exploration of the private worlds of the two people rather than on their relationship. In working this way it was of the greatest importance that the focus be systematically brought back on to the inner experience of the partner who was working, to avoid talking about or interpreting the other's behaviour and attitudes.

The following interaction is an example of how the counsellor would typically deal with such an occurrence.

Pamela: Yesterday we had another row. Paul wanted to spend another day in Norfolk [one of his favourite bird-spotting areas] and I just couldn't stand it and shouted at him. We had promised some other friends that we would probably spend the weekend with them and I thought it very unfair of Paul to spoil the occasion for me. I couldn't very well go there alone, as he claimed, because everybody else would be in couples. Paul just doesn't understand how I feel. His birds are more important than I am to him.

Counsellor: Now wait a minute. There is no point in us speculating about what is or isn't important to Paul; that's his territory. Our task is to find out what your experience of the situation is. So let's look at that. You wanted to spend the Sunday with Paul, as a couple visiting friends.

Pamela: Yes. Together, as it used to be.

Counsellor: The togetherness is what is most important to you now, isn't it?

Pamela: Well, yes, that's what marriage is all about, is it not?

Counsellor: Is it?

Pamela: Yes of course, without that you might as well give up and get a divorce. You've got to make an effort and stick by each other's side. That's what Paul should do more often.

Counsellor: Like you?

Pamela: Ehh, yes. [*Hesitant and defensive*] Well, at least I try to.

Counsellor: You try to do what?

Pamela: *I* try to be with him as often as possible.

Counsellor: Even when you don't want to do what he wants to do. [*This is said in an affirmative and appreciative way.*]

Pamela: Well, no. [*Thinks for a few seconds*] Not really. Oh, well. [*Looks embarrassed*] Yes. I see what you mean.

Counsellor: What do I mean?

Pamela: That I am not prepared to do for him what I expect him to do for me.

By systematically focusing on the experience of the partner who was talking and refusing to collude with any complaints about the partner who was observing, it was fairly easy not only to gain the trust of both partners but also to make them interested in each other's perceptions and experience.

Paul and Pamela discovered that they had not allowed themselves much time to live for themselves and that neither had had much of a chance to develop an inner centre of reference. Yet they were amazed at the richness of their partner's inner world once this private landscape started to unroll before their eyes.

Though it took Pamela considerably longer than it took Paul before she felt secure in her own inner world, both partners eventually developed a sense of inner awareness and private understanding of themselves which gave them the required peace and confidence from which to advance back in the direction of their spouse. They rebuilt a relationship between them and decided to start a family. Unfortunately, Pamela was in the low-fertility range and they were unable to have children when they wanted to. This led to more difficulties between them as they had different views about how to remedy the situation. They had more counselling and eventually decided to go their separate ways, which they did to mutual satisfaction.

Couples' relationships are often built on a lack of intimacy with themselves and others. In fact relationships can become an excuse for the avoidance of intimacy with oneself. In order to create a full existence on the personal-world dimension one has to dare to be alone first. An intimate and secure relationship with oneself can only be generated if some basic facts of life and death get faced. Building up a sense of confidence and courage in oneself can only be done by exposing oneself to the raw realities of living, without hiding in the comforting company of the social world. Knowing that one is capable of standing alone even in the face of fate and disaster gives a sense of private reality which makes the world a less frightening and more rewarding place. Only from the security of this inner reality can others be approached and merged with in the intimate manner of the private world. When this happens relationships are formed which are secure and basic, rather than ephemeral and artificial, as are those on the social dimension of the public world.

Making connections with the final fourth dimension of human existence will help people in putting down deeper roots in the personal world or indeed in the physical or social world. This fourth dimension is that of the spiritual world of ideas, values and meanings. In fact strength and flexibility of personality and character are almost invariably connected to a strong sense of what one values in the world and values are what define the spiritual dimension.

When clients are hesitant in their relation to themselves on the private dimension, it is often helpful to encourage them to reflect on what it is that really matters to them or is most deeply meaningful. This in turn will bring them closer to themselves in a spiritual way, as they define their own purpose.

The spiritual world

In any therapeutic work, sooner or later the client's relationship with the ideological level of her beliefs and values will become the central focus. Just as the first dimension of the natural world referred to a person's connection to the concrete aspects of living in a physical environment, so the fourth dimension of the spiritual world refers to a person's connection to the abstract and metaphysical aspects of living.

For many people this dimension can be understood to represent the religious element of their existence. For others any reference to spirituality or religion is off-putting. Most people will be able to relate to the notion of a dimension which represents their ideas and beliefs about life, the world, themselves and the beyond. The spiritual world is the domain of experience where people create meaning for themselves and make sense of things.

Often people are hardly aware of this dimension, especially if they are convinced that they have completely abandoned childhood religion. They then may live their lives simply taking one day at a time and not attempting to make sense of what appears to them as the plain requirements of everyday life. Of course even such a pragmatic outlook on life represents a philosophy and an ideology. Every person has an implicit worldview.

Existential therapy always aspires to cast light on the implicit ideological outlook of the client and will gently urge her to uncover her values and make them explicit for herself. The discovery and revaluation of old ideals, which were there all along, hidden away under the polish of adaptation to social world values, is often an experience of great relief to clients who thought themselves incapable of believing in anything, for lack of a purpose or self-direction and independence.

Current therapeutic approaches often indirectly encourage people to find role models and pattern themselves after an example, particularly the example of the therapist. The existential approach advocates a return to the unfashionable practice of shaping one's life after one's ideals. Not imitation of the socially desirable but aspiration to the ideally valid is seen as the motivating force *par excellence*.

When people rediscover their inner connectedness to something greater than themselves, to some ideal which will lift them beyond their everyday struggles, a new motivation flows inside of them, which can carry them through difficulties with unerring purposefulness.

Clients often feel hesitant to claim back this dimension of their experience as it is clearly not one that is currently given much credit. In a scientific and materialistic era physical and social world relations are in the foreground. The personal dimension is often pursued in a rather limited and self-centred manner, but the spiritual dimension is quite often considered taboo and outdated. We have thrown out our ideals together with our religions and people's values are often muddled and confused (van Deurzen, 1998).

The spiritual revivalism of some transpersonal approaches does not contribute to giving this dimension a good press either. Clarifying a person's way of relating to this spiritual dimension is not about the cultivation of mystical and transcendental experiences (even though it might be that for some people). It is about making explicit a person's existing views on life. Understanding the ideal world of a person means grasping how this person makes sense of the world and what it is she lives for and would be willing to die for.

Formulating the values that one lives by is often the first step in the direction of solving problems on the social, personal or physical dimensions as well. When it becomes obvious that certain ideals and values are very important to a person, she will often find a new strength to implement those ideals and values regardless of external or internal pressures and impediments. Having to overcome public opinion, physical obstacles or character weaknesses can suddenly seem like minor challenges against the background of the worth-while enterprise of fulfilling one's aspirations. Rising to the challenge of one's own ideals can instil a whole new meaning to life and with this sense of purpose comes a vital aliveness and passion which are commonly considered unattainable (see Frankl, 1955, 1967).

In working on the spiritual dimension with clients it is important to realize that the moral principles they need to discover are not necessarily the same as those of the practitioner or those of contemporary society. The thing that is most important to one client may be relatively unimportant to another client or to the therapist. What matters is to help each individual in establishing her own priorities, helping her to reach for her particular elementary motive (see Midgley, 1981). In doing this, the practitioner must be careful to assist the client in distinguishing between values picked up from conformity to external reality and values expressing the individual's internal truth. Sometimes the two may be intertwined or even identical.

For Douglas the purpose and value of life had always been neatly regulated by an external order into which his existence had fitted very nicely. He was brought up in a strict Catholic family in a large Australian town. His parents were both part of the medical establishment, and his father was a well-respected surgeon. Douglas, like his elder brother before him, was ready to tread in his father's footsteps, when the opportunity arose for him to come to England for a two-year specialist medical training which would prepare him for a non-surgical career. Without much doubt about the rightness of this move, Douglas decided to take this 'once in a lifetime' opportunity and without further ado, even though his family disapproved slightly of his change of direction, he travelled to Britain.

At first he enjoyed his stay in Britain very much. He had never been out of Australia before and he made the most of his move by visiting all the sights up and down the country, whenever he had a free moment. He kept so busy with his work at the hospital and his trips and visits that he, as he said, hardly noticed he was away from home. Then, after the better part of his first year in Britain was drawing to an end, it suddenly dawned on him, one day, as he was sitting in Southwark Cathedral, that he had not really been able to pray to God since he had been in England. At once he felt a sadness, which he had never before experienced and which would not let go of him. He tried everything he could to rid himself of this melancholy: he tried praying in various churches; he tried cheering himself up partying with his friends and colleagues; he tried drinking; he tried writing home; and he tried anti-depressants. All was to no avail. He was sad and remained sad.

In the therapeutic counselling sessions Douglas tried to brush off his sadness as mere homesickness. He believed that perhaps working even harder than he already did might make the time go by faster so that his two years would be over quickly and he could go home and get back into a normal routine and feel fine again. However it was disturbing to him that he was wasting valuable time abroad in this way and that he was now unable to enjoy his escapade away from home any longer.

It was this reference to his stay in England as an escapade that first set him searching in the right direction. He admitted to himself for the first time how his two years in England were meant to be a mere holiday from the strains and stresses of his Australian life. He had never seriously considered taking to this new career, but he had every intention of returning and stepping back into the groove at the exact place where he had left off. What surprised him was that he had taken this whole adventure so seriously and that he had started feeling guilty about having a good time away from home.

Douglas felt particularly guilty towards God. In Australia he used to be a faithful and committed Catholic; church-going had been a family practice which was taken seriously. It was unthinkable that he should not have taken Communion for nearly seven months for instance, but he hadn't. At first he thought that the guilt was there because he had sinned, because he had gone against the law of his religion and of his family. Later he thought that the guilt was there because he had not been able to find forgiveness after confession for such a long time. He thought that therefore a sense of guilt had accumulated which normally prayer and absolution would have regularly dispelled.

It was obvious that whatever rational explanations Douglas could find for his sadness and feelings of guilt, he would nevertheless still be immersed in the same strong emotion. He was clearly not receptive yet to the message of his conscience.

Gradually Douglas started to recognize how his sadness was not just about loss. Though he regretted the sense of enveloping security in which he had been wrapped when he lived in Australia and though he missed his former life and established routines, he also knew with absolute certainty that things could never be quite the same again. What was more: he knew that he did not want things to go back to what they had been and also that he had made the decision of breaking with the established patterns because he had to do it.

He realized how easy it would be to flee back to Australia, even before his two years were up, and to get back to normal, pretending that this escapade had only been an adolescent adventure. He was not cut off from his old securities; he could gain access to them whenever he wanted and he would not lose face if he did. On the contrary, everyone would cheer and welcome him back. No, his sadness was definitely not about loss of the old. It slowly started dawning on Douglas that he was sad because he was afraid that he was losing the one and only chance he would get to discover the world that lay beyond the boundaries of the old and secure homestead.

As soon as he got this first glimpse of his own longing for more than the familiar and secure world, he started making sense of his guilt in terms of existential guilt. His guilt, far from indicating that he had done something wrong, was a reminder of how he was in danger of omitting to do what was right for him to do. He had been on the brink of new discoveries in himself and in the world, but he had kept on protecting himself from the full impact.

He had reserved his commitment, by not fully engaging with his life in Britain, by remaining a tourist, by waiting for his two years to pass so that he could go safely home again.

Yet of course he wanted to engage. He was the one who had undertaken this trip in the first place; no one had forced him. He was the one who had known that the set pattern of the Catholic surgeon's son, surgeon-to-be, had not been sufficient. He was the one who had abstained from going to church while he was in England. He was the one who had wanted more. He was the one who had looked for a greater challenge. He was the one who had wanted to find wider horizons and who had yearned for a greater depth in himself. And then, as soon as things got rough, he groped for the old securities and stuck his head in the sand. No wonder he felt sad, disappointed, depressed. No wonder he felt guilty: he owed himself better than that. He had an existential debt to himself.

When Douglas began to formulate his difficulties in these terms, he cheered up almost immediately. No longer did he fear that he could not stand being away from home. Now he remembered with greater precision what it was he had come to England for. He rekindled the spark of vitality and determination in himself, which had originally made it possible for him to undertake this project in the first place.

Leaving the authoritarian God of his childhood behind was now no longer something to be afraid of, it was a first step in the direction of rediscovering an inner authority and an inner sense of right and wrong. Leaving behind the values of the family and the social group he belonged to no longer led him to despair but opened the door to the formulation of his own values.

Over long months of struggling with himself Douglas began to understand how he need not totally accept his old framework of life, but neither need he totally reject it. There was not one set of standards that ruled the world in Australia and another, contradictory, set that ruled life outside. It was possible to pick and choose what suited him amongst all these: he need not either totally conform to or totally negate any one set of values and standards. Broadening his horizons and gaining strength in himself allowed him to make up his own mind about what it was worth living for.

Not long before he had to return to Australia, Douglas went to see a British priest, whom he admired, and he discussed the story of the Garden of Eden with him. After this he found a renewed faith in God, because he had concluded that God would not necessarily disapprove of people who wanted to think for themselves. Choosing to eat from the forbidden tree and gain knowledge about right and wrong was not necessarily a sin. In fact, he thought, God had put the tree in the Garden of Eden and He had thus Himself introduced the potential for aware living. All in all, God would probably not have wanted to keep people dumb and content in paradise forever anyway.

While it was clear that Douglas was preparing to find some compromise, which would allow him to slip back into the pattern in Australia without becoming an outcast, it was also clear that he did not intend to erase his experience in Britain. In fact, his letters, written respectively two months and a year and a half after his return, indicated that his independence of thought took an initial nose-dive, but increased steadily over time. In his second letter he formulated his own thinking about the purpose of his life in a more definite and precise way than ever before. This was to a great extent consequential to his increasing dissatisfaction with the spiritual life and the ideals he had found at home. While he had made an attempt to fit his own thinking back into the current trends, he had eventually decided that he must take the risk of following his own road.

In practice this meant that he considered himself a free-thinking Christian and ceased to practise as a Catholic. He also tried to bring his own ideals to his work, by relating to patients as thinking people rather than as cases of gastric ulcer or duodenal cancer. It sounded as though Douglas's tree of life had started to come to fruition, as he so strikingly put it himself, as his depression lifted.

Many people, like Douglas, have difficulties in making sense of their own ideals and values. Coming to terms with one's own aspirations and purpose in life is only possible in so far as one is able to gain sufficient distance from the trends and fashion around one. Sorting out one's social world relationships is therefore often a necessity before the ideal or spiritual dimension can be tackled. In doing this it can be helpful to find oneself in an isolated position from one's culture and reference group. Travel and cross-cultural experience can be a trigger for this kind of experience. Any other occurrence or situation, which brings alienation from one's direct support system, may also provide an awareness of the lack of reference to personal ideals and inner values.

When confronting the spiritual dimension it is also of great importance already to be at ease in one's personal world. Without a sense of inner confidence and trust in your ability to cope with the responsibility of making your own moral judgements and decisions it is hardly possible to start looking for guidance within yourself. At the same time, inner strength and clarity on the social dimension will dramatically increase when the ideals of the spiritual world are being cultivated. People also often report how an improved ideal-world relationship enhances their natural-world experience. Tuning in to the absolute values that connect one to the larger pattern of the universe can redefine the concrete realities of the physical world and heighten sensory awareness and appreciation of the given.

Thus in actuality all four dimensions of human experience are interlinked and interrelated. It is not possible to work exclusively in one sphere and neglect all other aspects. Though clients frequently emphasize their struggle in one particular dimension, it is usually essential to ensure that difficulties in living get worked through on all four dimensions.

Chapter summary

1 Human beings experience the world on different dimensions. Existential work takes care to explore a person's experience on all of these.

2 There are four dimensions that can be distinguished. They are:

- Physical dimension (*Umwelt*).
- Social dimension (*Mitwelt*).
- Personal dimension (*Eigenwelt*).
- Spiritual dimension (*Uberwelt*).

3 The physical dimension (*Umwelt*) is that of our relationship to the material world around us, the natural environment. It also involves our own embodiment in this world and our relationship to the factual limits and challenges that are thus presented to us.

4 The social dimension (*Mitwelt*) is that of our relationship to the other people that live with us in the world. It represents our insertion into a public domain where cultural norms, social conventions and the power relations of interpersonal dynamics influence our behaviour and experience.

5 The personal dimension (*Eigenwelt*) refers to our relationship to ourselves in the very private manner that is generated by self-reflection. This is our own world and it may include our relationship to things and animals or people that we experience as part of ourselves.

6 The spiritual dimension (*Uberwelt*) refers to our relationship to the beliefs, ideals, values and principles that we live by. This is the dimension of our overall worldview and ideological perspective, which determines how we operate on the other dimensions and how we make sense of the world.

7 On each dimension we are confronted with a number of possibilities and opportunities as well as with a number of predictable limitations and challenges that we have to learn to face up to and take into account.

8 On each dimension we can pursue our own aspirations or create illusions about our own capacity for overcoming obstacles, we can also despair over the ultimate concerns that we encounter on each of these levels. Finding a constructive and realistic way to deal with these polarities is essential for good human living.

9 In terms of the physical dimension it is important to attend to the way in which clients are embodied or disembodied in their engagement with the world and to enhance their security and ability to confront reality and take appropriate risks.

10 There is no point in working on the other dimensions as long as people have not learnt to come to terms with a basic sense of being able to manage their own physical existence autonomously.

11 On the social dimension we need to monitor whether clients tend to approach others by attempting to dominate them, by submitting to them or by withdrawing and avoiding others altogether. We can facilitate an understanding of the person's difficulties in dealing with the social world and juxtapose the competitive mode of operating with a more co-operative mode of relating.

12 Overcoming the conflicts of the social dimension requires insight into the distinction between I—You and I—It relating. It will enhance a person's ability to seek relationships where mutuality and reciprocity allow for a more dynamic and contributive form of interaction.

13 On the personal dimension becoming aware of individual strengths and weaknesses can lead to the discovery that what seemed like a negative personal characteristic can hold a positive potential that can be developed.

14 Focusing on a person's inner experience of identity can take a person beyond a sense of being at the mercy of physical or social determinants.

15 People can become aware of being the centre of balance of their own world and claim responsibility for their own lives.

16 This always needs to be counterbalanced with an overall awareness of the wider implications of human existence, so that the person is robustly located as a centre of gravity in a universe that is much wider-reaching than any individual can be.

17 On the spiritual dimension ideals can be uncovered or discovered for the first time. This can lead to a complete change of perspective or direction and existing predicaments or dilemmas might take on a new significance in light of these changes.

18 It can take quite a bit of courage to acknowledge what one wants to live or die for. But the passion that is generated by recognizing personal purpose overcomes any previous apathy or lack of spirit.

19 Constructing one's life around deeply felt values refocuses attention and enables a new engagement with the world on all dimensions.

20 Purpose and meaning in everyday living enable one to contend with difficulties much greater than one previously thought oneself capable of taking on.

4

Taking Stock

Defining assumptions

The previous chapter showed how the existential approach hinges on an understanding of the client's worldview. Now we need to address the way in which clients can be helped to come to grips with their experience of the world. Some of the illustrations in the previous chapters simply described clients' quandaries or crises and their eventual solution or conclusion. The actual labour clients needed to complete before difficulties could be resolved was only mentioned in passing. This chapter pinpoints with greater precision how the existential practitioner is to proceed in assisting the client through this arduous process.

Taking stock of one's life, which is the initial task of existential work, requires attention to be paid to three aspects in particular. First, assumptions about the world, on all four dimensions, need to be recognized, defined and questioned. Assumptions are the things one normally holds true without questioning. They determine one's perception of things as real or unreal. Second, values need to be recognized or determined, in order to establish ultimate and vital concerns, which make things worthwhile and meaningful. Third, personal talents need to be recognized, defined and elaborated, as they are the source of what makes life possible and actual for a person.

All three aspects need to be taken into account if a personal worldview is to be explored and translated into a dynamically reflective and satisfactory lifestyle. Gaining clarity about assumptions will increase a sense of reality; gaining clarity about values will increase the ability to make life worthwhile; gaining clarity about personal talents will increase one's ability to make life work in actuality.

It is the therapist's task to make sure that the client's attention will be directed to all three aspects. Often it will be necessary to remind the client over and over of the importance of focusing on these salient features of her mode of being. Some approaches to counselling and psychotherapy, in an attempt to encourage the client to do just that, place the emphasis on the client's feelings. Other approaches, with a similar desire, stress behaviour or attitude. Still others stress personal responsibility. The idea is always the same: to enable a client to become aware of herself as the centre of her own experience and action.

Many clients initially present their problems in living as entirely brought about by external causes. They consider it to be the circumstances that determine their unhappiness and misfortune. They will sometimes refer to the physical situation as limiting them. At other times they will blame the cultural or social context. Most people sooner or later will also blame specific relationships they are in for most of their troubles; partners or parents are often the target for such fault-finding. Again, when people see their own character as the source of their misery, they often see this in relation to their early childhood experience. Traumas they suffered through no fault of their own will be referred to as the explanatory cause for their current personality or emotional problems. Finally, for some clients fate or the hand of God is perceived as the origin of their suffering and distress.

It is rare that clients come to therapy with an insight into their own responsibility in contributing to their difficulties. Although they almost invariably hope that they will discover ways of becoming more in charge of their own destiny, they rarely have an inkling of how to proceed in gaining such insight and mastery.

By the time they finally ask for help, most clients have spent a considerable amount of time struggling with their own difficulties without much success, feeling increasingly lost and usually also lonely and isolated. Nothing is easier for the counsellor or therapist than to fall for the notion that all the client needs is a shoulder to cry on and some human understanding and empathy.

Many counsellors or therapists see their role as being there with the client and allowing her to air her feelings and express her pain. They have learnt to provide a warm environment of empathic understanding and they are often accomplished listeners. Their complaint is that they will start to feel at a loss by the time the client has been saying the same things for several sessions without there seeming to be much progress or movement. They frequently get a sense of being trapped with the client in a vicious circle that they do not know how to break out of.

At times like these practitioners may turn to suggesting homework to the client, in an attempt to incite her to change and get out of her rut. In supervision the professional will begin to express feelings of impatience with the client's self-indulgent behaviour, harbouring a longing for some new technique or gimmick to get the situation unstuck. Yet the more the practitioner actively tries to remedy the situation by producing one new device after another from a bag of tricks, the less the client will be inclined to take any responsibility for her own life.

Therapists who up to this point may have been a paragon of positive human interaction may now become irritated with the stubbornness of this client who refuses to respond to either empathy or suggestion. The practitioner may decide to throw in the towel or indicate to the client by her attitude that she is at the end of her rope. Clients will often oblige and decide to stop coming to the sessions just when they sense that their counsellor or therapist is fed up with them. Sometimes they may even pretend that all will be well. Sometimes it may even be that all they needed was to be left to their own devices.

In many cases, however, the whole process has miserably failed when it ends on this note. In fact all too often counselling or therapy can become a mere substitute for an ordinary caring human relationship. It must therefore run dry when it becomes apparent that it is only a substitute and that the practitioner will never genuinely be prepared to exchange affection, but will only be capable of limited professional concern.

If you are to work with professional integrity, it is crucial to make it clear from the outset of the therapeutic encounter that the client is not buying your affection. What is sold is not part of yourself, or even your empathy or unconditional approval, but your expertise in the art of living and your craft in unravelling difficulties and overseeing problems.

Therefore, the existential method consists of scrupulously responding to the client from a position of acting as a catalyst for transformation and clarification. The process is one of reminding the client how to conduct her own investigation into her mode of living, thus bringing her back to herself and her own conscience. Never in an existential way of working does the therapist comply with the client's demands for sympathy or pity, nor does she fall in with the client's assumptions about life.

The existential attitude is one of constant alertness and acuity. The client is encouraged not to take anything for granted, but to question, clarify, explain, define and explore, not for the benefit of the counsellor or therapist, but in order to learn to reflect. She is taught to reconsider and think through her reactions rather than passively slide along with the feelings that have landed her in this trapped position. When the client begins to give her account of the predicament she is in, the existential practitioner is ready to intervene as soon as a clear theme is developing. Nothing is to be gained from preventing the client from following her own free flow of thinking and speaking about her difficulties and distress. But as soon as a complete picture emerges the therapist will begin to point in the direction of those aspects that may usefully be explored further.

In doing this the key is always to bring the attention back to the client's experience of the world. If the client says: 'Every Christmas it's the same story; everybody expects me to organize the party,' the counsellor might say something like 'Do you mean, you get the impression that you are being exploited?', thus shifting the focus onto the client's inner experience and to the essence of what is implied in the statement.

It is important to indicate systematically to the client how she can start to re-examine her own experience, by shifting the focus back onto herself as the centre of this experience. It is crucial to do this in such a way that the client is not pinned down to an interpretation of her experience. She is simply encouraged to look at it again from a different angle. The effect of such prompting is often that the client will correct her previous statement to something more accurate and more closely related to herself as the protagonist of her own experience.

The client may now say something like 'It's not just an impression, I know that I am being exploited, but it is only because they are dependent on me for things like that.' And this is now a clear statement about the client's view of her social world relations, which can be explored. The therapist does not have to empathize with the client's feelings as this might reduce the richness of the experience to one single, negative aspect. The experienced practitioner will know how to open up every statement to invite the client to consider what it expresses in terms of her perception of the world, instead.

The simple statement 'everyone expects me to organize the party' could have been heard as a complaint but it could also have been heard as a disguised boast. The therapist could have jumped to the conclusion that the client needed to be challenged and suggest a remedy for the unacceptable situation. She might also have interpreted the statement as another illustration of typical behaviour and pointed out an underlying motivation. Either way, the opportunity for further reflection on this issue in terms of the client's underlying assumptions about herself and her world would have been missed.

Ordinarily counselling and therapy imply that the professional should take a certain stance towards the client's difficulties. She might implicitly approve of the client, supporting her no matter what with empathy and unconditional positive regard. Or she might implicitly disapprove, confronting the client with challenging questions or evocative and equally challenging interpretations. She might also come up with suggestions of alternative solutions and possible new forms of behaviour. Many counsellors and therapists try to include both a supportive empathic element and a challenge. This can often have a confusing effect on the client, who does not know in the end where she stands, whether she is liked or disliked by the therapist, approved of or disapproved of.

While clients may respond with feelings of confusion to the eclectic approach, with feelings of despondency to the supportive approach and with feelings of inferiority to the challenging approach, in all of these instances they would be likely to become increasingly dependent on the professional. As long as the practitioner operates from a framework that implies approval or disapproval the client is kept in a dependent position. It is therefore hardly surprising that a recurrent complaint from professionals is that clients seem incapable of taking responsibility for themselves and their lives. The therapeutic enterprise often encourages dependency.

Even the most incisive and outspoken humanistic or cognitive approaches, which might overtly insist on the need for clients to take responsibility for themselves, may still covertly encourage dependence. These approaches may find themselves in the position of double-binding clients by inciting them to become responsible. They are in this like the double-binding mother who declares that the child must do as she says and become independent. By imitating the professional's desire for their own independence the clients may learn to mimic the role of the self-responsible person to a degree, but without necessarily having discovered the motivation for genuine autonomy in their own hearts.

The only road that leads a client to discovering such internal motivation is through a relationship to a therapist who maintains a balanced position. A balanced position is by no means to be confused with a distant or aloof position. Only a professional who is genuinely and passionately concerned with human nature and with the difficult task of living in the human condition will be capable of being sufficiently involved to achieve a balanced position. This will stem from her deep interest in finding out what motivates each person and how different people handle their specific predicament. This passion will be obvious to the client from the warm and enthusiastic energetic attention the practitioner will bring to the therapeutic dialogue.

So, while the practitioner's attitude towards the client is balanced, her passion and interest for her profession and for the pursuit of truth is unlimited and obvious. This philosophical ardour will be apparent through the practitioner's consistent and supportive querying of all that the client, and indeed the therapist herself, takes for granted. This makes the therapeutic relationship into something quite different from ordinary human relationships. Sessions become a time when a particular person's dealings with living are all-important and receive full and constructive attention. These dealings are seen as neither good nor bad nor as necessarily typical or characteristic of this particular client. The specific circumstances of the client's life, in the same way, are not considered primarily good or bad but they are viewed as a particular sample of human conditions providing certain learning opportunities and challenges, which are worth exploring.

The therapist's aim is to be able to consider the client's issues and dilemmas from a fundamentally open stance. She never assumes that she knows or understands the client's point of view completely. She will need to elicit clarification of many concepts that the client seems to take for granted and on which she appears to expect agreement with the therapist. When the client realizes that the practitioner does not automatically assume understanding, agreement or disagreement, she becomes free to investigate her own assumptions more carefully.

A client might, for instance, begin a session by saying that she has been wondering on the way here what she might talk about so as to use the session properly and not to be seen to waste valuable time. The existential therapist does not assume that she understands the client's quandary without first investigating the underlying assumptions. The implicitly approving counsellor or therapist might immediately respond with an understanding nod and a reference to the client's feelings, along the lines of 'you seem anxious to get a lot done today'. The implicitly disapproving counsellor or therapist might respond by proposing a structure for making an agenda, thus indicating a basic mistrust of the client's ability to use the session properly. In both cases the practitioner would have taken the client's words at their most commonly accepted face value.

The client in both cases will have received confirmation of her assumption that she ought to perform a certain role in the therapeutic session, namely that of the compliant client. The existential therapist will be on the lookout for such traps of ordinary dependency and compliance, and will read the client's communication as an expression of a number of basic assumptions well worth investigation.

The existential therapist might want to invite the client to consider what she calls 'using the session properly' or what she has in mind when she thinks about 'wasting time' or what in her opinion makes time potentially 'valuable'. In this way, following the client's own lead and expression of what is of concern to her right now, the session will start to take shape around issues which are likely to throw some light on this particular client's view of the world.

The client, when realizing how important her reconsideration of her own assumptions and opinions can be, will often find much to talk about and examine. She will be fascinated with this reflection on her own world and views and will cease to feel at a loss for significant material, seeing how each and every facet of her experience expresses her expectations and standpoint. The session is thus in full swing from the first moment: nothing is insignificant, nothing is needed other than the client's very presence and communication.

The counsellor or therapist remains constantly alert for implied assumptions and she keeps querying these and encouraging further exploration and definition. She indicates by this focus that the client is perfectly capable of using the session fruitfully, as all she says is of value and worth investigation. She also demonstrates how she assumes that the client is able to make sense of her experience for herself, eliciting rather than providing answers. The professional in this way creates a climate of trust in the client's competence to address her own issues and gain her own insights and she stimulates the client's desire for autonomy while letting her experiment with the skills required for the successful exercise of such autonomy.

Existential psychotherapy or counselling is here again similar to education. It points the client in the direction of paying adequate attention to those aspects of life that she is currently taking for granted and of which she is neglecting to see the salient features. The art teacher might draw the student's attention to a shadow she has overlooked, in the same way as the existential practitioner will draw the client's attention to the assumptions and implications of her attitude that she had thus far not even noticed.

In doing this it is crucial to abstain from immediate value judgements on the truth or worth of these assumptions. It must be remembered that the aim is to get a clear picture of the client's universe rather than to change it. As long as a client is unready to give up an assumption, however blatant the error of this assumption may seem, it is important to allow the client to stick to her guns. Probing and exploration of the consequences of any assumption should sooner or later allow her to abandon mistakes on her own initiative.

Alison was the client who started her first session expressing her concern about using the session properly and not wanting to be seen as wasting valuable time. Alison was twenty-eight years old and had been seeking counselling because of her paralysing bouts of jealousy of her thirty-two-year-old husband, John. John was himself in the health profession and he had been instrumental in Alison's referral, because he was, as Alison put it, 'fed up with her making a nuisance of herself'.

Alison, who used to work in the hospital catering service, had given up work at the birth of their first and only child, six years previously. Now that her daughter was in school she did not really know how to fill her days, but there was no question of her returning to work, for John 'wouldn't let her'.

In the initial interview Alison had indicated how her 'pathological' jealousy was more John's problem than her own. She herself was more concerned that John appeared to be increasingly ashamed of her being his wife, now that he had worked himself up to a distinguished position. She thought that it would not be long before he would try to make a fresh start for himself, getting rid of her and marrying someone more 'proper'. Although Alison believed that John had sent her on to a counsellor only to make her stop bothering him, she soon took a liking to the idea of counselling when she realized it involved her having someone to talk to all by herself.

Most of the counselling work with Alison consisted of a process of focus on her assumptions about herself and her relationship with John. Discovering the ability to clarify and define her views gave her a completely new insight into her own intrinsic strength. Once she sensed this strength the rest followed naturally.

When Alison started the first session with her remark about wanting to use the session 'properly', the counsellor was immediately struck with her using this word, which had also been used several times during the initial interview. She therefore responded to Alison by saying: 'When would you consider yourself as using the session properly?' Alison now embarked on her first attempt at defining her own assumptions. At first she was a little hesitant, but she soon got the hang of the method. Before long she began to stop herself sometimes in mid-sentence in order to reconsider what she actually meant to say. Sometimes she was rather taken aback by the discoveries she made about her own presuppositions.

In response to the counsellor's first intervention Alison determined that using the session properly would mean doing whatever was expected of her. Rather than challenging this assumption, the counsellor pointed out how Alison seemed to doubt her own ability to be successful at doing what was expected of her. Alison confirmed this notion enthusiastically and went on to describe how all the other women in her neighbourhood and all the women at John's work were generally far more 'proper' than she could ever be herself.

After further exploration it became evident that a 'proper' person to Alison was a person who had something to offer, unlike herself who could only do things to please other people and most of the time without succeeding even in this. She concluded that she saw herself as at the mercy of other people's liking of her and she disliked that position very much.

She now described the various ways in which her own position of being at proper people's mercy had been evident over the past few years, after the counsellor had simply encouraged her to do so by saying 'In what ways have you been at other people's mercy?' She spent a lot of time airing her frustration with her husband's increasingly long hours at work, now that he had obtained a senior position. She was convinced that the reason he would not have her working was that he was ashamed of her doing cleaning and because he did not want her spoiling his new relationships at work. She would certainly have been able to return to her old job in the hospital where John worked, but then she would have been too close for comfort to John's 'hobnobbing' with the medical staff.

Alison thought that John might be having an affair with one of the female doctors. She felt at his mercy and she dared not go against his wish for her not to return to work. She feared that if she did he would ask for a divorce and take Joanne, their daughter, with him. She felt at the mercy of having to accept his long hours at work because he always made it seem as if his job was far more important than anything else, as it involved helping other people. She herself clearly assumed that 'proper' work like John's was based on a person's ability to do things for others and that her own merit would never reach this far.

She also felt at her daughter Joanne's mercy because the girl was becoming less and less interested in being at home with her mother. Not only did she want to play at a friend's house nearly every day, but at weekends she would be off on excursions with John quite frequently and she would make it clear that her mother was not a desired presence on these trips. Alison felt sure that Joanne would prefer to live with her father rather than with her if it came to a separation.

Most of all Alison felt at the mercy of the doctors who had advised her to be sterilized after Joanne's birth. Though she had been very ill with pre-eclampsia during her pregnancy and though she understood that there would have been a serious risk if she had another child, she had not been ready to be sterilized. She had given in because they had 'forced it on her' and because she dare not contradict the opinion of these professional people. She had wanted to discuss the matter with someone before making up her mind, 'but they seemed all so busy'. She had decided to give in and 'not waste their time any more'.

At this stage the counsellor who had thus far only responded with a 'Who else?' or 'How?' now and then, intervened in order to bring another assumption to Alison's attention.

Counsellor: You seem to imply that people paying attention to you would be wasting their time.
Alison: I don't know. I suppose I do waste people's time.
Counsellor: I didn't say you waste people's time, but that you are implying that you consider yourself as wasting their time.
Alison: But I do waste people's time.
Counsellor: Whose for instance?
Alison: Well, John's mostly, he always complains about me bothering him. Joanne as well; she hates me fussing over her. The more I try to do things for them, the more I am with them all the time, the more they try to rid themselves of me.
Counsellor: So that's not *their* time you're wasting then.
Alison: What do you mean? [*Silence*] You mean it's mine. It's my time I'm wasting?
Counsellor: Is it not?
Alison: I'm trying. I do my best. It's no good. [*There is a ten second silence during which she gets out her handkerchief; she blows her nose.*] It's no bloody good. [*She hides her tearfulness behind her hanky; elbows resting on her knees.*] I'm doing all

these things for them. They are all I've got. [*Sobs*] They don't even like it. It's no bloody good. It's all for nothing. It doesn't do no one no good.

Counsellor: So you are wasting your time?

Alison: I've nearly wasted my *life* on them. He wants to take Joanne with him when he leaves. That will be the end of it. There will be nothing left. Nothing. [*She cries audibly now for a little while.*]

Counsellor: So that's what you are desperately trying to prevent: being left with nothing. That's why you hold on so tightly to what you've got for the moment.

Alison: [*wiping tears energetically and nodding enthusiastically*] I can't give up. They're all I've got.

Counsellor: So you hold on really tightly.

Alison: I've got to. They are my all.

Counsellor: And they hate it; the tighter you hold on to them, the more they struggle to get away from you.

Alison: They do. It's like what John said the other day, he said: 'The more you are suspicious of me and Heather, the more I feel like proving you right.'

Counsellor: So it is as if you are digging your own grave; you are making your own suspicions come true.

Alison: It seems like that. But I don't know why that should be. It's like when John says that he thinks I want him to leave me. I honestly don't; I want him to stay. But the more I want him to stay the more he wants to go.

Counsellor: You don't *want* him to go, but you certainly *expect* him to.

Alison: Yes. Yes, I do. I can't even understand how he could have stayed this long.

Counsellor: Somehow he must really care for you, to stay so long with someone who has got nothing to offer.

Alison: Well. He likes the food. I am a good cook, you know.

Counsellor: Ah. You've got some redeeming talent?

Alison: I could have made it big in catering, if I hadn't had Joanne so quickly.

Counsellor: You mean you could have made it big, like John has, quite under your own steam?

Alison: In my own line, given time. Oh yes.

Counsellor: Now there is something to ponder on till next time. It's time to stop for today.

At the next session Alison's attitude was predictably much less submissive. Though the work was only starting and many assumptions needed still to be explored before she could start freeing herself of some of the shackles she was holding herself down with, the tone and mode for this exploration were set during this first session.

What the counsellor did during this first session and continued with in the subsequent sessions was to function as the voice of Alison's conscience. She incited her to express her own views on her situation as fully as possible and then think through the implications of her assumptions once these were sufficiently clear. In doing this the counsellor was consistently on Alison's side, with her, like a real ally, reliably reminding her to consider things from her own perspective rather than speculating about other people's perspective.

The counsellor's task was to keep Alison on a straight track and to remind her to get back to the issue at hand rather than wallowing in emotion and jumping from one complaint to the next. In doing this, the counsellor had to be tough, without reproach, without animosity, but always work-oriented. The counsellor's attitude here was comparable to that of the art teacher.

Sometimes in trying to come to grips with the art of painting a student may burst into tears or get angry, realizing how all her efforts so far have remained in vain. Instead of encouraging the student at such times to immerse herself in this emotional discharge the teacher will simply accept the emotion as a side-effect of the learning that is being engaged in most intensively. The teacher will draw the student's attention to what she is doing and to what she is neglecting in the most straightforward and matter of fact manner. Sometimes it can be done with humour.

The counsellor assumed that Alison, although she needed to express her frustration and upset with her difficulties in living, would be capable of coping with a realistic look at the implications of her own attitude. She was thus conveying to Alison that she considered her basically strong and capable. Because of this it was possible to point out how Alison herself constantly assumed how she was at the mercy of others and with no strength of her own.

Often when clients' bluff is called in this way it becomes obvious how deep down they have a much stronger faith in themselves than they let on at first. Alison was quick to remember how she did have assets to offer to John when she became aware of the negative way in which she had thus far been presenting herself. If the counsellor had been all-empathic of Alison's pain at finding herself so worthless or if she had attempted to inspire her with some good feelings about herself, the message conveyed would have been that Alison was incapable of sorting herself out. Then, as she could not rely on her own strength, positive feelings and courage, the dependency on the counsellor would have become established once and for all.

Existential counsellors or therapists decline to do the work for their clients. They assume that the clients will be able to cope by themselves once the basic monitoring and reflective skills become accessible to them. While professionals have to be always open to be corrected in their statements about their clients' assumptions and their implications, they will be very definite in the way they show clients what it is they have been saying and assuming. They make no value judgements on the client's perceptions, attitudes and opinions, but help her to examine their consequences and implications.

In this instance the counsellor helped Alison in making her assumptions about her relationship with John and Joanne explicit first. Alison's blind holding on to what she assumed to be her only strength was thus highlighted. Then it was pointed out what the consequences of her attitude and behaviour were for herself. It was found that the whole process was based on Alison's assumption that she would be left eventually because she had nothing to offer that would make people want to be with her. Making explicit what was implied in Alison's own words was the way in which this was brought out.

Alison's own need for correcting the erroneous assumptions that she had been expressing was then called into action and a whole new picture started to emerge. Rather than developing this new theme for her, the counsellor encouraged her to pursue this thought in her own time, indicating by this that this was her thought and that she was quite capable of taking things further on her own.

Clients do not gain much from getting pampered by professionals. Clients on the whole are quite capable of handling life on their own, given some instruction in how to reconsider their own ways of living. It helps enormously if therapists can remember to have a basic respect for clients and simply help them to expose the truth they are currently living, but which has been obscured. The professional assists the client in bringing her viewpoint out in the open by small interventions such as: What is your perception of that? How do you see that? What is that like for you? What is your experience of that? What does that evoke for you? What does that mean to you? How does that strike you? What do you make of that? How do you respond to that? These and other questions aimed at encouraging clients to declare and develop their standpoint openly, replace the usual and often offensive: How do you feel about that? This is a question to which clients often dismissively respond with 'OK' or 'Terrible'. Although feelings can sometimes be appropriately looked at (see Chapter 5), it is often more important to get to the root of what brought the feeling about in the first place.

Once the client's truth is starting to become explicit the practitioner enables the client to begin to examine it by shining broad daylight onto it, thus exposing its internal contradictions and its implications. When doing this it is important for the professional to be blunt and perhaps even a little ruthless, yet always gentle and open to correction by the client. The existential practitioner is always entirely serious and earnest, but when possible uses humour, without malice. In a playful way she signifies to the client that although her mistakes are to be taken seriously and need sorting out, nothing prevents her from doing this in a light-hearted and basically joyful manner. However difficult life may become at times, it is always possible to face up to the truth of the moment. Realizing that one has made a mistake is no big deal; it even may be worth smiling about.

Of course this approach rests on a philosophical attitude to life, which entails recognition of the fact that all human beings operate with certain assumptions, some of which are likely to be erroneous and will need revising. Assumptions are therefore never seen as wrong or bad, they are not being condemned or dismissed, but they are examined and tested for their current use to the client.

The existential therapist does not pretend or imagine that she knows the specific assumptions of the client. It is crucial to approach each session with a fresh and naive curiosity about this person's world. The therapist is like someone from outer space, foreign to the country the client inhabits. At the same time she should be capable of more insight into what is directly relevant for survival than the client herself, who is likely to be lost in a corner of her own country. As a foreigner the professional asks for explanations on the salient features, habits and rules that are characteristic of the client's world. She might sometimes need to ask for more detailed information on things that the client takes absolutely for granted. The practitioner's naive approach will take the client aback and force her to rethink for herself. If a client, for instance, says: 'I am suffering from not having enough sleep at the moment,' it is obvious that she expects her therapist to understand this and agree with her on the basic assumptions underlying the statement. The therapist will naturally be tempted to be drawn into falling in with the client's assumptions, especially if she is trained to be a good listener. Many counsellors or therapists will naturally respond with a nod and an understanding or empathic smile, a welcoming 'Mmmm'. The existential therapist might, on the contrary (though not necessarily), respond with an ingenuous enquiry into the need for a certain amount of sleep: 'What do you mean, not enough?' or 'I'm not sure I understand; what would be the right amount of sleep?' or 'Ah, tell me then what would be enough sleep!' This type of intervention should come forth from a genuine openness to understanding and wanting to comprehend another's worldview, never from a wish to implement a certain technique or play a clever game with the client.

While this phase of piecing together the client's ideas about life, herself and the world around her is going on, the ultimate aim always is to assist the client in grasping the principles that will turn out to withstand questioning. These will form the basis of her reappraisal of herself. Some assumptions will almost immediately fall by the wayside and be abandoned by the client as soon as she faces their implications. Other assumptions will stand the test of time and investigation and will be recognized as having a certain ultimate value for the client.

The source of the assumptions, ideas and norms has little bearing on their ultimate reality and usefulness. Assumptions and habits stemming from conformity with parental or cultural standards may still be useful and valuable. They need not be rejected out of hand. No one can be entirely original. No matter how the person first came into contact with an assumption or an idea, what matters is whether she wants it in her life now. This depends on the way she wants her life to be.

Some clients will feel well served by holding on to the assumptions and habits of their childhood. Others will feel happier making a shift to ideas and beliefs they discovered later on. As long as people are able to reflect on their assumptions and understand their implications and consequences and still feel at ease with them, everything will make sense and be satisfactory.

When clients get to this stage of awareness of their own intentions and assumptions a new insight into the purpose of their life can be gained. Deciding on which assumptions to hold on to and which to let go involves a process of increasing sensitivity to the ultimate direction one wants one's life to take. Assisting clients in finding this direction is the next level of existential work; it requires the sorting out of individual values.

Determining values

When clients define and examine their own assumptions about the world it soon becomes obvious which of the assumptions can be abandoned because they represent old views and errors that they no longer need to hold on to.

Some assumptions will be almost instantaneously discarded after they have been scrutinized closely.

The remaining assumptions, even though they may seem wrong sometimes, will be tenacious and clients will often seem unable to come to reason as far as these assumptions are concerned. Almost invariably this kind of tenacious assumption is rooted in a much deeper and more important aspect of the client's view of the world, which concerns her beliefs about what really matters. It is this area of the client's experience that the existential approach stresses. Although many cognitive approaches emphasize the importance of examining assumptions, all too often the assumptions are then either seen as the negative result of some learning process which needs to be corrected, or they are simply challenged as wrong. The existential method seeks to encourage clients into further examination of their assumptions and their underlying value system. What ultimately matters in existential work is to determine what it is that really matters to the clients, not what ought to matter to them.

Often people are unsure about the values and principles that lie at the source of their assumptions and views about the world. They think that they do not have any special or hidden motivations. Though people are often not reflectively aware of their own motivations, beliefs and desires, they make no mistakes in their discernment of likes and dislikes. What is not attractive, appropriate or desirable to them reveals their intrinsic internal guidance. This is what people often refer to as intuition.

They sense in some mysterious way precisely what it is they like and what they dislike, without quite knowing where their judgement came from. Every single action, person, situation and thought is compared to the blueprint of individual standards, values and ideals. If it falls short it is disliked automatically even without a conscious thought-process having to take place.

Alison, the protagonist of the previous illustration, knew very clearly all along that there was something she disliked about herself so strongly that it made her feel certain that no one else would want to be with her either. This dislike of herself, far from being irrational and far from being susceptible to being overridden by some sessions of assertiveness training, was based on her failure to live up to her own expectations. She knew there was something wrong, but she did not know what it was. She would not accept any suggestions involving the rejection of her own intuition which told her that she was in some way unlovable.

Alison also assumed that she could not directly challenge John, her husband, on his long working hours, as his work was clearly more valuable and important than anything she would have to offer him. The only option open to her was to challenge him excessively on something that she did think was wrong: his having too friendly a relationship with one of the junior doctors. Alison's lack of determination in claiming her husband's attention was not in the first place a problem generated by a cultural female submissiveness to the male. It was based on a different type of assessment of the situation.

Alison's value system did not dictate that males were superior to females.

It did dictate that people who were doing proper jobs were more valuable than people who were not. In fact it said more precisely that one of the most important and valuable things in life was for people to fight for a good cause. Alison perceived work as one possible way to fight for a good cause, though she did not see it as the only way by any means. She sensed therefore that John was engaged in the sort of life that was valuable and that she had no right to interfere with this. It would have been against her principles to try to keep him away from his work as long as this work was such a challenge and so valuable. She just knew she could not stop him, without consciously being able to explain why this was. She also just knew in this same intuitive manner, that her own life at the moment was being wasted and that she herself had therefore become totally valueless to herself and to anyone else.

Instead of trying to contradict Alison's beliefs about the world, it was of the utmost importance to help her to recognize them herself. She needed some assistance in formulating out loud to herself what her conscience was telling her in a direct and non-verbal manner. As always, one of the guiding principles here was to look with Alison at what seemed to draw her motivation and energy most right now. In order to get an idea of what her own views were on what in life really mattered she had to establish what she was most serious about.

It was obvious that her energy was mostly directed towards trying to keep John faithful to her and avoiding a divorce. She could see how clumsily she was doing all this and how she was having results that were in contradiction with her intentions. Yet she remained adamant that her intention definitely was to fight for her marriage and for keeping the family together. If the result did not match her intention then at least she would be able to have peace with herself for having tried hard enough. This was very significant in that it indicated Alison's commitment to the value of putting up a fight for what seemed to be a good cause.

When she explored this idea of the good cause further it soon became evident that the cause itself mattered little, but that the principle of total involvement in an accomplishment was the significant factor.

To Alison a meaningful life would be the life lived in the pursuit of some worthwhile cause. She could imagine living without John and Joanne and still live a fulfilling life. But she could not imagine herself content by simply continuing along the lines of her present life, in other words with her husband and daughter but without a real challenge.

When she started to see the implications of what she was finding out about her own intentions it occurred to her at once that her jealous outbursts had been the closest she could get to the pursuit of a worthwhile cause: keeping her family together. But now that her own intentions were clear she could forthwith dismiss this particular course of action as a miserable and useless substitute for some real battle.

Stories of the golden days when she used to be the heart and soul of her troop of Girl Guides were interspersed with tales of her accomplishments in the catering department of the hospital. Alison appeared to be a self-assured and vigorous person when she reflected on her various successful deeds and actions. She seemed to have lived a particularly challenging life until quite recently. Her first years at home with her baby had also been well filled. She had been an active member of a mothers' and toddlers' group for several years, in charge of the tea and biscuits, but also setting up ventures of selling home-baked cakes and sweets.

She stopped actively participating in anything outside of the house around the time Joanne first started attending primary school. It emerged after long reflection and evasiveness that Alison had felt embarrassed to take part in school events because now the more intellectual parents were becoming more prominent and she felt inferior. She feared that with Joanne growing up other skills would be required than the ones she had. Hence her fear that John would take over.

The counsellor pointed out that there seemed to be a worthwhile cause here that Alison was letting slip by. What about fighting for the success and dignity of people such as herself, who had much to offer and had a lot of energy with it, but who felt defeated by the system as a foregone conclusion. This remark did predictably not fall on stony ground. The counselling sessions continued the further exploration of the underlying values involved in Alison's desire to stop feeling inferior for not having completed her schooling. But at the same time she got herself involved in assisting with the preparation of school dinners in Joanne's school.

As happens so often, this initiative provided further material for the understanding of her subjective value system. At the same time it afforded an opportunity for her to get a glimpse of what she would herself consider worthwhile. She found herself envying the lady in charge of the school dinners in almost as intense a way as she had previously been jealous of John. The pursuit of this issue threw up a new perspective, which linked all her previous concerns.

Alison discovered that she had experienced discontinuing to work outside the home as an escape from something that she needed to face now. This was the fact that though she was a good, or even an excellent cook, she would not have been able to pursue a career in catering in the way she desired, for lack of the proper training and schooling. She could not imagine herself ever making up for this lack. Once her career at home had also become blocked by only being able to have one child, there had not seemed any avenues open to her. Therefore she had grown bitter and had started feeling that she had to try to hold on to John and Joanne desperately.

She could now see that she was living a life totally in contradiction with her own values and that she must therefore more and more despise herself as long as she continued in this same trend. Her envy of the head of the kitchen in school thus led her actually to reconsider her own mistrust of her abilities for further training. It was only because she recognized her wish to do well in catering as an eligible cause worth fighting for that she found the courage to apply for the relevant course.

Getting onto this course was half the struggle. When she succeeded in this she realized that she was perfectly capable of handling the training, not only in its practical aspects but also its theoretical component. She recovered a sense of dignity in herself that she had given up on as an option.

Alison's discovery was that of many clients who start getting an insight into their own value system and who learn to act accordingly. It was that of discovering that the external world suddenly becomes much more real and meaningful when internal subjective reality is adhered to rather than dismissed as not feasible.

In working with clients towards their understanding of what it is that has ultimate value for them, the objective is always to enable them to find ways in which they can implement their values and their subjective reality in some concrete way. They are encouraged to cease to submit themselves blindly to the assumptions they have been making about the requirements of objective reality. However, it is of the utmost importance that the therapist does not make direct suggestions about how to proceed with this implementation. Remember that where clients do not find their own motivation to take action this almost always indicates that they have not yet unearthed their motivating values.

When people do become aware of what it is that they would be willing to die for if necessary it is usually also immediately obvious to them what it would consequently be worth living for as well. Though in many cases this something involves some direct action or activity there are also instances of people's values having been betrayed by overemphasis on action and activity.

Sonya's plight well illustrates this point. She approached a counsellor on a friend's advice because she had been unsuccessful at combating a powerful insomnia, by various means. Her difficulty in sleeping kept her tossing and turning till four or five o'clock in the morning, only allowing her two or three hours of actual sleep every night. She had to be at work by nine o'clock and she would often have great trouble in getting up and being ready on time because she would be absolutely exhausted and heavy with sleep when the alarm sounded. This pattern had been going on for nearly three years.

In the first session Sonya insisted that it was nonsense to take sleeping tablets or use other artificial means of getting to sleep such as hypnosis, which she had tried for a while. She dismissed these as so many 'fool's traps', which was a polite translation of a rude French expression. Sonya was a very successful thirty-seven-year-old French lady working in the fashion industry on an international scale. She was the living image of the glamorous career woman: poised, sophisticated, well-groomed. She announced that she had no time to squander and generally indicated that she would not take lightly to being used in any way. She had an extremely lively manner and a sharp tongue.

What she wanted was a sure-fire quick remedy for her insomnia. She felt that her life would be fine if this minor but irritating and irksome habit of wakefulness could be bridled in some lasting way. She had opted for existential counselling because she believed herself to be an existentialist; she viewed existentialism as an action-oriented philosophy, which would allow people to have total control over their lives.

The counsellor simply indicated to Sonya how the aim of the sessions in her eyes would be not necessarily to take control over life, but certainly to understand why taking control would seem such an attractive option. The counsellor added that while the insomnia would be an obvious place to start exploring her way of living and her views on life, it would undoubtedly lead to the investigation of everything else as well. She then stressed the importance of Sonya's commitment to honesty in looking into herself and her own attitudes. She emphasized how the work to be done could only be done in absolute loyal co-operation. Sonya replied that she liked the clear-cut business arrangement and that she would hold her end of the partnership.

She began the next session, which was really the first counselling session, with the announcement that she had a confession to make. She felt that the counsellor needed to know that she had not been quite honest with her, in that she had omitted various details of her present situation. First of all her real name was not Sonya, which was merely her trading name, but Anne. She still preferred to be called Sonya, but thought it best to let the counsellor know that this was an assumed name.

She went immediately on to relate the misery she had gone through a few years previously when she had had three miscarriages in a span of fifteen months. Having described the horrors of this experience in some vivid detail, she dismissed this episode of her life with a swift wave of her hand and a nonchalant 'C'est la vie . . .' She now pursued her account of herself with a mention of her disturbed and disturbing relationship with her husband of ten years, Peter, himself a busy professional as well.

Sonya spoke for over twenty-five minutes without interruption and without any encouragement from the counsellor. Her story was clear and to the point. Her language was colourful and her tone of voice extremely emotional and even theatrical. She demonstrated an extraordinary ability to express deep despair one minute and to disengage from it the next moment almost in the same breath.

During all this time the counsellor felt constantly drawn into some sort of competition. It was as if Sonya was testing her ability to match this vitality. She was signifying to her with every sentence that she, Sonya, was a superior human being, who was totally in charge of herself and of the counselling situation and therefore not really in need of counselling at all.

Although the counsellor was tempted to stop Sonya several times in order to make some clever remark about the obvious, she stopped herself from doing so because she was aware of the competitive element in her motivation to speak. She waited for Sonya to have finished entirely. Even then she simply sat and looked at Sonya in a friendly but quiet manner. The following dialogue ensued:

Sonya: *Enfin*, aren't you going to say something?
Counsellor: Should I?
Sonya: I was supposing you would now tell me what to do, where to look, how to work out these problems . . . [*Ten-second silence, Sonya lights a cigarette.*]

Counsellor: Let's suppose that I wouldn't.

Sonya: [*looking slightly puzzled*] I definitely think you should. This is what I am paying you for.

Counsellor: [*after some reflection*] Let's suppose you are paying me for staying silent.

Sonya: [*looking dramatically horrified*] Ahh no. I don't need an audience. I have that in my work.

Counsellor: So what if I did remain silent?

Sonya: I would go elsewhere, to someone who would tell me how to solve my problems.

Counsellor: You are assuming that there is a specific recipe to solve your problems? [*This said slowly and soberly.*]

Sonya: Yes, yes [*said rather quickly and impatiently*]. . . . No. No. [*She looks more reflective now.*]

Counsellor: What if you took some time to think through your own problems, rather than rushing around for solutions?

Sonya: This is precisely what I find difficult to do. I can plan my work perfectly well. I can handle my staff, my travelling arrangements, the rushing around at busy times of the season, the shows. It's no problem. As long as I am on the move, at the job, in the middle of things I can handle almost anything, I enjoy it, I thrive on it, I revel in it, I love it, even at the worst of times. It's a game and I'm good at it. It's so absorbing. It's with me day and night. There is no time for personal problems.

Counsellor: So even at night, when you can't sleep, it's your work you're thinking of, it's your work that keeps you awake?

Sonya: Always my work. I never think about my personal problems. I am not the self-indulgent type. Even at the time of the miscarriages I spared no thought for my own unhappiness; I was just worried about the way in which the business could deal with my absence.

Counsellor: This is clearly something you are proud of.

Sonya: Hmm [*nods emphatically*].

Counsellor: So let's see what it is that makes your work so valuable to you. What about it is so important that you let it take up all your nights and days.

Sonya: [*immediately ready to provide the answer*] It's . . .

Counsellor: [*interrupting*] Why not take some time to ponder?

Sonya now proceeded to explore her reasons for liking and even worshipping her work and her own role in her business. She needed quite a lot of assistance in keeping focused on her experience of her own situation as she tended to wander off into picturesque descriptions of events and people around her.

As is the case with many clients, she was quick to express feelings about things. She would get quite worked up over the recounting of certain interchanges with members of her staff in particular. She expressed extreme disgust and loathing for their stupidity and lackadaisical behaviour. It was a different matter when it came to thinking through her sentiments and reflecting on her experience. She was unused to taking time to orientate herself in her own inner world. Her attitude was all action-and reaction-oriented. The social dimension with its public demands dominated her worldview.

Sonya soon picked up the principles involved in existential exploration. She would come to sessions reporting for instance how she had stopped herself in the middle of a fit of anger against one of her employees, simply by wondering which project she was defending, which of her intentions she felt was being thwarted. There were many small events that she reported to illustrate her typical way of approaching life and other people and she was gratified in being able to locate her own mode of being in this way and gain some distance from it in the telling.

Slowly a map of her worldview emerged. On it 'influence' figured as the central avenue towards value and a meaningful existence. Sonya recognized her own desire to command respect in a position of authoritative leadership as her main motivating force. She had organized her whole life around the attainment of this goal. She had in fact achieved her goal, for she was in a position of great influence and respect. The only problem was that now that she had achieved this central value, as she had determined it for herself, it was no longer meaningful in itself. The flaws of her philosophy of life were starting to show up. The insomnia was the most potent reminder of her weakness and of her inability to be in total control. The eagerly forgotten miscarriages were an even more eloquent witness of her failings.

The evidence was accumulating against her way of life. She was experiencing grave doubts about her position in the world and the significance of what she had managed to achieve. Although she was apparently in total control of her firm and her own life, it was slowly starting to sink in that the more she gained external control the less she was her own person. She increasingly felt compelled to achieve more and more; it was, as she remarked, like a drug-addiction.

From the moment she first expressed this fear of her dependency on her external success and control, Sonya became open to her inner world. She grew less preoccupied with the effort of projecting the image of the professional lady in charge.

It now became possible to take a fresh look at her value system, as she had now genuinely started to take stock of her life rather than defending it. It was particularly one day after she had had another blazing row with husband, Peter, that she admitted to herself that she feared that her marriage was a total failure. She thought that this was directly related to the way in which she did or rather did not, relate to Peter as a person. The row, as usual, had been one for dominance and had involved a group of friends whom they were taking out. Sonya's experience had been one of public humiliation. This had roused her temper to such an extent that she had ended up leaving the restaurant where they were dining, in the middle of the meal.

Her sense of humiliation brought her face-to-face with her own limitations. Her immediate reaction was to deny this and run away. She knew one hundred ways to pay Peter back and to convince the friends of his wrong. The following extract from the ensuing counselling session gives the flavour of the way in which this minor crisis became a breaking-through point for her.

> Sonya: [after a three-minute account of the ways in which she will punish Peter for his behaviour] No one, absolutely no one should be left to get away with such a conduct. The humiliation. Ahhh.
>
> Counsellor: That's the crucial point, isn't it: your experience of humiliation. It destroys your whole reason for being. It goes against all you strive for.

Sonya: Oh, my God. I could have killed him. Then and there. I could have strangled him. I still could. Just the thought of it again. He humiliated me, with them there. Humiliated me, what nerve.

Counsellor: What nerve indeed to humiliate you. Perhaps you should be grateful for his pluck.

Sonya: Pardon? [*She looks outraged but interested.*]

Counsellor: At last we have a chance to see you at work when you're down. From the sound of it you were already planning to get up and on top again.

Sonya: Are you suggesting I should remain humiliated?

Counsellor: Is that unbearable?

Sonya: [*lighting a cigarette*] Hmmm, no, I would not be inclined to bear it.

Counsellor: You would fight back and make sure you win, but in doing so perhaps miss an opportunity for recognizing your own limitations and for discovering new aspects to things.

Sonya: My God, you don't make it easy for me.

Counsellor: [*shaking her head*] No.

[*There now follows a three-minute silence, the first long period of silence in Sonya's sessions ever. She is obviously touched. Eventually she puts her cigarette out vigorously.*]

Sonya: I shouldn't smoke either.

Counsellor: Why not?

Sonya: It's just all part of the same thing, isn't it. I just run and run on. I never stop. I never really stop to think about me.

Counsellor: Not even when you lie awake at night.

Sonya: No. No. I just plan my running for the next day then.

Counsellor: Not even when you get humiliated. Not even when you lose something that's precious to you.

Sonya: That hurts. I don't want it to hurt. I don't want to lose.

Counsellor: So you just keep running away from the hurt, faster and faster, until no one can keep up with you any longer, not even yourself: you run so fast that you can't even find time to rest and recuperate. As if there is no time to lose.

Sonya: But the faster I run, the faster time is running out. People can't keep up with me, but I can't keep up with time.

Counsellor: What does that mean, keeping up with time?

Sonya: Ohh. My God. [*She wrenches her hands, then stretches her arms out to the sky.*] Have pity on me. I have made so many mistakes. I was wrong. I was wrong [*She sobs rather dramatically.*]

Counsellor: How were you wrong?

Sonya: I ran after illusions. I was trying to be like God. I was trying to control everything. I controlled nothing but my illusions. Such arrogance. Then there was no peace. That was the price. I couldn't find peace: no sleep, no love, no babies. I wanted everything. I got nothing. They despise me. I didn't even fool them.

Counsellor: You fooled yourself though.

Sonya: I did not know. I was the last to know.

Counsellor: That sounds like you have been unfaithful to yourself in love.

Sonya: [*thinks this one over for a little while, then in an almost inaudible voice murmurs*] I betrayed Anne.

This was the end of the session and at the same time the end of the first phase of the counselling process. Sonya after this began to explore a much deeper sense of value, which she had buried deep down in herself with the life and name of Anne. She now understood that the thing most precious and important to her was to live a fulfilling life. She defined this as being able to signify something for other people. Her frantic pursuit of success in business was an expression of that desire. She was trying to obtain that which would make life worth living. She craved confirmation of her own completeness through other people's recognition of her success.

Having come to this conclusion the paradox of her own situation started to stare her in the face. She seemed to be getting quite the opposite of what she was looking for. There was no sense of completion at all. Her definition of completion was a sense of peace in the knowledge that one is well and truly alive. She experienced her own life as a constant rush, chasing after acknowledgement from others and with a constant doubt about her own existence. The insomnia was the perfect expression of this paradox. Instead of being able to give in to a basic trust in her own ability to renew herself in sleep, she frantically tried to mastermind her continued aliveness by planning for tomorrow, thus keeping herself awake.

The basic theme that started to emerge was that of control versus abandonment and trust. This became particularly acute when she contemplated the meaning to her of the concept of fulfilment, which she considered to be so significant. It occurred to Sonya that fulfilment would come with abandonment and surrender to something one cannot control but that is basically benign and creative. The sort of fulfilment she was producing for herself was only second best; it came through incessant effort in an endeavour to master and control her environment.

Sonya now discovered how and why her efforts must remain vain: instead of giving in to sleep she was trying to master it. Instead of drifting off to sleep she was trying to drive herself to sleep; instead of surrendering and trusting she was controlling and forcing. She would not be able to go to sleep, not for a lack of wanting it, but for a lack of trusting and believing that she would be able to. She expected nothing to come easy; she expected to have to work hard to gain sleep at night. Her expectation made her proceed accordingly with a control orientated approach towards sleep where only a yielding approach would work.

Of course sleep was only a very small, almost incidental example of Sonya's misunderstanding of herself and her world. It soon became clear that she made precisely the same mistake in her relationships with other people as well. With her husband, Peter, in particular she had not once allowed herself to yield. She feared that he might abuse her if she let him think that she needed him in any way. She was constantly on her guard: always ready for attack or counter-attack, ever doubting the possibility of finding understanding, compassion and real intimacy.

Sonya, having started counselling in the belief that her life was nearly a complete success, now began to wonder if it had been a total failure. Somehow she needed to go to extremes in order to feel alive. She plunged herself into despair over her failure and in this way allowed herself to let go of her tight control. She became willing to contemplate what had previously been swept under the carpet. She began to consider her distress over her childlessness.

She soon established for herself that having children would have been her ideal of a fulfilling life. Procreation, she felt, especially for a woman, was about yielding to nature and principles far beyond humanity. In the process a woman received the blessing of her own flesh coming to life in a miraculous and wondrous way.

For Sonya, however, procreation had not worked out anything like that in practice. She had first had two abortions to accommodate the demands of her profession. Then she had had three miscarriages, when she tried to have children. She was left with a sense of destruction and suffering. She soon declared that she felt a deep sense of guilt about all this. It was as if she had killed her babies by not being able to surrender to the natural process and remaining tightly in control. Instead of receiving and welcoming what nature had intended her to take charge of, she had rejected it. She had pursued a wild-goose chase after fame and fortune and so she had neglected the source of life inside her. She saw the miscarriages as a just punishment for her own arrogance. She had paid the price for remaining in control. Now she had got even with herself.

Her attitude was very different now from that of the person who had begun working towards some understanding of her own life five months previously. She decided to stop coming for sessions for a while because she needed to get on with living her life for a bit and try to digest her new insights. She knew that therapeutic counselling was not about attempting to plaster over the cracks and get rid of symptoms such as sleeplessness. She felt ready to try again on her own without assistance and see what would happen. She also confessed to wanting to experiment with the life she had created for herself. For now that she understood what she had done wrong she thought she might be able to do it right.

For about eleven months Sonya gave herself totally to her career. She exhausted herself entirely in the process, for she no longer tried to make herself sleep unless she could not keep her eyes open. Instead of tossing and turning she sat up at night and worked or prepared new strategies for her career. She was extremely successful in what she undertook.

After this time of all-out devotion to her second best choice, she returned to the therapeutic process, to work out what she wanted to do with her life. She felt that she had proved to herself that her social success was indeed not fulfilling in the sense that she would like it to be. The idea was to find out how she could learn to surrender, so that she would discover the secret of human relationships and of childbearing. It took her nearly a year before she started to realize that once again she had been trying to discover the magic formula by which she could manipulate and control her fate.

Noticing the slowness of her own progress was in the end the only way in which Sonya could learn about surrender. It was soon after she made a remark to this effect one day that she reached an important conclusion. It did not really make that much of a difference what precisely she would do with the rest of her life, she found, as long as she could discover value in it just as it was.

She became pregnant within two months of this shift in her experience of herself and she kept the baby. She left her work, to almost everybody's astonishment and horror, and she began a phase of her life which was marked by a very different, though not less problematic, state of affairs. Insomnia was no longer a problem as she gave in to the tiredness accompanying her pregnancy and later the care for her baby. She became quite at ease with bodily experience, which before had usually been centred on appearances only. She gave up smoking and marvelled over the rediscovery of her sense of smell, which she now also found, was an important part of sleeping and feeling comfortable. But as private world relations were coming more to the fore, a new range of problems had to be dealt with. Her relationship with Peter and her relationship with the baby caused considerable distress.

Sonya discovered how life's challenges are never tackled overnight and how understanding the values that one wants to live by is a process that is to be renewed and questioned over and over again. While finding a deep fulfilment in herself through committing herself to what she felt was worth living for, she still had to uproot the mistaken assumption that doing this would make everything all right once and for all. Eventually Sonya grasped the notion that values can only be guidelines and not guarantors of bliss and happiness. She tried to find a way of life that satisfied her various needs and made room for both her career and her home and personal life and this search continued to occupy her quite fully. She had learnt to keep searching and not expect to ever find a permanent or definitive answer.

In assisting clients in determining the values they want to live by, it is essential to help them in thinking through the implications and consequences of the sort of life they are setting out to live in accordance with these values. Often this raises the issue of the client's ability to stick by her own intentions. Examining and exploring the talents that she can draw on in this process is therefore frequently indicated.

Exploring talents

Once the client has been able to identify her motivating force, by determining what it is that really and ultimately matters to her and is worth living and dying for, the remaining question is how she can implement and realize this value in practice.

Paradox reigns here as much as in other areas of human experience. Clients will often discover that they tend to apply their talents in ways that are diametrically opposed to what they intended. Sonya's experience was an illustration of such a paradox. She employed her basic talent for creativity and organization in such an exclusive and controlling manner that she deprived herself of the enjoyment of the fruits of her labour, depleting herself without replenishment, making fulfilment impossible.

As was the case for Sonya, this kind of paradox frequently rests on a misconception about self and the world. It stems from a lack of insight into what is involved in living. People are naturally inclined to stumble blindly around in their lives. They apply their talents in whichever direction they happen to be drawn at any time and without much thought about the implications and consequences of their actions. Reflective living does not come naturally; it has to be acquired. Gaining insight into one's own abilities and the ways of managing them takes experience and active deliberation. Gaining understanding of human existence, and awareness of the directions in which one can go takes even more experience and more reflection and deliberation. Passive living comes easily; one can always fall back on it. Active living requires much practise and study, as does any art.

Many clients will expect a fairly easy progress. They will be prepared to work to find the root of their difficulties if this puts an end to their suffering. But they will expect rewards fairly soon. The only reward that will provide sufficient motivation to carry on is when they uncover strengths that were unsuspected or that were previously used in self-destructive rather than constructive ways. With the discovery of such hitherto hidden forces and strengths, a new sense of power will be experienced which will make further learning and exploration seem desirable rather than just necessary. To reach this self-motivating dynamism it is crucial that the therapist insistently keeps the focus on the client's inner experience of herself and her world. In doing this the emphasis will be not on what the client is doing wrong and how miserable she is making herself, but on the talents themselves, implicit in the mistakes that are being made.

One way of going about this is to use the already described method of a 'why not?' enquiry. When a client keeps harping on certain elements of her own disastrous habits or characteristics, the counsellor may stimulate her to take a fresh look at the underlying qualities involved. She can do this by encouraging the client to look for the basic principle at the root of the negative behaviour or experience and work out the talent which it implies and which could be put to better use.

If a client, for instance, complains of her seemingly inevitable propensity for rationality, a suitable intervention might be to encourage her to reconsider her instant rejection of the quality, by simply asking 'Why not be rational?' This type of examination of implied value-judgement and assumptions is almost always productive.

First of all the therapist clearly indicates by such questions that she genuinely stands on the side of an exploration of truth rather than on that of blindly relying on opinion. In doing so she makes it easier for the client also to consider herself in the light of a search for truth rather than with a negative bias or from an assumption of her life being fixed.

Second, the therapist takes the investigation into the arena of what is already acquired, rather than that of what is missing. In doing so the seed is sown for a rehabilitation of prized but hidden characteristics and existing but misused talents.

Third the client is thus encouraged to think twice about her own usual way of dismissing certain things and finding certain other things attractive. She is reminded in those few words that her own views on why or why not to be a particular way are important subjects of consideration and investigation.

The client may reply from a stance of wishing to comply with other people's standards and norms, saying something like 'but everyone tells me it is wrong to be so rational'. In this case her assumptions about compliance with social world reality will be worth investigating. She may on the contrary reply that she feels herself handicapped being so overly rational. In this case it will be useful to get some definitions of what rationality means to her, so that an underlying positive principle and talent can be unearthed.

It may in fact become obvious that although the client is complaining of being too rational, she in fact only feels obliged to pay lip-service to this kind of disapproval of a characteristic, that she deep down values as a major asset. The therapist will only be able to help the client acknowledge such a conflict in so far as she herself is sufficiently detached from immediate value-judgements on qualities. This type of detachment and open-mindedness is the result of an insight into the complexities of human character and inclination. It is based on an understanding of the paradox of human experience rather than a dualistic either/or view of human abilities and characteristics. The existential therapist will be able to view each characteristic against the back-ground not only of its counterpart or opposite quality but also with the awareness of their binding and unifying principle.

The client may, for example, repeatedly report incidents that indicate a certain rigidity in her approach to life. If it then happens that she complains of others accusing her of stubbornness, a search for underlying basic principle and talents is clearly pertinent. By assisting the client in an exploration of her own experience of these events it may come to light that she does not see herself as stubborn or rigid but rather as faithfully sticking to her guns. She thus rejects the label of 'obstinate' for her behaviour and prefers to see it as insistent or even more positively as determined and resolute. This is not a mere matter of linguistic subtlety; being able to pinpoint the client's positive interpretation of personal characteristics is the key to a person's willingness to work on her own attitudes and perception of reality.

It is crucial that people feel at ease and confident with their own basic positive qualities and abilities before they can start questioning the negative counterparts. Also it is a fact that most people have enormously good intentions; they deserve some credit for the positive part of their efforts at making the best of life. After that it will be much easier for them to start contemplating what is amiss and to begin to balance out distortions. Once a client has started reflecting on her personal talent for determination, she will probably indicate how she despises people who lack firmness or steadfastness: she might dismiss them as weak or unstable, perhaps even as unreliable. This demonstrates her consistency of outlook and makes it possible to point out the implications of such a one-sided, though consistent, view.

People typically do attempt to make life more liveable by holding on to such one-sided notions about reality; coping with the inherent paradox of life requires much understanding. Gaining that understanding is made easier by referring to the unifying principle. In this case the unifying principle is 'will'. The paradox involved is the principle of will embodying two polarities, which each have positive and negative qualities and which therefore have constantly to counterbalance one another.

Ultimately, total and exclusive wilfulness will lead to destruction of self and others, but so will total absence of will, complete indecision or indifference. Neither pole is good in itself, nor bad in itself. The secret of constructive use of the principle of 'will' lies in the ability to apply the continuum of its possibilities flexibly. This must be done appropriately according to the situation and always through dynamically balancing the opposites rather than in a static manner.

This client may slowly begin to grasp how, in opting consistently for one end of the spectrum, she is excluding her experience of the positive qualities that exist on the other end. She may also begin to see how in doing so she is condemning herself to having to bear the consequences of the negative implications of her end of the spectrum, without the ability to balance these by veering to the other end.

Concretely, the client may recognize how she is able to make constructive use of her will, in sticking to tasks or getting her own way at times. Then she may see evidence of how she is also condemning herself to being inflexible or rigid. She will also recognize how she is automatically protected against lack of wilfulness. She is unlikely to slide into limbo, which she can observe happening to some other people. But by the same token she is losing out on the use of adaptability and flexibility. By her one-sided upholding of wilfulness as positive she also condemns the positive sides of pliability.

The basic talent that this client has already acquired is thus seen as the first step towards managing the whole spectrum of the paradox of human experience. Whatever the client starts off with, there is always an indication of some human ability and talent that is already acquired. If the client complains of her indecisiveness for instance this automatically indicates her already acquired ability to be adaptable or to be open to different possibilities.

It is just like the old trick of recognizing that the glass of wine which is half empty can also be viewed as half full. It is like the useful habit of counting one's blessings, referred to in the Bible, which is not a mere matter of optimism but the only starting point for an improvement of the situation. Interestingly clients almost without exception take to the suggestion of their existing talents like ducks to water. All too often their secret longing in coming to counselling or therapy is that it will confirm their own best hopes about themselves. All too often all that is on offer to them is a miserable confirmation of their own worst fears. The latter can only be tackled by a solid and lucid building on the former.

People seldom have trouble with acceptance of the notion that no one is perfect: they are usually quite willing to recognize the ways in which they can expand their existing repertoire. They must first, however, be allowed publicly to establish this existing repertoire of merits. It is easy to miss a client's implicit request for acknowledgement of her talents. People are often very shy about the recognition of their abilities.

Clients may, for instance, list their failings, whilst implying the merit of honesty by doing so. They may report having been cruel to someone they care for, thus implying their usual lovingness. They may report that they are inevitably stuck with a certain area of their life, dying to receive praise for their noble commitment to sticking it out no matter what.

The most humble person is often deeply convinced of her own grandeur in humility. It is the task of the therapist to bring these hidden qualities and this veiled self-confidence out in the open, without malice and without condemnation or ridicule. There is nothing more valuable and essential than this making explicit of the client's essential belief in herself and her basic ability to live. Denying it or denigrating it will make the client unwilling to work any further.

This demonstrates once again how the existential practitioner is to be a companion on the road towards further self-discovery. She is an ally, the voice of the client's good conscience, in the very best sense of the word. She thus enables the client to make the most of what is already there and to continue expanding the repertoire. Pointing out pitfalls and short-sightedness on the way will be the natural and logical counterpart of this role of guardian angel. As soon as the client has come to think of this monitoring as an essential and familiar function, she will cease to shy away from relating to herself in a similar fashion. She will then be far more at ease with the full exploitation of her own talents and more capable of facing life with confidence.

Frequently clients are raring to go back to living a normal life without help of the counsellor as soon as they get an inkling of the new possibilities in store. In this they are rather like children who have been shown a new skill and who can hardly wait their turn to try it out for themselves. Sometimes the professional will be inclined to want to remain too closely involved at this stage. Psychotherapists and counsellors often do have an inclination towards protectiveness. However, it seems as if once clients gain confidence in their own ability to undertake a new leg of life's journey under their own steam, it is often preferable that they do so straight away. With some insight and understanding there is no better teacher than experience itself. Old sayings are often based on good sense and in this case there is no doubt that practise indeed makes perfect.

Karl's story illustrates these points quite nicely. Karl was a young German who wanted some help in sorting out the mess he felt he was getting himself into in his life. He had come to England at a time when new European regulations had provided the opportunity to find work in Britain, whereas his past political activities had made remaining in Germany particularly unattractive. Karl was not permitted to work as a teacher in Germany even though he had the relevant qualifications, because he had been involved in subversive left-wing action during his student days. He was quite bitter about this state of affairs and spent much time criticizing German bourgeois morality. He had, however, known ahead of time that this would happen and he had chosen to continue his ardent political provocation because he strongly believed in the cause he was fighting for.

It soon transpired that though he currently felt as if he were in exile and though he hated every minute of this, there was nevertheless a certain satisfaction in the experience of having become a martyr for his ideals. Karl quickly elaborated on this theme of his pride in his own heroism. He was obviously gratified by the notion of his complete loyalty to his ideas. He felt as if he had remained in one piece, because he had not given in to pressure from the establishment, he had not sold out for the sake of saving his own skin. Therefore he could look himself in the eye and feel self-respect, even pride in his own fidelity to the cause and to himself.

Once this side of things was clearly established, it became possible to consider the paradox of the situation and examine the implications of such heroism for his current everyday life. The picture here was less satisfying. Karl felt miserable; in fact he had begun to doubt the sense of his previous attitude altogether. He had left his friends and companions behind in Germany. Some of them were still students, some were involved in full-time political activities of an illegal kind and some others had now begun their teaching careers. He himself was only doing freelance work as a German teacher as well as some occasional translating for a publishing company. He disliked London and despaired of ever again being part of an in-crowd.

It was this experience of being the alien in a foreign culture that had shocked Karl most. He had not expected it to be so tough to have to live in a foreign country, where everything was different and he was always the outsider. To his horror he missed the very things that he had revolted against whilst in Germany. He started doubting his own good sense in having gambled away his career for ideas that were now starting to fade.

Yet, he could not just give up his old ideals: he had, as he said, to have something to believe in, if not he would 'go round the bend'. This is what made him so bitter; he felt stuck for a dignified solution out of an impossible situation and the obvious solution was to blame things on the people responsible for his self-imposed expulsion. He therefore hesitated between blaming the authorities and German bourgeois morality in general or blaming himself for being naive and idealistic. In practice these two attitudes implied two possible solutions to his dilemma. If he persisted in blaming the authorities he had the option of joining a group of political activists with whom he had been in contact already who would be happy to have him join their ranks. He was particularly attracted by the sense of belonging he would experience again and by the vehemence of the protest and revolutionary action that it would involve him in. He had grave doubts about the rightness of such action. His own ideals and values did not accommodate the extremism of this approach, however bitter he had now become.

The other, diametrically opposed, solution was to pack in his previous notions of right and wrong and to return to Germany with his tail hanging between his legs. He would then accept conforming to the establishment and taking up some job in private schools or in industry. This was attractive in that it would allow him to go back home and take up with his old habits and friends. It was despicable in that it would deny and annihilate all he had been committed to in the past.

Clearly, neither of these solutions was satisfactory. Karl needed to think through his ideals and values and decide where his talents could be most usefully employed in a constructive manner and how he could develop them in a direction that would accommodate his ideals as well as his realism.

Interestingly, one of his deepest beliefs was in the ideal of a dialectical society. He longed for a society where there would be no clashes of opposites, because there would be no holding on to set positions, but a dynamic integration of forces in the direction of constant change and growth instead. What Karl was not aware of at all was the possibility of applying such a theoretical notion in his personal life as well. He had simply not realized that his difficulties were based on a view of life in black and white, in either–or, rather than as a dialectic intertwining of opposites.

No sooner had Karl caught a glimpse of the chance he had been neglecting of practising in his own life what he had been preaching in theory, than he began excitedly to plan new ways of implementing the third strategy. He called this 'the new matured dialectical lifestyle', with a twinkle in his eye, which signified both his relief to be finding a decent and dignified way out of his impasse and a slight self-mockery of his own previous helplessness.

Finding an alternative lifestyle that could include the valuable elements of both rejected options became a challenge to Karl. Doing this in the right way and making a success of it would mean not only that he had a future to look forward to but also that his old ideals would have been proved solid and feasible.

Taking stock of the talents that he had already mastered and could further develop was the main objective of the following sessions. Karl viewed his own loyalty to his ideals as one of his main assets. He thought that it exemplified his ability to be steadfast and determined. He knew he would be able to count on himself to make the most of his life now that he saw a possibility for applying his determination again.

It was not so difficult for him now also to recognize how his determination could sometimes be negatively applied and turn into stubbornness. He found that this would usually occur as a result of his fear of new situations. It was mostly his experience of having to cope with living in a foreign country that had helped him to become aware of the stubborn side of his attitude. Previously he used to dismiss the thought of his being stubborn even though he was often told that he was. Funnily enough, he now became capable of identifying with some conservative attitudes. He could see how people would come to a conservative stance in politics; something that had seemed unbelievable and outrageous to him previously. In fact, he started to see how his own attitude had been conservative in many ways. With this insight came the understanding of the missing elements in his life: flexibility and adaptability, which he had previously rejected under the one heading of opportunism.

It became important to discover new roads; ways in which he might proceed towards implementation of his own values, without his former stubborn exclusive attitude. As is so often the case, while he was struggling to find concrete ways to apply his newly developed ideas, an opportunity arose which seemed to fit the bill perfectly, but which he would undoubtedly have dismissed previously as a bourgeois snare.

Karl was offered a part-time position in Germany with the publishing company he had been doing some freelance work for in Britain. Though the work itself was rather tedious, it was the first concrete offer of a job in his own country that he had ever had and as such it was very gratifying. Also it was situated in a town where one of his old friends had moved. This friend was one of the few that Karl still respected. He had joined a new – legal – political group, which was making significant contributions in line with Karl's ideals, even though it was far less revolutionary than anything he had been involved with previously.

Karl's hesitations about his new move were entirely dispelled after he made contact with this friend and was more or less invited into this party as a link person with British developments. Within six weeks Karl was settling back in Germany. While the therapeutic sessions obviously ended there, Karl remained in touch with his therapist at least once a year for five years and in this way confirmed his continued understanding of his own way of operating flexibly from a firm set of values and ideals. His progress was steady and rewarding. He said himself that he had learnt to search for a life in which he could feel both secure and challenged.

While much could be added to moderate this account, none of it would change the fact that Karl did make exceptionally good use of his sessions. This was not just because he felt a great urgency to come through the crisis in his life and because he felt very isolated and thus willing to look into himself more than normally. He also was able to take stock of what mattered to him and of what he was capable of and he did not refuse to consider abandoning some old assumptions in the process. He was thus freeing himself of the ways in which he had been employing his own talents against himself. He became ready to rebuild his strength in new creative ways rather than letting it go to waste through blind and misinformed idealism.

Some of the essential principles Karl did hold on to and kept developing over the years were his sense of wilfulness and his sense of specialness. He took particular pride in and strength from his ability to be resolute and from the belief in his own capacity to live a significant life in using his insights and experience to the full. One thing he had learnt however was to balance the power of his will by flexibility and openness to experience and to balance his sense of specialness with the awareness of everybody else's specialness as well. This was a direct result of his awareness that it was possible to apply theoretical notions such as dialectics in a practical and concrete way in his personal life by including paradox rather than trying to eliminate it.

Karl's story illustrates the importance of the recognition of personal talents as a key to the future. It indicates how talents can be uncovered and expanded by referring to the underlying principle and its so far neglected complementary elements. At the same time the work Karl had to accomplish was based on his having to recognize his original intention in order to locate and pinpoint the values and ideals that stood out for him as a guiding principle from which he could draw new motivation and strength as well. What became evident for Karl was that his values did not significantly have to change. There were numerous ways in which he could act in accordance with the same values. To a large extent this was a matter of gaining a broader perspective. His living abroad had a lot to do with this broadening of his outlook.

What Karl discovered was that it is important to have a general sense of direction in life, as well as a basic sense of one's own strength in pursuing this direction. At the same time it is useful to remain flexible about the specifics of one's journey as things cannot be completely planned and decided upon at the outset. On the journey one discovers new aspects to things, since they seem one way from a distance but quite another close up. Assumptions need therefore to be constantly questioned. Though it is impossible to live without building up certain expectations and assumptions about things, it is essential to remain capable of questioning these as soon as they are proved wrong or destructive. New assumptions will replace the old ones and therefore a continued alertness and questioning of these is ultimately necessary.

Values may change and be enlarged or on the contrary become more focused but very often people's general direction, as they intended it from the start, remains the same. They simply become more expert at orienting themselves and recognizing where they went wrong. Often values take on a deeper meaning when people mature; when the horizon of one's journey is reached, a new horizon has already replaced the old one. The goals of once upon a time are put back into perspective while one proceeds, though they will often still be understandable as useful and necessary intermediate milestones on the way.

The process of taking stock of the general layout of the person's lived world is thus set in train. Much of what is being discovered about what in the world matters most is due to a careful consideration of actions and reactions, moods, emotions, dreams and thoughts. Therefore more precise attention needs to be paid to the exact process of monitoring these in order to map out a person's experience of the world effectively.

Chapter summary

1   Existential work starts with a process of taking stock of one's life, which involves:

   • Clarifying the assumptions that we hold about the world on all four dimensions.
   • Establishing the values we hold and the ultimate concerns that preoccupy us.
   • Define and elaborate personal talents and abilities that have not yet been recognized and put to good use.

2   The existential therapist does not sell affection, empathy or unconditional approval, but nor does she aim for blind neutrality.
3   What is on offer is the therapist's expertise in living and her ability to unravel difficulties and make sense of them.

4   The emphasis of the work is on life rather than on the client's current predicament. The objective is not to soothe or accuse, but together to find truth. This means that all assumptions are investigated and value judgments are questioned.

5   Clients are not molly-coddled, but expected to do the work for themselves. They are helped to become aware of hidden strengths and encouraged to discover how they might be undermining and sabotaging themselves.

6   Recognizing one's likes, dislikes, principles, beliefs and motivations leads to working out one's value system.

7   Once a person's values become clear it is often evident that they are constantly unwittingly betraying the very things they hold dear.

8   Many people, without them being reflectively aware of this, live lives that are in flagrant contradiction with their own values and beliefs, so they need help in formulating their values and comparing and contrasting them with the implied values of their everyday actions.

9   Life is only experienced as meaningful if we feel we are in harmony with our own beliefs and are working towards making the structures and pathways of our life fit our sense of what is worthwhile.

10 People can be taught how to monitor their daily experience in order to become more aware of their worldview and of the goals and values that are most meaningful to them.

11 Concepts that are taken for granted often need to be checked and re-examined, questioned and redefined as a person starts on the road of discovery towards a more authentic direction in their life.

12 Consequences and implications of life choices need to be systematically explored and challenged and alternatives compared.

13 People often paradoxically apply their talents in ways that go against their original plans and intentions. They do not have to persist in pursuing the wrong direction if they become aware of this.

14 After determining what it is that ultimately matters to a person the next step is to establish what abilities and talents the person can draw on to achieve their objective.

15 Passive living comes easily, but almost inevitably leads to impasses and stagnation.

16 Learning to live deliberately rather than by default takes time and requires that we learn to reflect and self-reflect carefully.

17 Revealing the hidden strengths in clients' apparent weaknesses and the truths in their errors is the best way to build confidence and self-motivation.

18 Focusing on what is already acquired and working for the client is more effective than wasting time deploring what is missing and what has gone wrong.

19 Questioning negative traits can most effectively be done against the background of acknowledging positive ones.

20 Helping clients to be aware of the paradoxical nature of human existence can lead to helping them to find a dialectical way forward that draws on the strength in their weakness and takes account of the weakness in their strength.

5

Creative Explorations

Understanding emotions

Feelings play an important role in therapeutic sessions. Some clients simply cannot manage the intensity of their feelings. Others may not understand what it is they are feeling. Yet others complain of not being able to feel anything at all. For many clients feelings seem to contradict reason and they therefore become confused when emotions take over. Sooner or later with each client the issue of managing emotions has to be addressed. Understanding the message of emotions can be a powerful way of gaining further insight into your mode of being.

Many practitioners mistakenly assume that what matters is to encourage clients simply to express their feelings. They think that catharsis will bring relief of most forms of distress and they congratulate themselves when their clients cry or shout. There is no doubt that having a good cry or shout can make one feel better momentarily and that suppressing emotions can be harmful. At the same time the mere reactive type of emotional experience is in itself never sufficient to solve anybody's problems. What is needed is the understanding of what the emotion is indicating about the way in which you are conducting your life.

When physical pain is experienced it means that there is something wrong with your body and you know that you need to attend to it and remove the cause of pain. When negative emotions are experienced it means that there is something wrong in your existence and you know that you need to attend to it. Merely expressing the pain or the emotion will not in itself right the situation or improve your life. The same applies to pleasure and positive emotions. Merely expressing the experience will be no guarantee that you have learnt anything constructive about how to achieve more of the same in the future.

Existential counselling and therapy set out to help clients in learning to read the message of their emotional experience, so that they can master it rather than suffer it. Learning to live with your emotions is rather like learning to surf on a rough ocean. At first you feel totally at the mercy of the unpredictable waves. They come flooding in before you are prepared for them. You get submerged, overwhelmed, sometimes nearly suffocated or drowned. But with practise you gain a sense of the direction of the streams and it becomes possible to ride on the crest of the wave instead of being knocked out by it. Then a powerful feeling of mastery and harmony is experienced. The ocean will still remain indomitable, but now its power can be participated in because it is understood.

Emotions are the ebb and flow of human experience. They are always there and their currents and undercurrents need to be taken into account. When feelings run high you can easily get swept away, when they are low you can get a sense of stagnation. Understanding the tides of the emotions is the only way to benefit from and exploit the power that feelings generate. Emotions are the source of much energy. They move you and drive you to action. Tuning in to your emotions and allowing their energy to fuel your existence can make life more rewarding and more passionate. But if you are to remain in charge of this passion rather than feeling controlled by it, then the significance of each feeling needs to be monitored and trained in the direction of your choice.

The existential practitioner needs to provide clients with lucid guidelines on how to use emotions constructively. Raw feelings, once recognized, need to be translated into understandable messages. These messages need to be deciphered and turned into constructive action. In this way clients are taught to become conversant with their emotional life by learning the language of their own response. Instead of remaining on the level of pure reactivity their emotional activity can now become the source of a sense of mastery.

Dorothy needed to find just such a sense of mastery. To her the world seemed a place lurking with dangers and she attempted to deal with this hazardous world by tightly remaining in control. Her compulsive controlling behaviour had nothing to do with mastery over her emotions. It was totally reactive and based on her terror of losing her grip. She was terrified of anything going wrong and she tried to arrange things in such a manner that nothing possibly could go wrong. In this way she had become the slave of her own control and she was entirely controlled by it.

Dorothy was a fifty-one-year-old housewife, whose only son had recently married and moved to a different town. She came to therapeutic counselling on the advice of her doctor after she had told him about the way in which she had been feeling hampered by her recent obsession with hand washing. It was her new daughter-in-law who had first remarked on her excessive tidiness and compulsive ablutions and who had told her that she should consult her doctor.

Dorothy had always kept her house impeccably clean, to the great irritation of her son and her husband, but it was only recently that her tidiness had got out of hand. Especially when visiting her son and daughter-in-law, she would feel intense panic when confronted with dirt, dust or mess. Her daughter-in-law had told her off several times for interfering with her household and since then Dorothy had begun to feel compelled to go to the bathroom and wash her hands with excessive care. At first this had not seemed strange to her, but then other people started to notice and comment. She thought that there was something wrong as she could not stop herself from repeating the action up to six times in an evening visit.

Dorothy felt that her daughter-in-law, who had stopped her from doing what was natural to her, caused her compulsive action. It was only because she was not allowed to tidy up in the house that she felt compelled to clean the dirt off her hands instead. She had visions of germs crawling all over the house and she experienced the cleaning urge as a natural response to the threat of infection and chaos. In unravelling the feeling of panic that befell Dorothy when cleaning was not possible it came to light that tidiness was essential for Dorothy's well-being. She felt one could not survive without it. She also thought that she was a bit of an expert at it. She was quite proud of her ability to keep things organized and under control. She felt frustrated that her son and daughter-in-law did not recognize this.

It was only when a new incident occurred that it was possible to tackle the message of Dorothy's emotions and help her to understand what she was doing wrong. Her washing machine broke down and the kitchen was flooded. She was also left with dirty linen and the mess of the repairs. Her reaction was one of absolute panic and horror. She felt almost too paralysed to act at first and afterwards insulted her husband abundantly and unnecessarily. It was at last clear to Dorothy that her attitude was not too productive and possibly even destructive.

Her first remark in the counselling session after this incident was that she did not understand how this could have happened because she always made sure the machine was well looked after. This led to the exploration of her belief that it was possible to stay in total control of one's environment and avoid catastrophes entirely. Dorothy recognized that this was a desire rather than a belief, as she well knew that it was not really possible to remain in control all the time.

She was now encouraged to explore the emotional impact of imagining that she would have to contend with mess and catastrophe instead of being able to avoid them. Although she was at first rather reluctant to imagine this too vividly, she soon realized that there was something quite satisfying in imagining the worst. She usually spent so much time and energy on trying to prevent these things that she hardly let herself actually prepare for them. It felt like a great relief to think about getting her hands dirty in cleaning out the living room after pigs and ants and pigeons had been in it for some weeks. As these were the creatures that she thought most likely to cause havoc in a house it was like tackling her worst nightmare to imagine having to deal with that. She was surprised at her own reaction of satisfaction in working out that fantasy.

Once Dorothy realized that facing the worst would not imply losing control she started to relax somewhat. Thus far she conceived of her relationship to her environment in terms of either being in control or losing control. Now she began to consider that there might be a third possibility. This had never occurred to her before because she had simply not trusted her own ability to cope with anything unexpected and chaotic. She had always believed that she could only handle situations that were orderly and safe. Now that she began to think that coping with catastrophe or disorder might actually be a relief after the constant tension of trying to prevent it, she became interested in the idea of mastery. If she learnt to work with mess rather than trying to eliminate it, then it would not control her and she would not have to exhaust herself controlling it either. This notion of co-operation with her environment rang many bells for Dorothy. She started reminiscing about the days before her son was born when she used to do a lot of gardening. Her joy in gardening stemmed from the days of her adolescence when she used to work an allotment with her grandfather. He used to tell her about taming nature instead of dominating it. But all that seemed like a long time ago. She could not really understand where it had all gone. It had just gradually changed. Her whole life had become so much more ordered as she got married and when her son was born she had felt so overwhelmed with work that there was no time for gardening. They ended up paving over most of the garden. She felt quite tearful thinking about that.

Once Dorothy's emotional experience had thus shifted from covered-up panic and irritability to sadness she started to feel more truly herself. She felt again like the girl she had been. Her tears were for the loss of her closeness to nature as she had known it when she was young. Nowadays she was so cultured and polished, 'uptight' as her daughter-in-law had called her, it made her quite sad. She was unsure whether she might be able to do anything about all this. She was reluctant to listen to what her emotions were telling her as she had learnt to discipline and deny them.

Then fate gave her a little push as her brother had a mild heart attack. His doctor told him it was caused by lack of exercise and by too much stress. Dorothy, knowing her brother and herself, added that it had been caused by his up-tightness. Suddenly she was very decisive and she brought some builders in to remove the concrete in the garden and revert it back to soil. She was much exhilarated to find that she did not once feel like washing her hands when working in the garden. The amount of sheer enjoyment she got out of doing this was enormous. Wearing old clothes and her husband's wellies was an added bonus. She had not been this dirty for twenty-five years and she had not felt as good ever.

Dorothy had a long way to go before she could really abandon her habit of tight control, but she did loosen up considerably by taking up gardening again. At least her disturbing symptom disappeared and she was able to relate more positively to her daughter-in-law now that she was becoming livelier and less concerned about neatness. What Dorothy did was learn to listen to the message of her emotions instead of continuing to try to silence them. Just expressing the panic or the irritation would have merely increased them. Trying to convince herself that there was no reason why she should feel this way would have merely led to her becoming more controlling. What she needed to do was to realize that there was a good reason for her feeling the way she did. She had been going against herself and against her environment rather than with herself and her environment. Gardening was Dorothy's way to return to a more mindful interaction.

Dorothy used to feel panic and irritation at the thought of losing something that she valued very much: control. The message of her emotions was that she needed to consider whether there was a way in which she might attain what she wanted that would be more effective. What she found was that it was not so much control that she really wanted as a sense of mastery. In itself the message of the emotions was therefore rather crude and it needed to be thought through to make sense of it.

In general human emotions can be seen as a person's magical attempt to manipulate reality (Sartre, 1939). Emotions such as jealousy and anger relate to one's attempt to hold on to something that is valued and that is under threat of being lost. Fear and sorrow relate to one's having to give up or lose something that is valued. Guilt and shame are the expression of one's sense of absence of what is valued. On the other hand emotions like desire and hope indicate one's aspiration to something that is valued, while love and joy are the expression of a sense of possession of what is valued.

Any emotional experience that makes one move in the direction of what is valued is experienced as positive. Any emotional experience that makes one move away from what is valued is experienced as negative. In Figure 5.1 such a view of emotional experience is schematically represented. The emotional cycle swings downwards from possession of something that is deeply valued, and considered essential, to its loss and eventual absence. The emotional cycle swings upwards from the sense of emptiness of existence through a lack of what is valued to an aspiration to obtain what is desired and to fulfilment in its ultimate possession. Every affect can be seen to have a positive and a negative aspect. No emotion is in itself right or wrong. The diagram indicates the potential for transformation of destructive emotional experience to constructive emotional experience.

Similarly, there is no intrinsic positive value in an upward emotional trend, nor is there an intrinsic negative value in a downward emotional trend. Loss and gain are not synonymous with failure and success. Letting go is just as important in life as building up. What matters is that there is movement and

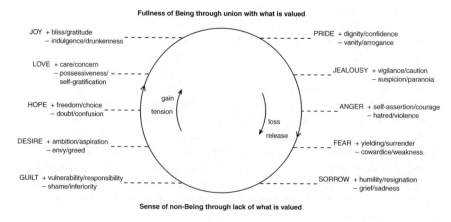

Figure 5.1   *The emotional cycle*

flexibility and that emotions are understood for the existential message they express.

Anxiety is not included in the diagram as it is a more general and basic experience, which accompanies any increase in existential awareness. As mentioned in Chapter 2, anxiety has a negative expression in *Angst* or anguish and a positive one in excitement and anticipation.

The task of the therapist is to help clients in unravelling all this aspecific emotional experience and in detecting its specific significance. The object is, of course, for clients to become able to interpret their emotional experience more and more clearly themselves. Dramatic revelations of hidden meaning of emotions will have little impact on clients other than making them feel dependent on the therapist. The therapist must resist the temptation to translate the messages of the emotions for clients until clients themselves are starting to participate actively in the process of investigation and uncovering.

The therapist will encourage close scrutiny of moods and emotions, indicating profitable ways of searching and giving some clues about what to look for, without ever forcing the issue or suggesting answers. Existential counselling or psychotherapy is in this way similar to the Socratic method. It is a way of gently prodding the client along into action, never allowing her to get away with laziness or lying, but always reminding her of how she herself can unveil the ideas and essential intentions that are hidden behind the apparent confusion on the surface.

Making sense of a confused whirlpool of emotions was exactly what Donald and Angela needed to do. They came to the therapeutic counsellor originally looking for advice in some essential decision-making, which they seemed unable to handle without their tempers flaring up and ending up rowing.

Donald was a forty-seven-year-old American, living in Britain. Angela was a thirty-nine-year-old British woman, mother of two teenage children from a previous marriage. Donald and Angela had been recently married after a brief but intense courtship. They now found that some of the realities of their new family life were extremely difficult and they were at a loss for solutions that would satisfy them both. After an initial session with them as a couple a decision was reached that they would each have some individual sessions to sort out their personal difficulties in relating to the other partner. Though at first they had presented their problems as based on cultural differences it was soon obvious that this was only one aspect of their disagreements.

Their rowing was generally a result of their discussions about the education of Angela's two children (aged fourteen and sixteen). The children were both in boarding schools but since the marriage Donald had started to try to convince Angela that this was an unnecessary expense and that they could just as well live at home and attend nearby schools, which had an excellent reputation. Angela would not hear of this and refused seriously to consider Donald's point of view. In the initial session they had presented their request for the counsellor to solve their disagreement, each obviously in the hope that the counsellor would take their particular viewpoint. When asked to express their respective views as fully as possible they soon began to realize that there were many emotional issues involved in their quarrel and that it might be useful to try to unravel these independently first.

Donald's first session started out like this:

Donald: I still want to know what you think of putting kids up in boarding school.

Counsellor: Right. So that is the first issue you want some help clarifying. Let's see if we can find out what it is you would have liked to hear me say. Let's take it step by step: What do boarding schools evoke for you?

Donald: Places for rich kids, whose parents have more important things to do than to raise their kids themselves.

Counsellor: Sophisticated dumping places?

Donald: Yes, exactly. Somewhere convenient for parents to dispose of children they should probably not have had in the first place and wouldn't have if they had not been such snobs, who could afford to have other people raise them in their place.

Counsellor: You disapprove very strongly, don't you?

Donald: Wholeheartedly. I hate the very thought of it. I wasn't raised in that sort of environment and no kids of mine will be either.

Counsellor: In other words, if they were your kids, there would be no problem; they would live at home. The problem is then entirely around how much your point of view is going to matter, around how well-established your authority as a step-father is.

Donald: Indirectly. Yes. I suppose so. [*Thinks for a while*] Yes. That is what gets me mad: not being able to influence the decision.

Counsellor: So, you feel powerless; your anger is a way to try to regain control.

Donald: [*nods in agreement; thinks and muses over this a while*] Unfortunately it doesn't seem to have the desired effect.

Counsellor: No?

Donald: The more I get worked up over this, the more she rejects my point of view.

Counsellor: As if your view didn't matter.

Donald: Yes – damn it. I get the impression of being treated as a schoolboy myself. Angela wants to remain totally in charge as the mother. The fact that I'm nearly ten years older than she is is being ignored. She thinks I'm not the father, so I cannot possibly know what is best.

Counsellor: So you are being forcefully reminded of the fact that they are not your own children and that you are not even a father yourself.

Donald: Does that matter? I don't want to be reminded of that all the time. I want to be a father to them now.

Counsellor: What if it did matter?

Donald: Well, damn it. She shouldn't have married me in that case.

Counsellor: You mean, if it matters that you're not a father, then you must also be unsuitable as a husband?

Donald: Yeah. You might as well throw in the towel.

Counsellor: How is that?

Donald: I gave up a hell of a lot to stay in this country, for her. I thought I was getting myself a nice family and all I've got so far is trouble.

Counsellor: So you are discovering that there is a whole lot more to being a husband and father than saying the wedding vows.

Donald: [*laughs loudly*] You mean, I did have naive ideas about fatherhood after all. [*He laughs some more.*]

Counsellor: Might that be possible?

Donald: [*still laughing*] You must be kidding. Not Don. Not the great Don. [*He suddenly stops laughing on a loud inward breath – almost like a sob – then sighs.*] Oh man.

After this Donald began to look into the significance of his own attitude. He recognized his anger against Angela as an attempt to try to hold on to and fight for his own illusions of instant fatherhood. He saw how he had moved towards fear of losing this illusion in his wish to run away and throw in the towel if he could not have it all on his own terms, holding on to his illusions. Then he had experienced sadness, when becoming aware of the way in which he was already losing his battle for his illusions and how in reality he was not getting what he had imagined he would. Finally the sadness had given rise to an abandonment and letting go of his own false pride; his laughter had been the result of seeing himself naked suddenly, realizing that he had never really possessed what he had tried to believe that he could and did possess. This laughter was a mixture of humour and sadness. In the following cynicism about himself his movement towards realization of his own shortcomings had begun and he was expressing his embarrassment with his own self-deception.

Whilst being able to trace back his own process of emotional letting go of the stuck issue, Donald was liberating himself for a renewed consideration of his aspirations towards fatherhood. It soon transpired just how important this was to him. In fact, having the children was one of the prospects he was most keen on in marrying Angela. To Donald becoming a father was a major hope of fulfilment of his existence. So far it had been an area of great frustration. He had often felt extremely inferior in comparison with colleagues at work who did have children.

In later sessions there were issues around his unreasonable behaviour with one of his colleagues at work, which he slowly traced back to the origin of feelings of envy towards this colleague, who was the father of three teenage daughters.

Angela's part in solving the disagreement from her side went through the exact opposite of the emotional cycle. She described her emotions since her marriage to Donald as initially centred on joy and gratitude for at last having found a man she could love and who would love her in return. She had felt as if at last, after much loneliness and isolation, her life was coming together. The children were now becoming more independent and were well settled in their respective schools; in a few years they would be ready to take off under their own steam and cease to be her preoccupation. She felt she deserved to start thinking about her own happiness now; things looked promising.

Then, when Donald had begun to become more and more insistent about wanting to bring the children back into the home, she started to feel on her guard. She began to wonder if he cared for her as much as she imagined at first or if he really just wanted to be part of a family. She felt jealous, not of the children so much, but of him. She did not want to share Donald with her children, she wanted him all and entirely to herself. She did not feel able to listen even to alternative solutions; the way she had arranged things with the children was working out fine and she was determined to protect her self-interest as she saw it, which was to keep her new husband away from her children, alone with her.

Her definitions of her own jealousy soon showed up another side of the reason for her feeling protective of her exclusive claims on Donald. While exploring her reaction to Donald's reiterated request for taking the children out of boarding school, the following dialogue took place:

Angela: I can't even begin to imagine Jennifer living at home with us at all. She is nearly seventeen now, she would not know how to adjust to there being a man in the house. She has her own ideas about the opposite sex now. You know what I mean.

Counsellor: No. I don't. What do you mean?

Angela: You know, she has crushes on people, as teenage girls will do: pop stars, teachers, anyone really. I think she is quite enamoured with Don as a matter of fact. They went out to the theatre together, over Easter, and she talked about it as if it had been a romantic escapade.

Counsellor: Reminding you of how she has nearly grown into a woman.

Angela: Yes. It's quite startling sometimes. She can wear my clothes, you know. When she was home during the break, she plundered my wardrobe. She actually took quite a lot of things; a lovely dress I treasured and some of my silk scarves. [*She swallows audibly and scrutinizes the ceiling intently with a worried expression on her face.*]

Counsellor: So you worry that she might rob you of other things you treasure as well?

Angela: As a matter of fact, I'm sure she would, given half the chance. If she lived at home, she would be all over Don. I would simply have to chaperone her constantly.

Counsellor: So it's not just Jennifer you don't trust. You don't trust Don's ability to cope with her infatuation either.

Angela: You know how men are. He is not even her father. She would wrap him around her finger. He would be at her mercy, smitten without even noticing it.

Counsellor: And you would lose him.

Angela: Right.

Counsellor: So it's not just Jennifer and Don you mistrust. You have absolutely no confidence in your own ability to create a stable and safe, trustworthy relationship with your husband.

Angela: I hadn't thought of it that way.

[*There follows a minute and a half of silence, during which time she intensively studies the ceiling.*]

Angela: I wish I hadn't said that now.

Counsellor: You don't usually think of yourself as weak, do you Angela?

Angela: No. (She studies the ceiling some more.) This is quite a blow really. I need to think about this. I think I would like to stop here for today.

Counsellor: You need to recompose yourself?

Angela: Yes.

Counsellor: What would happen if you didn't?

(Long silence)

Angela: [*with great effort to compose herself, voice hoarse and in a whisper*] I'd be lost.

The session ended here, but from there on progress was made in Angela's understanding of her own anxious avoidance of her weakness and vulnerability. It was months yet before she could begin to communicate these emotions to Donald and in this way start to contribute to a solution of the tension between them. Yet it was in this session that she for the first time let herself plunge down from her usual defensive stronghold into the depth of her fears of inadequacy and nothingness.

When Donald and Angela were able to let each other know what motivated their respective positions, rather than blindly wage war, their relationship moved on to a new level of understanding and mutual respect. Though that did not directly solve their differences of opinion, their discussions and struggle now tended to strengthen rather than threaten the relationship. They felt able to appreciate each other's emotional ups and downs rather than condemn them.

Making sense of one's own emotional experience, instead of dismissing it as a bother, often has this effect of enhancing interpersonal relationships. It is striking how similar people are in terms of raw emotions. As complex and individually different as thoughts and imagination can get, so simple and straightforward are the messages of people's feelings. Unfortunately feelings are usually subjected to much cultural prejudice and distortion, muddling up their basically clear messages.

All this makes it crucial that the therapist can stand aside from cultural norms and that she can put the confused picture of people's emotional experience back into sharp focus. Recognizing the basic colours of the spectrum of feelings and understanding their inter-relationships is a great help in this process.

Discovering meaning

Clients complain of not knowing what they want as often as they complain of feeling no motivation to carry on with their daily duties. Apathy is frequently experienced as the only alternative when the world seems to propose nothing of great interest. Detachment becomes the only remedy when nothing in the world seems meaningful or worth the effort (May, 1969). When people become detached and apathetic they embark on a downward spiral. They become incapable of making decisions as no choices seem to offer anything desirable. Life becomes meaningless.

Helping clients in their search for meaning and purpose so that they can find the true motivation that comes with the integration of wish and will is one of the objectives of existential therapy. It is the logical follow-up of understanding one's emotions. When it becomes obvious that one is keen on certain things and afraid of others, it is fairly easy to establish what the essence of one's aspirations is. In examining the latter it may come to light that the way in which one's life is structured does not allow much scope for what is most valued. If the aspiration or ideal that is being thwarted is given enough attention it frequently gives rise to an upsurge of motivation to make changes in one's life in order to make more room for what really matters.

A thorough analysis of the message of one's emotions can therefore lead straight to an increase in motivation through the recognition of what is valued and by finding ways to achieve this. But in many cases things are not quite so simple. If emotions are deflated or if life seems to offer little real opportunity for change in the direction of what is valued, then a total lack of motivation may ensue. People may experience a lack of will to live and the only way to help them forward may be to assist them with the difficult task of finding meaning in absurdity or suffering (Frankl, 1955). It has been suggested by existentialists that one can only really learn to live when life has first become meaningless (Sartre, 1938; Camus, 1942). In this sense the existential approach is particularly pertinent with clients who have lost the will to meaning and who feel trapped in an absurd life.

Lena was in just such a situation. She was seventy-two years old and had lost all sense of meaning, therefore letting herself become the will-less victim of deep depression. Lena had had a brief stay in a psychiatric ward but she was allowed to go back to her own flat fairly soon. There a social worker and a psychiatric nurse regularly visited her. It was finally decided that she would perhaps benefit from counselling as she always had a lot to say about what was generally wrong with the world.

In the counselling sessions many aspects of Lena's thus far rather secretive background were revealed. Although she had British nationality Lena was of Dutch Jewish origin. She had moved to England at the beginning of the Second World War, together with her parents, to escape from the Nazi regime, which would almost certainly have exterminated them, had they remained in Holland. Although Lena was thirty years old at that time, she lived with her parents until they died when she was in her early forties. Lena had no living relatives. She had had a very serious and sober life. She had once had a close friendship with a man, but he had disappeared when it had become obvious to him that she preferred to continue caring for her parents rather than making a commitment to him.

Lena had no contact whatsoever with her past in Holland. She knew nobody there and had only been back twice for brief holidays, which she had not enjoyed. Although she had had a very active professional life for thirty-five years, she had hardly any contact with any of her ex-colleagues. She had been an efficient personal secretary for many years and she felt rather betrayed by her past employer who had abruptly ceased to be interested in her from the first day of her retirement. She had existed for her work only since the death of her parents and with her retirement her life had stopped holding any meaning for her. Although she had become less and less interested in doing anything outside her flat, she was very preoccupied with the world's unfairness. She improved simply by having another person there to talk to about her pessimistic ideas rather than just keeping them to herself.

At first it seemed as if Lena was simply depressive, negative and vindictive. She blamed everybody else in the world for the woes of humanity. It was tempting for the counsellor to dismiss Lena's attitude as stemming from an intrinsically bitter and unpleasant character. But as soon as Lena's assertions about the world were taken seriously and explored from a philosophical rather than a psycho-pathological perspective a different picture emerged.

Lena's outlook on life was indeed pretty pessimistic. She could not see any valid reason for continuing to live or for the world to continue to turn round. She argued that people were miserable creatures who would be better off dead. But when her bluff was called, her negative arrogance turned to despair. It was pointed out to her that there had been a time when she must have thought differently about these matters, as she had thought it worth saving her own life by escaping from the Nazis and coming to Britain. At first Lena became rather defensive and said that she would not have bothered if her parents had not been alive then. But when she was asked to check this statement carefully and honestly by herself, her attitude changed at the following session.

She herself started out the next time with a timid reference to the previous session. She said that what she had meant was that she wished it could have been that way. When encouraged to be more specific she began to talk about the intense guilt she felt for having escaped from Holland all those years ago. It had only been possible because of her father's special connections with Britain and she felt that it had been an act of cowardice. She sincerely wished that she had had the courage to remain in Holland and fight the Germans in some way instead of fleeing, as so few people could afford to do. She was at the same time well aware that she would even now perhaps take the safe and soft option if the same dilemma were again presented to her. At the time she had calmed her conscience by telling herself she was doing this to help her parents, but she had since realized that this was probably a lie.

The only way to expiate her guilt seemed to be by remaining entirely devoted to her parents' well-being for as long as was possible. Her monastic and sober life since her parents' death had been the only way of continuing to pay the debt that she felt she had accumulated with the privilege of her British exile. What surprised Lena most was that she had always known all this on some level but had never formulated it even in her own mind.

When Lena talked about her life there was a faraway look on her face, as if she was not really aware of speaking to another person at all. She was clearly deeply preoccupied with the discovery of an inner reality, which had dominated her entire existence without her ever knowing this consciously. Everything that had been cause for bitterness now at once made sense. Her virginity and childlessness in particular were understandable in the light of her inner conviction of the unworthiness of her own existence. As she had believed that she really ought to have perished how could she possibly have affirmed her life by acts of procreation?

It was equally little surprising that she had never really been back to her native land or attempted to find trace of her past friends and acquaintances there. It would have been too shameful to discover the inevitable deaths and disappearances of so many of her childhood and young adulthood companions. By pretending to herself that there was no point in picking at old wounds she thus deprived herself of the confrontation with her own guilt and cowardice. She had therefore to continue to suffer isolation. One of the reasons that her contacts with British colleagues had always remained aloof and reserved was that she dreaded having to relate her past to them. She had preferred imagining that the slate had been wiped clean and that she simply was not the kind of person who made close personal relationships.

It turned out in fact that Lena had had a very different sort of life before the war. She used to have many close friends and an active social life. All this changed with the evacuation to England. At first she and her parents decided to keep a low profile simply because they feared that the Nazis would eventually catch up with them again. Then the habit of keeping away from others as much as possible became engrained and Lena never felt as if she really belonged in this new country. Going back to Holland after the war was out of the question for the reasons already mentioned, so that Lena continued to live a life of self-imposed exile, which could provide little deep satisfaction apart from a dutiful appreciation of sheer survival.

Now that her life was nearing its end, Lena thought that it had mostly been wasted and that she would have had more dignity and merit if she had bravely embraced the fate of deportation and death. And if that was not enough to make her feel desperate, there was the added difficulty of her sense of alienation from God. Lena had been a fairly religious person for many years even though her family had not been practising Jews for as long as she could remember. With her move to England she had given up any outward signs of religious life and contented herself with a very private relationship to God. But even that became disturbed by her guilty conscience and she felt unable to address herself to God without getting an uncontrollable urge to think of him as a Nazi. She had in the end preferred to decide that there was no God, as a true God would not have allowed the Nazis to cause so much desolation and destruction without at least redeeming people through their suffering.

This account of her position on spirituality opened the door for Lena's discovery of some inconsistencies in her thinking. She was asked how she imagined that people who suffered intensely in the war might have been able to find dignity or be redeemed. She answered that this would have happened if they had been able to face death and suffering without flinching and in the knowledge that they would be saved through their belief in the rightness of their own convictions. It was then suggested to Lena that evidently for herself there was no hope in this case as she had entirely escaped from this suffering. Lena saw at once what was wrong with that argument and for the first time acknowledged how much suffering she had herself been through in this strange exile from everything that mattered to her.

Now it became possible to reconsider her whole life story in a totally different light. It was no longer the story of deception and cowardly escape. It was the story of her own struggle with her inner conflicts and guilt. In this light her life actually seemed like a monument to human struggle with paradox. The way in which she had driven herself to the edge of the bearable in the past few years had a definite flavour of martyrdom.

When Lena started to respect her own share of suffering she became free to imagine the suffering that she thought she had evaded by fleeing to

England. In doing so she came to the conclusion that she would probably still have known the same contradictory aspirations of wanting to save herself and yet wanting to face the enemy with dignity. What Lena learnt in the process was that human struggle can take place in many different ways, but that it is bound to take place no matter how one pretends to the contrary.

In finding that her life could be seen to have a dignity all its own after all, Lena recovered the basic sense of meaning that had been absent for so long. With the retrieval of it a new purpose for her remaining days also appeared on the horizon. Now that she was liberated from her own Nazi occupation it became conceivable to enquire after the fate of some of the people in her distant past that she had never been able to forget. Once Lena had begun this arduous process of retracing the past she discovered a vigour and wilfulness in herself that she had not known herself capable of. There was no more time to lose, she said, for there was still much to be accomplished before she would be ready to die.

Lena's words describe the self-motivating willpower that comes with a sense of purpose in life. When the future is scanned for opportunities to accomplish what is worth accomplishing, purpose is created and motivation and willpower emerge. Such a sense of purpose is always closely related to the meaning that one is able to find in one's past and in life in general. Of course meaning can be found in many different ways. What is meaningful to one person is not necessarily so to the next. Discovering meaning is therefore always an eminently personal process, which the counsellor or therapist can only help along by keeping the client to the task and by highlighting aspects that the client seems to be blind to.

As a guideline for the practitioner who is working on this level the schematic outline in Figure 5.2 may be useful. The diagram highlights the paradoxical nature of human existence once again. It shows how people can find meaning in their existence on the four planes of experience. On each level the basic purpose is contrasted with an ultimate concern. The first represents the ideal value that a person knowingly or unknowingly strives for. The second represents the logical and inevitable shadow side of this aspiration in the form of a threat to the person's attainment of her ideal.

Many existential writers have referred to the ultimate concerns that people are inevitably confronted with. Jaspers (1931) spoke of limit situations, Tillich (1952) spoke of threats to self-affirmation, Heidegger (1927) referred to the same concept as care, or concern, followed in this by Binswanger (1963). None of the authors has systematically considered the correspondences between meaning and ultimate concern. Even Yalom (1980), who more recently proposed a framework for existential work based on the notion of ultimate concern, did not make explicit connections between concern and purpose.

In addition to recognizing the basic purpose and ultimate concern it is important to recognize the intermediate goals that most people settle for in a more realistic manner. It can be helpful to remember that if someone has arrived at such a compromise it is often a way to avoid the basic conflict

Dimension	Basic purpose	Ultimate concern	Realistic goal
Physical (body)	health	illness	survival
	strength	weakness	efficacy
	happiness	misery	comfort
	life	death	safety
Social (ego)	success	failure	recognition
	power	impotence	influence
	belonging	isolation	kinship
	love	condemnation	respect
Personal (self)	integrity	disintegration	individuality
	freedom	dissolution	autonomy
	authenticity	inauthenticity	specialness
	certainty	confusion	identity
Spiritual (soul)	truth	falsehood	understanding
	perfection	imperfection	virtue
	wisdom	absurdity	meaning
	good	evil	responsibility

Figure 5.2   *Dimensions of human experience.*

between human aspirations and the ultimate realities and contradictions of existence. In existential therapy however it is not compromise that is aimed for, but a dynamic exchange between the two extremes.

Purpose can be found on all four dimensions of experience, but it is crucial to contrast each possible purpose with its shadow side, which forms a basic threat to finding meaning. As always, people tend to operate with static views of themselves and the world; they think in terms of either/or. Either they will for example believe in God, or they will be stuck with a meaningless universe. Instead they may discover the need for a dynamic integration of their striving for absolute truth on the one hand and their basic sceptical starting point of doubt on the other.

No truth can ever be attained without reference to a basic doubt and a grappling with absurdity. But equally no ground of absurdity can fulfil a human heart. On all four dimensions the recognition of the depth of non-being has to be referred back to constantly if life is to be sparkling and full of movement. On all four dimensions striving for purpose has eventually to be undertaken for there to be any meaning to life at all.

While it is possible to live with a sense of meaning on only one dimension, getting stuck on any one of the four will be experienced as a nagging dissatisfaction at the background of one's experience. People often do not know in any articulate explicit manner what it is that bothers them, but they do sense something is wrong, when they feel stuck on one dimension, even though their life may seem fulfilling in an objective way.

Miriam was a twenty-six-year-old secondary school teacher. She was hospitalized after a suicide attempt and referred for counselling at her own request after having received various other forms of treatment and assessment. Though her suicide attempt had been relatively innocuous, she had in fact been extremely serious about wanting to put an end to her life. She did not herself understand this sense of despair that was sapping all her energy.

In fact she had experienced the first genuine surge of energy when she was plotting her own death. She admitted to feeling a certain sense of pride in her ability to cut her wrists. The second surge of energy had burst forth when her psychiatrist had informed her that she was to be put on long-term treatment for 'emotional instability'. She was well aware (having some medical knowledge) that he was implying that she was manic-depressive and that lithium would be used to stabilize her unruly melancholia. She became very angry and found the motivation to demand to have counselling instead.

Miriam described her life as flat and uninteresting. She had been teaching for three years now and while she was nervous during the first year, she had been at ease the second year and by the third year she had been bored. She was now married to Paul, with whom she had been living for five years. A similar pattern was evident in her relationship with him; at first she had been nervous about their relationship. During that time, when they were still both students, money had been tight and they could hardly afford the basics, but it did not seem to matter and life had been quite interesting. Sexually things had been difficult for her at first as she was quite inhibited. Then she read a lot of books about sexuality and they experimented together. For a time after this their lovemaking had been wonderful and they started to consider having children. As this had not worked out, Miriam gradually became bored with the incessant sex. She now knew that Paul could not father a child and she did not think there was much point in sex any more.

They lived in relative ease; they had bought their own house two years before and both had good jobs and comfortable salaries. Miriam was disgusted with her life, which now seemed entirely safe and predictable. Yet she did not see why she should feel so desperate, when she clearly, as she said 'had everything'. When asked to specify what 'everything' was, she replied: 'Nice family, nice husband, nice house, good job, good friends, good money: everything.' When asked if that implied that there was nothing missing, nothing she aspired to, she just sighed and said 'not any more'.

When the counsellor reminded her that there had been something apparently important enough to die for, Miriam became instantly livelier. She talked about her desire to maintain a sense of dignity and not just go under in the drabness and boredom. Her suicide attempt in this sense was the expression of her determination not to put up with the life that she seemed chained to and which was totally unsatisfactory to her. The following dialogue ensued:

Counsellor: So you were proving to yourself that you could take your own life back in your own hands.

Miriam: Yes, something like that. People here seem to think it is a stupid thing to do; they treat you like a coward and a fool. They really got it all wrong. It was really difficult. It took me a lot of courage.

Counsellor: And that's what really mattered; realizing that you have that courage.

Miriam: Yes, for the first time I started to feel really good about myself again and then they go treating me as if I'm insane and take it away from me again.

Counsellor: No wonder you got so angry; defending the little bit of private freedom you have just gained.

Miriam: I'd be insane to let that slip away again. I've paid my dues . . . [*holds up her bandaged wrists*]

Counsellor: Ahh, you had to pay the price first. You had to sacrifice yourself, before you gained the right to your freedom.

Miriam: I had to earn it. Show myself worthy. I wasn't sure I was brave enough to put myself on the line. So far I've always played it rather safe. You can see where that got me: terrific.

Counsellor: So playing safe wasn't satisfactory in the long run and now you know that you have it in you to be more daring?

Miriam: Mmm – but now they think I'm mad. Normal people are not supposed to behave like this; they just settle for boredom and more boredom.

Counsellor: But not you.

Miriam: I never thought I would end up like this. I used to be a real idealist, you know.

Counsellor: How do you mean?

Miriam: You know, believing in a better world. Wanting to change the world. I never even wanted to get married, too dull.

Counsellor: So what happened?

Miriam: I don't know. It just seemed to disintegrate gradually. I fell into the trap, like everyone else. And here I am: married, mortgaged and stuck in a rut. [*Silence*] My ideals seemed to evaporate after the first year teaching. It's just too hard. You can't fight it. You can't change anything. If you can't do it in education, how else can you do it? It seemed like there was suddenly nothing left and I got scared. I just clung to what was there.

Counsellor: So you settled down and gave up your ideals.

Miriam: Not completely though. I still thought I could do it by educating my own children. By the time you get them in secondary schools it is too late. You have to do it from scratch. Feminists have got it all wrong; it is the mothers at home with their children who are having the most impact on the world. The idea of being at home, raising three or four kids rather appealed to me. Then of course that didn't work out either. I told you: Paul can't have children. They thought it was me at first, but it was nothing to do with me; it's his fault.

Counsellor: So that was another ideal down the drain.

Miriam: God, it was dreadful. I felt shattered and Paul seemed really upset as well, so I couldn't walk out on him, I couldn't just leave him any more, that would have been terrible for him.

Counsellor: Right, so you felt too sorry to leave him and you decided to kill yourself instead.

Miriam: [*looks up into the counsellor's eyes for the first time and studies her face for a few seconds*] You've got a sense of humour, don't you? I used to be like that.

Counsellor: What was humorous in that?

Miriam: Well, you sort of seem to see the comical side of me trying to kill myself.

Counsellor: What comical side?

Miriam: Well, it's like watching someone slip on a banana skin. It's funny because they suddenly lose their dignity, their false pride. One second they walk along pretending to be wonderful, the next they're down on their bottom and everyone laughs.

Counsellor: So how does that apply to you?

Miriam: I was playing the part of the loyal and desperate wife – then you suddenly point out to me how I was just putting the limelight on myself and not really being loyal at all. I just realized that.

Counsellor: You mean, it would have been far worse for Paul if you had died, than if you had just left?

Miriam: Yes, but I wanted to be a heroine instead of a disloyal wife.

Exploring her desire for heroism led to a new burst of energy and motivation. It took many counselling sessions to cover the ground of her aspirations and for her to separate these in her mind from the category of illusions and lost illusions. In this area her emotions were indeed extremely unstable; no sooner would she build up enthusiasm for an idea or she would dive back down into despair about the possibility of implementing it. It seemed difficult for her to believe in anything that was really worthwhile.

It was evident that she feared she would have to be content with a life that could provide satisfaction only in the physical and social domains. Anything of the order of satisfactory private or personal experience seemed taboo and out of reach. Her relationship with Paul was devoid of a sense of closeness and kinship. It was entirely based on respect and friendship as well as having a competitive quality. It provided her with a sense of security and with physical comfort and gratification. But, it could not provide the sense of belonging and immediate understanding that she longed for. Paul and Miriam were as two, not as one, as she would have wished. She said that would not have mattered if she could have had children, for then they would have been close to her as he never would be.

While it was sad that she could not find the intimacy she craved, it was far sadder that she had decided that her very longing for this was the problem and therefore had deprived herself of the intimacy of her inner world as well. She had for instance stopped even reading poetry, while she used to write and read it avidly. She had adopted the, as she saw it, 'mature' viewpoint that poetry was 'for adolescents and dreamers only'. In her life there was no more room for dreams. Dreams were dangerous: they turned into nightmares, or you would wake up suddenly to find yourself back out in the cold everyday reality. Although she was determined not to dream any more, she was also convinced that without dreams life was hardly worth living.

It took her months to realize that it was possible to accept that dreams cannot come true exactly as one wishes but that nevertheless fantasies can bring the motivation to obtain some of the delights imagined and desired. Progressively she adopted a new way of thinking which allowed her to claim her rights to a private world of her own. She started writing a diary again (which she used to do but had abandoned as 'childish') and before long she was back to writing poetry.

Things picked up from there. Having re-conquered her private world, she went on to make new connections on a more spiritual plain as well. She joined a poetry-writing group and met someone who had just returned from three years' teaching in the Third World. Her enthusiasm for finding a cause to dedicate her life to was lit.

Now a different phase started, during which she tried desperately to hold on to what she had established whilst expanding in this new area. She tried to convince Paul of the importance of their devotion to some project beyond the scope of mere teaching and watching television. Predictably Paul was not too interested. Not without first having to tackle much guilt and doubt and confusion Miriam eventually decided to pursue her aspirations further alone. Within two weeks of this decision Paul had a new girlfriend and eventually moved out of the house.

While she was working through her understanding of what had happened, struggling with mixed and very intense emotions, she also filed her application for teaching abroad and at the same time began to process her papers for obtaining a divorce. Holding on to her personal sense of direction proved crucial for her sanity during those months. Emotions made sense as long as she could remain aware of her own motivation. When she eventually obtained a post overseas, in a developing country, she was more than ready for this new challenge. Proof of this were some letters she wrote after several months in the new job. The following extract from one of these speaks for itself.

> I can't understand now, how I ever could even have contemplated killing myself. I must have been purblind. I thought I was unable to cope with my own life and with the world the way it was. Now I know this was because the challenges weren't great enough. It wasn't that I needed fewer emotions (as they seemed to think), but on the contrary more of them, much more. Please tell them about this at the hospital, for I shudder to think of all the other lives that are being wasted through sheer lack of understanding. It wasn't Lithium, but passion that I needed. Though the world is far worse than I feared then, I have discovered it to be also a whole lot better. It is certainly not boring when your life has a purpose.

It is important to note that in her work with Miriam the counsellor did not refer to the actual categories of emotions and motivations described in this chapter. Throughout it was Miriam's words and concepts that were used and explored. It is also crucial to note that such a dramatic solution as Miriam's is clearly not always in order. What the counsellor or therapist does is to help the client to trace back her original intention, her deepest sense of what it is important to achieve in life. The implementation of this original project can be as quiet and stable as it may be adventurous and bold; the initiative must be entirely with the client herself. Only she can find her own direction. The practitioner can only push her to be faithful to her own aspirations and provide clarity where confusion obscures the view.

By tracing back the meaning of the client's emotions the purpose that the client's life is inspired with is uncovered. Then it becomes possible to begin to find ways in which meaning can be created more fully. Instead of letting the client settle for appropriate behaviour copied from the role-models of society, she is encouraged to take heart in her own ideals. Living in accordance with one's inner sense of purpose provides motivation beyond the mere fulfilment of duty. It makes one feel truly and passionately alive and it makes life all the more worthwhile.

It is evident that the pursuit of meaning implies confrontation with the existential dilemmas in which the human condition is rooted. Following the direction of one's ideals can only be done effectively if one is at the same time willing to face up to human limitations. Existential counselling and therapy are about providing the clarity and support required to people who are determined to discover meaning but are terrified to be exposed to the raw realities of life.

Working with dreams

In the process of clarification of the client's worldview and in pinpointing her original project and motivation dreams are an invaluable asset. Through the discussion of dreams it is particularly easy to establish what images the client has of what it is that matters most to her on the one hand and of what she dreads most on the other hand.

It matters little whether dreams are a random product of relaxing brain cells or a directly meaningful expression of a person's current preoccupations. When clients report dreams they can and do recognize their present concerns and characteristic mode of being in the dream images. The dream is like a microcosm inhabited by the same intentions and worries as the client's actual world.

If clients do not report dreams, it is still perfectly possible to apply the principles of dream work to their conscious fantasies and daydreams. In fact it is just as relevant to view any of the client's reported experiences of real and imagined events as if they were indeed a dream. Treating complex material with the same systematic approach that can be used with dreams makes it far easier to get a handle on the material. As people often say: life in some ways is only a dream. What matters for life just as for dreams is to be able to trace back accurately the subjective position, viewpoint and intentions of the protagonist.

It is easier for the therapist not to get entangled with the client's difficulties and remain capable of seeing things in perspective if she reminds herself that she is an observer. The client's life can be seen as a dream, in which the client is caught up but from which the practitioner can remain free to perceive its internal contradictions.

The aim of working with the dream is to assist the client in distilling the essential meaning from the reported experience, whether this experience was real or imagined. If the experience is presented as a dream it is easier to do this, because the event is well-contained within a specific frame. Thus the client is more likely to be able to remain alert to the various elements that seem significant without losing her objectivity and ability to gain insight into her subjective position.

When doing this it is essential to keep in mind that it must be the client herself who assigns meaning to the dream. In no case must the counsellor or therapist interpret or suggest what the images stand for. Any dream or image can be given multiple meanings, as can be seen from working with a dream or a drawing in a group setting. While it can be extremely useful to the client to be given new ideas about possible implications of the dream, it is often more important that she is allowed to explore her personal view more fully before she thinks in terms of possible expansion into new areas of interpretation.

Often the same dream or image will be endowed with new meaning for the client in the process of her progressive understanding of her own intentions. It is not uncommon for a client to bring a dream at the beginning of a series of sessions and to keep referring to it throughout the therapeutic process. The dream will thus become like a thread leading from one level of her experience to the next and gaining increasing significance and richness with every step forward.

Undoubtedly it is possible to discover new significance in every old dream as time goes by and one's perspective matures and deepens. The same thing can be said for works of art, which tend to gain different significance for a person at different times in her life. Books are also an excellent example of this process of reinterpretation. Many people are quite familiar with the surprising effect of re-reading the same book ten years later and discovering aspects to it that had not been evident previously. This amounts to saying that people can only perceive that meaning in an image which they are open to at that particular time. They are never condemned to remain caught in one exclusive point of view, but they are unlikely to be capable of integrating any aspects that can simply not yet be encompassed by their current perspective.

The therapist may detect meanings in a client's dreams that are pertinent and relevant for the client but for which the latter is not yet ready. Although the practitioner may wish to encourage the client to consider such possible interpretations, it is crucial to abstain from applying any pressure. As always, the client is the only ultimate authority on what her motivations are and how she wants to perceive her own reality.

If, for example, a client reports a dream about planting trees and growing flowers, she may wish to see this as significant in terms of artistic or intellectual creativity, or she may wish to see it simply as an expression of her desire to get more closely involved with a physical form of existence. The therapist may suspect that the dream holds a deeper meaning of aspiration to procreation, especially if the therapist has children or has aspirations to have children in the near future. While the client may eventually come to recognize such significance in her dream, it would be highly inappropriate for the practitioner to attempt to impose insights on the client. Some clients are quite capable of rejecting those explanations that do not yet suit them, but others will sometimes comply and adopt external notions without truly experiencing them as real for themselves.

Even if this client does have unacknowledged aspirations to procreate, her best interests will not be served by recognizing these before she is ready to act on them. She may be much better off sticking to her own interpretation of the dream as an aspiration to become creative in some other way, so that she will be able to act on her insight and find constructive ways to implement it.

It is with existential explorations as with any other form of preparation for a journey: it is important to know your general direction and intention, but it is unhelpful to fix your gaze on a distant horizon. You need concrete attainable goals rather than overwhelming confrontations with ultimate goals that may paralyse your immediate actions. Therefore it must be remembered that the client herself will indicate how far she wants to venture for the moment and that in no case should her own limitations be ignored.

At the same time the therapist will encourage the client to explore any dream that is volunteered as completely as possible and exploit its full potential of indicator of the client's present mode of living. In order to do this effectively, some simple guidelines will be useful.

In the first place the dream's basic message can be tracked down by simplifying the complex story of the dream and summing up its basic action in one sentence. Doing this will require the client first to pay attention to her own role in the dream and phrase her subjective intention, as carried out in the dream, in a few words. This in itself will often throw new light on the significance of the dream in terms of its indication of the client's basic existential stance. It will, for instance, be immediately obvious whether the client is active or passive, whether she is in command of the situation or overwhelmed by it. But more importantly it will put the emphasis on what the client was aiming for rather than on what stood in the way of her actually reaching her goal.

Brenda, a client from North America, dreamt about running through knee-deep snow and being pursued by wolves. Her first reporting on the dream did not mention anything about her goal; it did not indicate where she was going or why she was in this dreadful situation in the first place. The dream was full of precise details and exciting or terrifying unexpected developments which diverted the attention away from the obvious question about the original purpose of the journey through the snow.

As soon as Brenda was asked where she was going in the dream, she realized that all along in the background of her awareness had been the understanding of the absurdity of the dangers she was exposing herself to. She knew with absolute certainty that she had been running towards a grocery shop in order to buy a pack of cigarettes and that without this silly preoccupation with smoking she would have been quite safe since the wolves had only started appearing the moment she set out on this particular quest.

As it happened Brenda had stopped smoking several years previous to this dream and while she had settled down to a well-organized and quiet life she somehow always hankered after the wild smoking days of her life. It became obvious to her through looking at this dream that her aspiration to smoking had symbolized her spirit of adventure. Exposing herself to the unnecessary dangers of the natural world (snow and wolves in the dream in this instance) represented a challenge that was not currently part of her life, but had been so through her addiction to cigarettes. The dangers of heart disease or lung cancer had, far from making her want to stop smoking, been a real secret attraction, which had been hard to give up. She had experienced smoking as playing with fire and that was highly enjoyable.

These days there was very little fire left in her life and it seemed therefore appropriate that the challenges faced in her dream were wintry cold and wild animals, who would have been afraid of fire. Still the intention in the dream was to obtain that other challenge again: cigarettes and the playing with fire. In all these different ways she was clearly determined to expose herself to some concrete risk to her survival; her original intention seemed to be one of the pursuit of increased vitality even if this might present the hazard of her own possible extinction.

She summed the dream up as follows: 'In pursuit of the unnecessary but essential pleasure of fire, I brave the near fatal challenges of the elements, until culture comes to my rescue but knocks me out in the process.' This last bit referred to the ending of the dream, in which a snowplough full of people, books and statues appeared and chased the wolves away. Just as it approached her to save her, it hit her, leaving her unconscious and waking up from her dream believing herself to be in hospital after the accident.

It is clear that the dream is considered a metaphor for the client's current existential position and that the function of summing it up in one sentence is to sharpen the metaphor to its most essential images and actions. In this way the client's aspirations and basic motivations stand out as well as her ultimate concern and basic fear. While the first part of the existential dream work is thus concerned with focusing and simplifying, the second part is concerned with amplification and exploration of the various elements in the dream.

As it was by now quite obvious to Brenda that her dream was the expression of her longing for an element of challenge in her life, it was necessary to explore in greater detail how she perceived that challenge concretely. It was evident that her ultimate concern was about being insufficiently strong to reach her destination or being knocked unconscious and failing in her quest altogether. It was necessary to elaborate this basic idea and examine how it would apply to Brenda's everyday experience. This amplification can most effectively be done by systematically examining the four different levels of experience as represented in the dream. With Brenda's dream this process revealed the following aspects.

In terms of the physical world dimension Brenda's playing with fire was already pinpointed as her basic aspiration; smoking in this sense had represented her experience of her body as concretely her own. Inhaling smoke was like breathing fire and feeling extra-alive; exhaling smoke was like seeing her own body's power being projected out of her mouth. Carrying cigarettes and fire on her every minute of the day used to give her a sense of oneness with the substance of the natural world; it was like possessing the secret power of some magical ritual. When smoking she was in command of the physical world, she was master of her own destiny. The knowledge that smoking involved her in physical dangers only added to the thrill of it all. Its being potentially lethal proved its potency and importance and increased her sense of being in charge of her own destiny when smoking.

In her dream Brenda was not succeeding in getting to the shop to buy her cigarettes in the same way in which, in reality, she now no longer did obtain the satisfaction of playing with fire. What came as a revelation to Brenda through thinking about this dream was that she had experienced her giving up smoking as a personal failure instead of as a personal achievement. The smoking symbolized this mastery over the physical aspects of her existence, a real playing with life and death. As such she had been unable to replace it with anything else. She had given up smoking largely for professional reasons, but she felt deep down that this had represented an act of cowardice rather than bravery.

This aspect of things was represented in the dream by the snowplough, which she saw as standing for culture. This was the expression of her relationship to the social dimension. Brenda experienced other people as ruthless and unstoppable machines. Although endowed with beauty (statues and paintings) and with knowledge in the form of books, in the end culture could only come to her rescue by such inhuman methods that it would not only scare the wolves away but would eventually crush her in the process as well.

What the dream expressed on this level was Brenda's awareness of having given up her aspirations of mastery over her own world. For the safety of culture's rescue she had given up her independence of thinking and let herself be knocked unconscious.

This independence of thinking was the first direct reference to the personal world dimension. The dream did not leave much room for this dimension. Brenda reported an awareness of terror whilst confronting the wolves and a sense of urgency for the snowplough to arrive. Neither of these feelings left her much opportunity to have a clear sense of a relationship to herself, since they were feelings directly related to material world concerns. The only moment a personal world started to emerge is when the dream ended; the moment when she realized she had been hit and she withdrew into herself, expecting to wake up in hospital. Interestingly, this also signified the end of the dream.

Brenda realized that in her actual life it was just the same; there was no room for a personal life, for time with herself, unless she was ill. In fact she had just spent a few days in hospital recently and had experienced this as an opening towards herself. She began to wonder whether the building of a more solid personal world might remedy the sense of emptiness of her current life. It became evident to her that only through making more space and time available for a personal world would she ever be able to solve the mystery of her aspiration to smoking. For the moment the natural world connotations of this seemed clear enough. Yet she was well aware that the playing with fire, the getting to the shop for a pack of cigarettes even though it exposed her to intense danger, was significant in a deeper way as well. She needed to become more familiar with her own inner world before she would be able to understand the meaning of her aspirations and before she would also grasp the full strength of her motivation in terms of what really mattered to her in a spiritual sense.

For the moment she simply concluded that it would be wise to expand her horizons in the direction of a personal dimension, rather than being entirely driven by physical world obsessions and at the same time being at the mercy of social world interference. She acted on this insight and began to reserve time to be by herself, when previously her life had been dominated by work and social engagements.

At first Brenda found it very hard to be at peace when not busy in some way; the temptation to start smoking again was particularly violent during this time. She gave in at first, but at the same time she began to investigate new ways of getting the fire back into her life. She was particularly concerned with the bleakness of her existence; she really did feel as if she were wading through cold snow by herself. She also wondered why other people seemed always so threatening (as wolves) or so unaware of her vulnerability (crashing into her) and why she seemed unable to include other human beings in her private world.

The dream remained a constant point of reference for her and many events of her everyday life kept illustrating aspects of the dream. Eventually she came to the conclusion that she wanted to make a new sort of contact with people around her. Instead of having only professional and impersonal social relationships, she wanted the warmth of confidence in another creature. After trying to obtain this from several people in her near surroundings without getting much more than physical response, she opted for a new approach.

She got the idea for this new approach through another dream, which was quite similar to the original dream but for the presence of other lonely travellers through the snow. This dream gave her the notion that she must somehow find these other lonely and isolated people running from the wolves, instead of herself howling with the wolves or riding on snowploughs that crashed into things.

In this second dream she had suddenly found herself on the snowplough, which had now become a sledge and which dispersed the wolves, but killed the people running through the snow and she felt intense guilt for this when waking up. The guilt was that of her realization that she was trying to escape from her original plight of being a runner through the snow, by joining the public, safe, but ruthless camp. Her guilt reminded her of her aspiration to mean more to others than she had seemed to be able to for the moment.

She concluded that she must take the initiative of being with others in a more caring way and totally unexpectedly decided to join the Samaritans, as a befriender. It was not surprising that this entirely fresh addition to her way of being in the world had a considerable impact on her. Although she had originally only taken up this new challenge as a way to extend herself to others out of her own social world isolation, it soon grew into something far more than just that.

Brenda discovered that she was adding an aspect to her relationships with others as well as adding a dimension to her personal life. But more than that she started to feel as if for the first time in years there was something in her life actually worth living for; the thus far rather neglected spiritual dimension had at last been integrated. She could now imagine living for something, which would enrich not only her own life but other people's as well. This gave her a source of energy and enthusiasm, which she likened to an internal bonfire, which would provide the warmth and sense of importance that she used to find in smoking.

Not long after this remark, Brenda had a third dream on the snow theme. This time she saw herself walking or wading through thick snow towards some people who were camping out in small tents. She felt worried at their vulnerability and wanted to shout to them that she was coming to help them, but when she tried to, her voice was like that of a wolf. She turned around and saw a pack of wolves approaching in a threatening way, so she ran towards the tents and fell down exhausted in or near a large fire. When wanting to warn the tent people of the approaching wolves she remembered how her own voice had sounded and she fell silent for fear of their rejecting or killing her. She began to cry in despair about this and to her amazement noticed that her tears fell onto the snow like fire drops, which were melting the snow and starting little fires. She thought: now I will know how to keep warm and how to be safe from the wolves. She woke up with a great sense of confidence and joy.

The first step, as usual, was to sum up the dream in one sentence in an attempt to grasp its essential significance in terms of her mode of being in the world and her original intention and ultimate concern. Brenda did this as follows: 'I intend to save some needy people from tough conditions, which I seem at ease with myself, but I find that they end up saving me instead.' Through closer examination of the details of the dream the different dimensions of her experience were then amplified. Brenda noticed particularly how certain she felt of her ability to cope with the natural world's harsh conditions. The snow did not scare her in the least and, as in the other two dreams, she felt perfectly at ease proceeding through the cold and snow as long as she was faced only with physical discomfort. This corresponded to her attitude to everyday life, where she was inclined to make do with a minimum of material comfort. In fact she had often discarded her own health as a very secondary consideration, by excessive smoking or by ignoring the symptoms of physical ailments and thus ending up in hospital.

Brenda realized now that her ability to stand pain and brave discomfort was one of her main assets. She felt rather heroic in this attitude and took great confidence in it. She realized that one of the reasons the Samaritans had appealed to her was because of their name, which reminded her of the biblical story. She liked the notion of becoming like a good Samaritan, giving up some of her physical comfort to contribute to the well-being of someone more vulnerable than herself. Braving the elements made her feel strong, just as smoking had made her feel strong.

However, as the dream indicated, this basic material confidence was undermined by the approach of a pack of wolves. Brenda had always been sure that the wolves were other people. In the first dream this public aspect of her world relations was mostly represented in a negative way, as a threat in the form of wolves and snowplough. In the second dream there had been an additional element of fellow human beings, who seemed as needy and scared as she. In this third dream it was apparent how these fellow human beings who were perceived at first as in need of her assistance turned out to be potentially scared of Brenda herself (when her voice was like that of a wolf). So there was an important shift in the public-world dimension. Not only was it clear now that some people might be worse off than she herself, they might even fear her in the same way as she feared others stronger than she.

The second discovery she made was that although she had initially thought these people might need her help, they turned out to be the ones to save her instead. Of course the reason for their superior position was that they, unlike herself, had access to fire. As soon as Brenda was aware of the fire's presence she was irresistibly attracted to it and she ended up almost jumping into it, in despair of her ability to be safe from the ravening wolves. At that moment she felt as if all was lost. She had been unable to fend for herself, too scared of other people. She had been unable to help the people she wanted to help, because they would have been scared of her. She had also found that they possessed the longed-for fire which she herself lacked, but she did not as yet belong to their group.

The moment she realized all this in her dream, she abandoned her usual stoic behaviour and broke down and cried. Only then did she discover that the very tears she cried began the process of melting the snow and her isolation. She had unveiled the secret of fire; she had discovered the source of it in herself. It was this discovery that made her feel part of the group of tent-people; she had now found a temporary home. By finding her own vulnerability and tears she had found her inner fire and could now belong with these other people.

Clearly for the first time this dream expressed some hope and comfort on the social dimension. The wolves would no longer be a real threat; she was part of a group and she had a home (however temporary) and most importantly she had the secret of fire, which would avert any attack by wild animals.

In terms of her personal world this dream also indicated definite progress. First there was the much more explicit reference to personal thoughts and emotions. There was an intensity of subjective experience, which had been absent from the previous dreams. The epitome of this intensity was of course the experience of actual emotional release in tears, leading to the discovery of personal potency, in the form of fire. This discovery of her own access to fire from the inside, rather than by having to borrow it from cigarettes or from other people, was what made her feel so joyful on awakening. She could now influence her natural surroundings, melting the harsh snowy conditions, and be safe from the cold. She could also scare off others, who would previously have been able to devour her. In other words, power in the private sphere also increased her autonomy in the physical and social arenas.

Brenda was able to hold on to these ideas and to build on them in real life.

Although the dream had only been an expression of a glimmer of new hope, she made its images into realities by believing in them and acting on them. So she stopped thinking in terms of her Samaritan work being some sort of mission, for her to save others, and started to see it instead as a journey towards others for her own development and expansion. Admitting to her previous arrogance helped her in making some friends amongst co-workers who started to appreciate her as a person capable of humility and generosity. This was an entirely new experience in Brenda's life and equalled the joy of the dream's ending.

While the third dream had been looked at in much greater detail than the first two, there was still little reference to the ideal dimension. Brenda was simply not at ease on this level. Earlier attempts to find the ideal significance of her dreams led to her belief that she wished above all to help the needy, which clearly turned out to be based on a lack of acknowledgement of her own needs and vulnerability. This indicated that Brenda had other tasks to attend to before she would be prepared to find a direct purpose in her life. For the time being, indeed, sorting out her personal world and more solidly establishing her physical and social relationships was enough of a challenge. Her ideal for the moment was simply to be able to keep the fire burning inwardly and keep herself warm and safe, especially with the developing friendships she had now engaged in.

Her main motivating force was the possibility of now gaining some potency in the social sphere of her relationships instead of feeling at the mercy of others. Secondly, it was in the discovery of her ability to influence her external situation through taking initiatives and finding comfort where only coping had been possible before. Gradually what came to the foreground was her newly discovered motivation to find a sense of inward reality and richness in her personal world, both with her thoughts and feelings and through increased intimacy with some close others.

Corresponding to these values and aspirations were her ultimate concerns of losing grip on the social dimension and being excluded and isolated again, reduced to the role of social commodity for others. Second came her concern, now growing with her increased comfort, that she would fall ill or be weak. It was interesting to note how she had previously hung on to the lower end of the physical world emotional spectrum, by inviting illness and hiding in her ability to put up with it as an alternative to health.

The same thing was true of her personal world; as long as she had kept herself unaware of her inner existence, there was not much fear of losing anything. As soon as she began to develop her aspiration to greater depth of inwardness and increased closeness with others, she became aware also of her confusion and her vulnerability. But then of course becoming aware of that and being able to express it both to herself and close others became the very strength for her moving forward towards greater intimacy with self and others.

As is so often the case, Brenda had had to make a move forward and get into the swing of things before she could start benefiting from the circular and self-perpetuating increasing strength of the motivation now driving her.

The dreams had the function of providing the images, which made it easy to find her bearings. In holding on to some simple images of her own situation and position she had been able to decide on the best course for her to set out on.

In developing these images and in allowing the dreams to become a map for guidance and inspiration she instilled in herself the hope of clarity and positive movement forward that had eluded her when trying to sort things out through reflection on her actual situation. The dreams, more than just expressing a factual situation, had been seen as an illustration of her particular approach to living. Thus she got a handle on the complexity of her experience. Looking at the implications of her attitudes toward the world, as expressed in her dreams, had then allowed her to recognize areas of short-sightedness and notice obvious room for improvement.

Focusing on the positive potential of the dream's point of view encouraged her to start seeing things from a different and altogether more constructive angle. Thus Brenda became the author of her own constructive images capable of turning these into a self-fulfilling prophecy, which could carry her forward logically and naturally.

Working with dreams in this way is about allowing people to realize which images and fantasies about the world are holding them back, so that they get ready to start undoing these or complement them with more helpful ones.

Without creative use of one's dreams and imagination the world becomes centred on the stale images that one absorbs from the external world. Reanimating the images one can live by with passion and hope is therefore a crucial step on the road towards greater vitality. Designing one's dreams as blueprints for reality is the beginning of a life, which brings fulfilment. From the centre of one's inner strength, thus built, reaching out to the world around one and towards other people will be far more meaningful.

Playing with imagination

As dreams are the expression of the way in which people orientate themselves in the world, so imagination is the origin of this orientation. It is the force of imagination that inspires the world with a certain reality. What is perceived in the outside world is inwardly processed and made meaningful in terms of the images of reality that each person has created. Reality is shaped and interpreted in this way.

Many images are culturally or socially shared and thus a kind of objective reality is reached which enables communication and understanding between people. Yet even within one culture there are many different interpretations of those shared images of reality. Concepts like death, personality or success can be defined in many different ways by different groups of people. Individual connotations on every concept and every aspect of life determine the outlook of the person. This outlook in turn determines the range of options available to that person.

The person who imagines that a nuclear war will destroy the world within the next decades is unlikely to undertake any project with much hope or energy. The person who imagines that her intelligence is subnormal is unlikely to take up public speaking or studying maths. The person who believes that she has been treated unjustly may discover an unexpected ability for self-affirmation. The person who imagines herself to be related to the royal family may adopt an attitude so regal that it creates an atmosphere of respect and reluctance in those around her.

Imagination creates an atmosphere and has an effect on the world. Everybody is engaged in imagining their world every day of the week. Few people are aware of this as they take on board the same images over and over again and have come to see them as truth rather than as a representation. As cultures are based on this type of commonly agreed repetition of images and representations it is possible to live one's life without ever realizing that it would have been possible to immerse oneself in a different reality. Many people have very little sense of their own creative abilities of imagination. It is comforting to them to think of reality as based exclusively on facts.

When people come to counselling or psychotherapy it is often because they have suddenly come face to face with the fictitious character of their reality. They want to find out if they have gone mad or if the world was never as certain a place as they imagined it to be: people may complain of having lost their illusions or of having woken up from a dream. When they experience this sense of relativity of reality and truth they are often only one step away from the discovery of their own capacity for the creation of reality. It is this that an existential approach will stimulate and support.

George needed support in his struggle to make sense of the world after his wife, Nelly, had suddenly died. They had been married for twenty-three years and their life together had been such a well-regulated life that George had been entirely soothed into believing that there was no other life possible. He had taken Nelly absolutely for granted and he had liked their way of life enough not to desire another one. There had been no great passion between them. They were childhood friends. There had been total agreement about what mattered in life and they had found fairly straightforward ways of dividing the tasks in the house. There had been few rows between them, as each of them knew what was expected. George had a steady and unexciting job and Nelly took care of all the housework. They had no children.

When Nelly was run over by a car and died within two days of the accident George's world simply stopped. He could not believe what had happened and he would not carry on living his life as before. He just sat at home pining away. He was physically and psychologically unable to adjust. He felt at a loss in feeding himself properly and relied entirely on his neighbours to take care of him and do all those things around the house that Nelly used to take care of. Although the neighbours were happy to help out, they started to get rather fed up and a little worried when George did not change his attitude as time went by.

Five months after Nelly's death George was referred to an outpatient clinic, after the neighbours had decided to talk about their worries to the visiting physician from the insurance company. A team of people treated him and therapeutic counselling was part of the treatment, even though George himself did not think talking about it would make it any better. He complained of the absurdity of life and wished that he could die. He looked fifteen years older than his actual age and behaved like an old man. As he soon refused to go out to the clinic, because he could not be bothered, it was decided to attempt home visits before sending him on to residential care.

The counsellor built a friendly and supportive relationship with George over the following months, during which time George became more ready to talk. It was soon obvious that he was not pining for Nelly as much as for his own life that had been lost. Nelly's sudden death had brought him face to face with the ephemeral quality of the things that he had previously believed to be reliable and stable. It was this change in his own world that he could not come to terms with.

He was himself rather surprised at how little he actually seemed to miss Nelly. He hardly ever thought of her at all. What he did miss very much was the regularity and comfort of his previous life. He had wondered about finding another woman who might be able to provide this for him, but he had dismissed the thought when he realized that things would never be the same again anyway. It was not just Nelly who had gone. It was not just the presence of a woman in the house that had gone. It was his faith in existence that had gone. With all its limitations his life with Nelly had provided a shared sense of meaning. When she was there his work made sense, because he had to provide for the two of them. Weekends made sense because they had both liked sampling country inns. Life had seemed like a reasonable and pleasant sort of experience. Now it seemed like a booby-trapped war zone.

It was when George began to express himself with these metaphors that the exploration of his world became more productive. He soon became aware of the fact that it was he and Nelly who together had created the pleasant atmosphere in life. This atmosphere was not inherent in a particular situation, it was brought into life by the way in which they had thought of the world and acted accordingly. In a way it was therefore illusory and unreal, because you could not count on it just to go on forever. The world was not intrinsically a reasonable and pleasant place. Yet it was by the same token also not an intrinsically booby-trapped and war-like place. Either experience was brought about by one's own created images.

It took George a while to grasp the idea that something imaginary is not necessarily unreal and that reality is always to a certain extent created actively by a belief in ideas or images, which are then acted upon. He gradually gained some understanding of his own active interpretation of the world. He could see how he construed life as basically dangerous since he had learnt that comfort and routines couldn't simply be taken for granted. As he experienced Nelly's death as a sudden unwarranted attack on his security, he had created an image of life as a war zone, where nothing is safe and where things can explode in our faces when we least expect it. He acted in accordance with this view of the world, by not venturing out any more and by not getting attached to anything that might again be taken away from him.

It was evident to him that he was indeed creating this kind of experience for himself when he felt great excitement for the first time in many months while watching an account of the Second World War on television. This sort of war experience matched his own imagery and he found satisfaction in the recognition of his private world in the documentary on the screen. It now became possible to create a positive sense of life, as it occurred to him that the war zone image need not be exclusively his own or absolutely negative. He became fascinated with the heroism of people in the situation of war and deprivation and he started reading avidly on the subject.

Once George began to create a new meaning in the world around him, the recovery from his depression was almost immediate. Eventually he even went back to work and he built a friendship with one of his male colleagues who was a collector of war memorabilia. Together they went on tours to Normandy and Arnhem and George found great pleasure in his new interest and companionship. It had been suggested to him many times during his depression that he ought to take up some hobby or do something of interest to him. But all this good advice was to no avail until George could create the right atmosphere and image to fit his actual experience.

Imagination is not an isolated process. It is one aspect of a person's whole mode of being. It is as useless to prescribe fantasies and images for clients as it is to prescribe new behaviour or feelings. Healing images must be compatible with the person's entire outlook if they are to become significant. This compatibility can only be reached if the client has generated the ideas or fantasies. No one else can determine what is to be meaningful and how this meaning can be created. The starting point must always be that of the person's already established imagination. The therapist can only assist in the process of elucidation of the significant images and in the transformation of negative into positive. She cannot change the client's basic orientation.

It is easy to overlook some of the less obvious ways in which clients use their imaginative powers and conclude that they are unimaginative. Imagination does not always manifest itself in fancy or original ways. It is, however, just as potently employed by the tidy conventional company director who actively pursues the image of her success as by the quaint original artist who pursues the image of her own creative genius. Everybody uses imagination although not always in the most constructive manner. Regret about the past and worry about the future are two less obvious ways in which people imagine themselves into a certain way of being. The positive counterparts of these are joyful reminiscing and daydreaming about the future. Of course any of these can be constructive or destructive. The person who keeps internally repeating an image of the past as the source of all her troubles or comforts is doing herself a disservice by creating a restrictive view of her own creative powers. The person who worries or daydreams about the future may be unaware that she is actively designing the time to come.

Much can be gained in all of these aspects of imagining by becoming reflective of the process that one is engaged in. The person who is compulsively worrying can turn passive worrying into active worrying and then into planning for the future. Worriers often are people who have a strong imagination and who have not yet learnt how to let it serve rather than harm them. The same can be said for compulsive daydreamers. Both can turn their strong imaginative powers to good use by learning to reflect on the creative process that they are engaging in. Letting the mind wander to days to come and contemplate their potential hazards and opportunities can be one of the most creative occupations as long as you remain in charge of the process. Imagination can in this way play the role of rehearsal of reality, shaping and moulding it until you feel at ease with what is to come.

In the same way going over the images of the past can be constructive in as much as you shape and mould them to provide a sense of peace with the present. An understanding of what you have done wrong or right yesterday can only be an asset in planning for the future. If you find yourself with a destructive self-image from yesterday's experience it is only by becoming reflective about it that you become capable of amending it. A regular routine of reviewing the images of the past is therefore crucial if you are to proceed towards a more constructive process of creating images for the future.

Of course many people are unused to consulting themselves on these matters. Current living practice in Western society does not encourage such reflection on the images with which we shape ourselves. Rituals like prayer or meditation are hardly practised regularly. The closest many people get to the fabrication of new images and stories to live with is when they watch television and follow other people's imagery. Unfortunately there is little opportunity for many people to process those images and to pick and choose the most constructive ones. Without such a process of reflection, imagination becomes passive rather than actively reflective and the person misses out on its visionary quality and gets overwhelmed with the sheer quantity of contradictory story lines. This is where existential therapy can help the person in waking up from the dream of passive imagining and learning to monitor her own visions and fantasies in order to cultivate her inner reality. An existential approach encourages the person to mind her own imaginings and re-create them in a playful manner.

Tina needed just this kind of assistance. When she came for therapeutic counselling she was in a state of great confusion. She had been given the telephone number of the counsellor fifteen months previously and had kept it in her purse in case of an emergency. Only now did she find the courage in herself to speak about what had been bothering her, because she had always hoped that her confusion and feeling bad would magically disappear. It had finally become plain and obvious to her that things were not improving but deteriorating and she needed help.

Tina was twenty-three years old. Her father was a West Indian and her mother was white, born and bred in South London. Tina had been raised by her mother and her stepfather, who was also white. She had two little half-sisters. Her father and her paternal family were very much in the background, although she did see them sometimes. Tina's self-image was extremely confused. She had grown up imagining herself to be white like all the other people in her close family, but from the age of thirteen or fourteen she had started to be teased at home for having a chocolatey colour. Her little sisters were particularly pale in comparison to her darkish complexion and she had at first imagined them to envy her for tanning quickly in summer. When her stepfather started to make nasty remarks to her and tried to get her to leave the home to go to live with her father's family, she understood what was really going on.

With the vivid imagination of a lonely fifteen-year-old, Tina began to make up the story of her own misfortunes. She created the fantasy of being a slave-girl who had been purchased by her stepfather to do all the work and take care of the other two girls. She imagined that they were now tired of her as she no longer complied with their demands. At first she tried to find refuge in her father's family, but she felt even less welcome there. She also felt that they hated her for being half white and having been raised by her mother. Now the slave-girl fantasy did not fit the bill any more either, as she clearly was not black.

After this double disillusion Tina did not know any more where she belonged or who she was or where she could find an image of herself to please her. By this time she was sixteen and had left school to do a typing course. As soon as the course was finished Tina started working as a temp and got herself a bed-sit in the area where her father's family lived. For several years she lived like this, making a living moving from one temporary job to the next and without any stable friendly relationships. She spent all her free time watching television and smoking and she fancied herself to be entirely different from other people.

Tina now began to build up a fantasy about being stuck on a desert island and waiting for a ship to come and save her. She hated her jobs and her family, who had become less and less interested in her as she became increasingly self-centred and eccentric. She hated everything around her except for her television set, which was her lifeline to the outside world. There were numerous incidents in her work that convinced her of the basic unfairness and toughness of the world and of her own weakness in dealing with this. She began to imagine that they were all out to get her because she was the ideal victim. She realized that she needed to be rescued from a desperately down-winding spiral. As always her television set was there to save the day and provide her with just the image to accommodate her. This image was that of a pop star with whom Tina fell desperately in love.

At first this new development rather energized her. It was the second time only that she had been in love and it had not been this intense before. She felt herself quite uplifted and hopeful. She saved up quickly for a video-recorder and began a diet of non-stop watching of the pop star's performances. In this way she also discovered the pleasures of masturbation, which added considerably to her growing belief that there was an actual connection between herself and the star. Never before had Tina felt so good. Now she had a fantasy all her own, which she could return to every day after work and wallow in whenever she liked.

Tina felt as if she were walking on clouds. She knew that she was special. She was not inferior at all, but superior. If only all these silly people knew that she was really his secret lover. The illusion was nearly perfect for several months. But then the magic spell was broken one day when she went to a live concert by this artist.

She experienced a sense of extreme humiliation in having to share the star with so many other people. It was at once clear to her that she had been fooling herself and that she had been playing a childish game, which had come dangerously close to reality. There she was in this huge auditorium with thousands of other girls and women screeching out the words and the tunes that she had imagined to be her private property.

Tina fainted at the concert and when she came to the ambulance people were talking about her before they realized that she had regained consciousness. She was looking for some support for her legs, which were most uncomfortably spread out on the stretcher, and when the ambulance people saw her jerking movement they made a wry comment about her. They called her another hysterical wench who was probably going to have an epileptic fit. Tina was shocked to hear herself referred to in this manner when she was at her most vulnerable and the remark started a new series of fantasies about herself.

Her fantasy about the pop star had been mercilessly crushed that evening and the fantasy about herself as hysterical and possibly epileptic took its place instantaneously. From that moment Tina's life became totally miserable. Her joys had gone now that the video-recorder had lost its appeal. All her thus far suppressed worries about her sanity came to the fore and she began torturing herself with constant negative self-observation. Within months she had convinced herself that she was mentally ill and she obtained the name of a professional through an acquaintance who was involved in the medical profession.

When Tina finally did contact the counsellor she had gone through another year of self-torture. It was because she had now reached the stage of not daring to go out to work any more for fear of betraying her mental illness to colleagues that she felt she must try to get some help. Tina's first few sessions were spent almost entirely in uncontrollable sobbing. It took another two sessions for her to tell her story as she had experienced it. Then, very gradually, some work could be envisaged.

The focus was initially on her image of herself. It was evident that in spite of her great suffering and negative feelings about who she was, she deep down believed herself to be a very worthwhile or perhaps even an outstanding person. It was not difficult to encourage Tina to find the root of truth in the fantasies about her own specialness. She gratefully accepted any encouragement in the direction of an honest account of the story of her own exceptional existence. Finding the recognition that she craved for her efforts to remain free in herself and not give in to the difficulty of her situation, Tina grew less keen on the image of her own inferiority. Thus it gradually became possible to review the past history of her troubles as an account of a learning experience. To distil out of it those elements that provided a proof of her strength and courage was the first objective. Recognizing the errors that she had made were the necessary, but gently introduced, next step.

It was perfectly clear to Tina that she had a strong and powerful imagination. Many people had remarked on this in the past as they had caught her out telling little fibs or white lies. She was also acutely aware of how she was in the habit of letting that imagination run away with her. She used the image of a bolting horse to describe the feeling she would get when this happened. Although she did not really want to go so fast and lose her sense of grip on reality, she felt as if she could not do anything about it and she experienced great exhilaration at letting it happen.

Tina was also deeply proud of her accomplishment of having lived by herself for so long without ever counting on anyone but herself. She knew that her life had not been an easy one and that her ability to manage in spite of this was proof of her basic toughness and resourcefulness. Given these fundamental positives it must be possible to draw on her strengths in a more efficient and rewarding way for the future. Once Tina had been reassured on the subject of her sanity and capacity for managing her own life successfully, her imaginative powers came into their own once again. She began to make plans with great enthusiasm, as she fantasized her way towards the future.

During this phase Tina needed a lot of assistance in monitoring her imagination, which would easily go on the run again. She had to learn to let her mind wander to wherever it wanted to when this was feasible and then to check it back and reflect on the actual possibilities of implementing the products of her mind's playfulness. She for instance came to the conclusion that her infatuation with the pop star had been an expression of her yearning for a more glamorous existence. She then went on to build a wild fantasy of her own future achievements as a pop star and had weeks of daydreaming about the wonderful outcome of such a state of affairs.

Learning to settle for a fantasy that might actually hold a chance of fulfilment she eventually transferred this image of her personal fame and fortune to an image of herself working in the world of pop music as a personal assistant. Some further trimming and pruning of this product of her imagination led her to come up with the desire to take a secretarial course. This of course was entirely feasible, especially as she had saved up enough money over the years not to work for a little while. Although she did not particularly enjoy this course, she made some significant contacts with other young women and she moved into a flat with one of them. As this friend was also a pop music addict, they often went to concerts together. This transformed Tina's life.

Once Tina's life was stabilized in this way, modelled after her own imaginative planning, other areas of disturbance came to the fore. Specifically her sexual fantasies needed to be considered, as Tina was in the process of building up an image of people suspecting her of being a lesbian for living with her girlfriend in a rather intense manner. In the course of her exploration of the images of her own sexual pleasures and disgusts, a long forgotten desire for her stepfather came to light. Tina was by now so conversant with the method of distinguishing between fact and fantasy that she could report several incidents of her childhood without getting caught up in the false beliefs that had long been part of them.

It now seemed to Tina as if the images that she had herself created about her stepfather stood in the way of her enjoying herself freely in a sensuous manner. She had believed that her stepfather wanted to abuse her and she interpreted many small events as a confirmation of this idea. All this had been part of her fantasy of being the family's slave-girl and although she had abandoned the latter she had never really considered whether she had been right in her belief that her stepfather wanted her. At first Tina decided that there must have been some truth in her imaginings and she developed the notion that all men were pigs. This freed her bad feelings about living with the girlfriend and she even came to the conclusion that she was no longer afraid of people thinking her a lesbian as she probably was and should be proud of it.

Acting out this new image of herself as a lesbian gave her much pleasure and excitement. She thought of herself as liberated and emancipated and this provided her with new energy and enthusiasm. But while this experience was very rewarding in some ways, it still left Tina with a very restricted notion of her relationship with men. She was dissatisfied with this as she meant to have children of her own one day. Thus she began the long exploration of her fantasies about her relationship to her stepfather and her father. This proved to be by far the most arduous of investigations and there were many occasions when she felt like resorting to destructive fantasies. Eventually she made up her mind to transform such a fantasy into a feasible reality and she went home to both father and stepfather and spoke to them about her suspicions and resentments.

Tina was rewarded for this act of courage by an inner sense of strong independence and determination to make the most of her life. There was at first little positive response from the father and stepfather. While Tina was pleased with herself for having talked to them, she was irritated with the lack of definite response. In examining what made this so very important to her, she came to the conclusion that these two men were each the symbol for one half of her background. Recognition from at least one of them would give her a sense of belonging. Letting her imagination run free again on the subject, Tina came up with the idea that she wanted them to indicate to her who was her real father so that she would know whether to call herself white or black.

She designed what she called 'The Solomon's test', which consisted of her writing letters to both her families in which she told them that she was going to kill herself because she felt that she did not belong anywhere in the world. She had no intention of really killing herself but she wanted to find out how people would respond to the threat. She was absolutely cool-blooded about the whole project and determined to carry it out.

In the event she succeeded in drawing the attention of both her families to her need for their support and recognition. She had herself only hoped that she would be claimed and chosen by one set of parents, but both rallied round and her sense of belonging was greatly improved. She began to visit her mother and stepfather regularly and she also struck up a good relationship with her half-sisters who were now teenagers. She gained much satisfaction from this new self-image of big sister and confidante and started to think of herself as very mature and responsible.

At the same time she was invited into her father's family and attended the baptism of her father's new baby. At the ceremony of her half-brother's christening she felt extreme elation and created the fantasy that she was herself being baptized and officially accepted as part of this West Indian family that had so far cared little for her. For the first time in her life Tina felt at peace with her mixed-race background and she cried tears of relief as she vowed to become as good a sister to baby Jason as she had now become to her sisters.

It was taking care of Jason on a regular basis that really brought Tina's life into its own. She discovered that she loved babies and she enjoyed being part of the extended family that she now belonged to. Within a few months she also fell in love with a friend of the family and she started her first relationship with a man. There were many other facets to Tina's journey of discovery into the land of her imagination and fantasies. There continued to be a number of serious obstacles to the full enjoyment of her creativity, but she was now able to manage her longings and fancies sufficiently to put them to constructive rather than destructive use.

Tina's experience illustrates the point that imagination is an extremely powerful force in the shaping of people's lives. With each new fantasy Tina's life took a new direction. Tina's task was to find ways to structure and slow down her quick imagination. By assisting her to do this without attempting to make her conform to the standards of a less fanciful society it was possible to help her draw on the creative abilities of her imagination. All too often people like Tina are condemned or dismissed for being too confused or hysterical.

Not everyone uses their imagination in such a volatile manner as Tina. Not everyone uses it in the constricted manner of George. In working with clients' imaginative powers it is important to gauge the level of their creative flexibility and to adjust the task to what is required by each individual. There is no better or worse in the area of imagination. What matters is to enable the client to move from passive to active use of images and from destructive to constructive creativity.

Chapter summary

1   Feelings are important guides to what matters to people. They illustrate their mode of being in the world.

2   Understanding and mastering emotions is like learning to surf the waves of the ocean, since emotions are the ebb and flow of human experience.

3   Emotional expression is not as important as deciphering the messages of one's moods and feelings, moving away from re-active emotionality towards active emotion.

4   Emotions indicate our position in relation to that which we value or dread.

5   Pride shows a certain taking for granted of what we value and enjoy. As the saying goes, it almost certainly comes before a fall.

6   Jealousy shows that what we value and enjoy is under threat and we try to guard it desperately, lest we may lose it.

7   Anger shows our sense that what we value is dangerously threatened and that we feel entitled to try to retrieve it with a final push of energetic effort.

8   Fear indicates that we do not believe we can save that which we value, and that we are wanting to remove ourselves from the threat to our prized possession. The experience of loss takes over from that of possession.

9   Sorrow is the expression of loss and shows that we are letting go of the valued possession, letting ourselves become empty of it.

10 Guilt indicates that we still experience the emptiness of loss but that we have swung back towards comparing ourselves to what might be and that we already aspire to regaining what we value, but are failing to do so for the moment. Guilt is our own sense of falling short.

11 Desire indicates our aspiration to achieve a new value without a definite sense of whether it will be concretely feasible to do so.

12 Hope is our awareness of the possibility of attaining that which is valued, whilst still maintaining a fair distance from actual possession of the object.

13 Love is the experience of going out of ourselves towards that which is prized in a commitment of care for it.

14 Joy is the emotion that accompanies our grateful achievement of what we value, in a movement of unification. It leads in turn to pride, so that the cycle can start all over again.

15 Every affect has positive and negative forms and the entire emotional cycle can be repeated endlessly or even at the same time for different values.

16 When no emotional attachments are made, there can be no aspiration or desperation over anything and so apathy results.

17 Meaning is created out of a person's engagement with what is valued and this commitment provides the purpose that makes life worthwhile.

18 The absurdity of life has to be appreciated before it is possible to create meaning in the world.

19 People can be helped to reconsider their life stories in ways that make more sense and that enable them to discover and create meaning and purpose where it previously was lacking.

20 For every basic value and purpose that we pursue there is also an ultimate concern about the loss of this value. We have to learn to take these limits of existence into account as much as our values.

21 Dreams can express our relationship to our values and ultimate concerns particularly graphically. They illustrate our relationship to the world on each dimension of reality and they can be deciphered to show what is meaningful, has value and is of concern to us.

22 Existential dream work is a co-operative venture in which world relations and personal motivations are described and explored for their meaning to the dreamer, but they are never interpreted in terms of an external system of meaning.

23 The client's dream world is to be made sense of by the client, so that she can better understand her own preoccupations and motivations in real life.

24 Dreams express our current orientation in the world, but our imagination can shape and reorganize this orientation for the future.

25 The stories we tell ourselves about the world, the past, the present and the future determine the possibilities or blockages we create for ourselves in the world.

26 Understanding how to make creative use of imagination rather than letting it influence us destructively is an important part of the art of living.

6

Coming to Terms with Life

Facing the world alone

The entire process of existential counselling and psychotherapy is centred on the issue of self. Nevertheless, from an existential perspective the notion of self is radically different to that of most other therapeutic approaches. Existentially a person's world relations define her sense of self. Self is the centrepoint of a person's entire network of physical, social, personal and spiritual world relations. We become that which we do and are preoccupied with and care about. Our various roles and functions define our sense of identity. It is therefore no wonder that many people are confused about who they are, since their sense of self can sometimes change drastically as their circumstances and world relations change. The therapeutic session is therefore seen as a moment of quiet when the client has the opportunity to come to terms with herself and her life. Because of this the emphasis is not so much on the actual interaction between therapist and client as on the encounter of the client with herself.

The practitioner functions as an alter ego to the client, rather than as a parent, an adviser, a manager or a friend. Before anything the existential therapist is the client's ally, but an ally with a modicum of wisdom. She is available to the client as prompter to the voice of the client's conscience, reminding her of her inner truth and helping her to establish a sense of balance and clarity of direction, so that a dynamic sense of identity is arrived at. In every session the therapist therefore makes sure to systematically refocus the client's attention on inward reflection about what she is engaged with in the outside world. Although there is of course a social dimension in the therapeutic relationship, sometimes in the public, sometimes in the private domain, the therapist reaches always beyond the purely social and interpersonal dimension towards participation in the client's subjective world. This is done so that the client cannot hide in dependent or counterdependent interactional excuses for not conducting her subjective investigation. The session is treated as a moment of thorough self-examination. The therapist seeks to enable the client to be in the session as if she were by herself, alone and in truth.

Most other therapeutic approaches assume that the way in which the client relates to the therapist is a reflection of her relationships to significant others.

The existential approach is more inclined to see it as an expression of her relationship to herself. This idea is based on the notion that people are only getting out of a relationship what they put into it themselves and that they are only able to relate to that which has meaning for them. The assumption is that people perceive the world and relate to it precisely in the way in which they perceive and relate to themselves.

This principle of kinship encompasses the notions of both projection and introjection. In kinship we gyrate towards that which is familiar and expose those aspects of ourselves that fit the current situation or people we relate to. Similarly, other people resonate with what is akin in us and we can thus bring out aspects in them that are prominent in ourselves. People behave a bit like magnets and find themselves attracted to and wanting to merge with anything that they feel affinity with. We can become absorbed in anything we experience as potentially our own and so will gradually transform self or others so as to maximize similarity and kinship. This basic striving towards unity does not, however, have to be seen as a defence mechanism, but rather as a principal motivating force, a basic mode of human being.

When the therapist therefore recognizes that the client is trying to influence her attitude or she becomes aware of the way in which the client actually does affect her, she encourages the client to take account of this herself and understand the implications. In doing this the therapist needs to give no interpretations of what causes such motivation, she simply needs to encourage the client to observe her own attitude and to examine its intention. This process of re-establishing the focus of the session away from ordinary social interaction onto the reflection on the client's subjective experience takes place whenever the client slips back into non-reflective interaction. It is a quite simple but subtle procedure, which is commonly used by any astute interviewer who wishes to expose the interviewee's vulnerable side. After a brief, apparently polite and innocuous interchange of niceties, the issue is at once pointed by a brisk personal question of the ingenuous kind. Agatha Christie's Miss Marple is an outstanding example of the practice of this art of naive and benign questioning, leading to sudden and thorough exposure.

The therapist has to make sure that she is not engaging in a battle of wills with the client, but that she is the client's ally and is gently prodding her along on the road towards greater exposure to her own inner world and aspirations. The client's honesty is not viewed as a trophy but as an option that she must be reminded of. Whether the client feels safe enough to take that option is largely related to the therapist's apparent ease with the situation and with the extent to which she can abstain from personal vindictiveness towards the client.

An existential practitioner never refuses to participate in any topic of conversation, nor does she volunteer many topics herself. She allows the client to ease into her explorations of subjectivity through the back door of social conversation. All the same the therapist herself never lingers any longer than strictly necessary at this back door. At the first opportunity she invites the client to move on to an exploration of the home of her subjective experience.

Thus the client is continuously referred back to conversation with herself rather than getting caught up in a conversation with the therapist. If the client asks her therapist, for instance, where she is going on holiday, the latter may after a brief and concrete answer retort with 'Is that the sort of holiday you would want yourself?' The ensuing reaction of the client will almost invariably reveal much of her aspirations and dislikes. Focusing in on what makes this or that attractive or unattractive now will naturally lead to an exploration of pertinent issues.

If a client, for example, remarks on how she felt irritated at having to wait to begin her session for a couple of minutes because the therapist was answering an urgent phone call, the therapist might say something like 'Yes, I am sorry you had to wait a minute there, it was obviously frustrating to you to have to hang on.' But after that initial genial and sympathetic response it will be necessary to encourage the appeased client to examine what precisely was upsetting to her in this situation. The therapist might focus the issue by first asking for a general opinion: 'Is that the sort of thing that gets to you?', then by pointing in the direction of subjective elaboration: 'What was going on in you while you were waiting?'

Thus the client is invited to observe her own opinions, views, feelings, thoughts, impressions and assumptions without attaching too much of a value-judgement to them. Frequently clients are unused to this practice. Many people are passively involved with their inner experience without having much of a grip on it at all. As long as there is an external world structure guiding their experience they are at ease, but when they are alone they feel at a loss. For many people the first step forward out of the confusion of their thoughts and feelings when they are alone is to analyse them. This is a way of imposing a recognizable and familiar external structure onto something that seems intangible and chaotic. The sort of internal world that is created in this way can be rather oppressive.

The existential counsellor or therapist will generally have to initiate the client into the practice of self-observation. By paying attention to all the fleeting feelings and opinions without attempting to make them fit into a causal explanation the client will gradually discover herself as the source of this complex inner world. Instead of remaining caught up in particular aspects of her experience she will learn to stand back sufficiently to grasp its meaning and trace her original project and intention. Stopping to be at the mercy of one's inner world, and thus ceasing to be terrified of it, is the objective. For this it is necessary to start by facing oneself on one's own. The therapist can only play the role of mediator between the client and her inner world for a limited time. The sooner the client learns to trust herself the better.

The entire process of therapeutic work as described in the previous chapters is a way towards this inner source of experience. It will be evident by now that it involves deep thinking about one's way of being so as to reach to an inwardness, which will become the core of one's actions and outward relations. This thinking is not the thinking of cerebral analysis, but the thinking of reflective attention to what is already there; it bears great similarity with meditation (Heidegger, 1957). Bringing to light in oneself what is already there is a matter of paying attention and respect to oneself and it is not dependent on having a high IQ. Many highly intelligent people lack this kind of self-respect and attention to inner life. Many very ordinary people have a good intuitive understanding of their own sense of purpose and they are able to be at ease with and respect their inner world.

Approaches to therapy and counselling usually pay attention to a person's biological, social and cultural conditioning, but rarely to a person's existential conditioning. Yet it is the latter that most people find it difficult to come to terms with. This is evident from the sort of experience people have when they are alone. No matter how deprived or alienated they may feel physically, socially or culturally, they may often be able to think of themselves with a specific identity and gain strength from this, as for instance as 'a differently abled person', a 'career seeking man' or a 'black woman'. Being different in some way can become the most outstanding strength especially if the person is able to join ranks with others in a similar position.

It is far more difficult to come to grips with the basic human conditioning and learn to have peace with and find strength in the realization of one's finiteness or one's endlessly reiterated confrontation with limitations and failure. It is relatively easy to recognize biological or social injustice and to rally against it. Coming to terms with the notion that the very basis of one's humanity in the reality of constant need and imperfection will inevitably lead to new injustice and renewed inequality is far more difficult.

It is not surprising that many people prefer a blind absorption in outward activity to a journey towards recognition of their own intrinsic humanity. The search for Self in accomplishments and external occupation can gratify one's wish for a better world and for personal merit for a long time. When a crisis strikes, inevitably the reality of existential conditioning will however be brought back to one's attention. Then we have to take into account the merciless progression of fate, which over and over again exposes our human vulnerability.

Some people are apparently so secure in their physical and social environment that the question of their basic humanity and finiteness does not seem relevant to them. It is only when they are confronted with misfortune that they begin to wonder how they could ever take so much for granted. A comparatively small crisis may throw them into sudden confusion because they have little or no deep inner security.

There are many men and professional women who live such outwardly focused lives. Even though they may spend time on their own regularly this time is typically spent in reading the newspapers or in some other activity, which keeps them entirely connected with that external existence. When suddenly faced with illness or the death of a loved one or alternatively with their own defeat through ageing or job loss or illness or accident, they may feel totally lost in the vacuum of their loneliness.

Crisis counselling is most often about such a sudden exposure of a person's inner lack of resources. It is therefore usually very necessary for people who have been used to taking a basic external security for granted until the crisis hit them, and especially if they have previously had little opportunity for coming to terms with themselves in isolation.

The story of Ivan Ilyich (Tolstoy, 1886) illustrates this point vividly. It describes the struggle of a wealthy and successful man in coming to terms with himself and his life when he is suddenly confronted with the imminence of his death. He comes to the staggering realization that he may have been wrong all along and that he has squandered his life in outward achievements without ever fully living in a deep meaningful way with himself.

Ivan Ilyich's discovery is similar to that of Kierkegaard, who used to assert that victory is man's greatest enemy as it alienates him from himself.

Yet it is very seldom that people turn to a counsellor or a therapist as long as they are successful in their material and public life unless some specific crisis occurs. Living in alienation from oneself seems perfectly acceptable to many people. It is only with hindsight that they can recognize how deprived their existence was during periods of ease and good fortune. It is only after having come to terms with their inner world through confrontation of a crisis that they can start to appreciate the positive aspect of this downfall. Only then can they begin to appreciate how inner strength and truth can be found only through a solitary grappling with adversity, failure and finitude. Finding an inner self-confidence relies on one's willingness to face the world alone with a basic humility.

This courage to be (Tillich, 1952) asserts itself precisely because of the basic lack of security. Resolute living from the centre of one's aloneness can only be achieved because of a confrontation of ontological insecurity (Laing, 1960). As long as the basic security of one's being is taken for granted, one lives in the expectation of being provided for. This entails a fundamental dependency on good fortune to continue to provide external comfort and achievements. Inner freedom can be obtained only through a process of liberation of these expectations. Quite often people only discover the possibility of inner freedom when they first face defeat on their own.

Many people, in spite of repeated defeat and crisis, remain hopeful that this is just a passing adversity and that life will be quite secure again tomorrow. Instead of rising to the challenge of their misfortune they may then attempt to ignore the opportunity and seek out salvation through oblivion or through reliance on others. The counsellor or therapist is in this case often appealed to in a last attempt to avoid facing reality and self.

The existential practitioner has to be watchful not to succumb to the temptation of playing the role of saviour. She will monitor her role as the client's conscience by checking whether her intervention is enhancing the client's relationship with herself or on the contrary making her more eager to flee towards external compliance. It is only if the client comes to terms with her inner freedom, through facing inner existential anxiety, that she will discover the ability to recreate herself inwardly. Without that capacity any external progress will ultimately turn out to have been in vain.

The client needs to find in herself an inner source of life that she can always rely on as a safe place where truth can be found, no matter what lies and deceit go on in the outside world. As long as the therapist tries to accommodate the client and attempts to ease her pain and anxiety, she stands in the way of the client's discovery of this safety in herself. The therapist must thus avoid playing the role of a drug or a television set or a kind neighbour. Though the client may need some oblivion as well, more than anything she deserves a chance to discover her own strength, her own intrinsic ability to face her existence alone.

It can be difficult to assist someone in this discovery if she is used to gaining a sense of self through continuous confirmation in action and public respect. Someone like that frequently has many avenues of escape from anxiety open to her. As long as she prefers the comfort of re-establishing the illusion of her safety to the struggle with insecurity and aloneness there is no point in forcing the issue. No one can discover new dimensions to life unless they are ready and willing to abandon old securities. The existential practitioner must abstain from missionary zeal. The client, if not pressed, will return when more illusions have fallen apart and the urgency of further investigation is confirmed.

It can be even more difficult to assist someone who is already entirely forlorn in inwardness. Yet those who are forlorn in themselves need to find inner freedom and resolution before they can turn to outward achievement of material comfort and respect. It is tempting to try to coax lost souls into action; often it seems as if all they really need is to gain some self-respect in being part of society. It is undoubtedly reassuring for the counsellor, for the therapist and for society if a quick re-adaptation and prodding into action can replace a characteristic eccentricity and withdrawal. Most often, however, there is very little gained in this way and very much is lost.

The withdrawn person who learns to comply with society's requirements for the sake of cure will usually end up functioning as a robot, entirely devoid of inner spark or personal freedom. Such adaptation is only obtained at a very high cost and inevitably with major recourse to means of artificial oblivion in the form of drugs.

Nobody who has been exposed to the intensity of distress that can accompany deep loneliness and alienation from the external world would suggest that madness is a better solution than re-adaptation. What is wanted by people in this depth of despair is invariably to escape from their isolation. More than anyone else these people are ready for the discovery of their inner strength. Their inability to handle external life however, makes them incapable of finding the freedom they are looking for. Unless they find a secure place from which to start facing inner chaos and confusion, they may be trapped in alienation both external and internal. Given a safe haven and some assistance in struggling through to an inner security they may find a very special level of insight and understanding. There is no question that those who have special sensitivity are in the greatest danger of getting lost in isolation, as they are more likely to experience external alienation and then withdraw.

People like this are often extremely resistant to any form of help, which can be identified as interference and an attempt to normalize them. They are just as quick to recognize any assistance which addresses the crucial issues and which is truth-seeking. More than any other client the forlorn person responds to existential therapy. Working with such a person provides an eminent test of the therapist's ability to work authentically. The person who is at the rock bottom of existence and who has nothing more to lose will instantly sniff out any form of patronizing or missionary zeal. Only the therapist who has faced this depth of self personally will be able to make a difference for the person so utterly lost at the edge. Yet any form of therapy or counselling worthy of the denomination existential will do precisely that.

Sean was twenty-five-years old when he began to see a counsellor. A psychotherapist had previously seen him when he had spent some time in a psychiatric hospital two years before. This was, however, the first time that he was taking the initiative to seek help himself. He had contacted the existential counsellor on a friend's recommendation. His request to the counsellor was to have tutorials on existential philosophy, not counselling. Sean was highly suspicious of any direct interference with his way of life. He had had very negative experiences with psychiatric help and psychotherapy, which he had suffered through only because he had been incapable of survival under his own steam. He felt certain that he would have gone under in his madness without this temporary psychiatric help. He felt even more certain that he would have gone under in the psychiatric help and the dependency on medication without the help of his friend and his parents.

Sean was living with his parents and spent much of his time in his own room. From the age of sixteen he had thus sought out solitude as an alternative to the interference of other people in his life. He was proud of being a 'loner' and yet he felt drawn into great despair and emptiness in the process. He had been a brilliant student for many years and he had an outstanding degree in philosophy from a well-respected university. Yet he had been disgusted with the curriculum that he had studied and he had come to the conclusion that life and the art of philosophy were lost on academic philosophers.

Although he much appreciated the support from his friend and his parents he felt unable to trust them. He suspected that their motivations for helping him were largely based on their wish to control him and his life. What he aspired to most was to achieve an inner clarity of understanding. Yet his inner world was in chaos. After he had completed his degree he had spent over two weeks locked up in his room at his parents' house, drinking nothing but tap water and occasionally eating cream crackers. When he had physically collapsed his parents had called in a doctor and Sean had been taken into hospital for physical, then psychiatric care.

It was only after a few weeks in hospital that his parents began to regret having taken him there, according to Sean's account of events. They were shocked at the way in which he seemed to be rapidly deteriorating, once he had lost himself through being 'drugged out of his mind'.

Eventually, with the support of his parents and his friend, who was in fact one of the psychiatric nurses at the hospital, Sean discharged himself from the hospital and began to come off his massively dosed medication. It had taken him over a year to find a new stability and a taste for anything other than sitting and staring at the wall or the television in his room.

His life at the outset of his existential tutorials consisted of a daily routine of getting up and getting dressed, eating, sitting, reading a little, exchanging some words with his parents or perhaps his friend, eating some more, having a bath, reading some more and going to bed. He was acutely aware of the discrete but insistent pressure that his parents were implicitly putting on him to perform in some socially useful manner. He was also increasingly alarmed at his friend's attempts to make him more active. He realized that everyone wanted to be reassured and see the results of their good works. Although he was critical of this, he also knew it to be natural and logical and so he was the more distressed at his own desire for further lonely meditation and withdrawal.

He approached the philosophy sessions with trepidation and scepticism, lest they should turn out to be a disguised attempt at indoctrinating him back to ordinary living. At the same time he was as eager for a challenge to his present life and as hungry for new insights and understanding as anyone can ever be. Though he was absolutely committed to his solitary life for the moment, he was also keen to find new ways to conduct that solitary life. It was clear to everyone around Sean that he needed action and human relationships. It was clear to Sean that he needed first to complete the task that he had started: coming to terms with himself and with life. No amount of skilful prodding and pushing would persuade him to get out and be normal. All he wanted was to confront the obliterating silence in himself.

Of course Sean was well aware that his philosophy tutor was also a therapist and before long he initiated discussions about psychoanalysis. He was particularly preoccupied with the view of his previous therapist on his need for isolation and withdrawal and he wanted to decide for himself whether the therapist had been right or wrong. His therapist had suggested to him that this need was based on his refusal of the struggles in the outside world. He had further indicated that Sean's withdrawal was a form of regressive behaviour and an attempt to return to the symbiotic world of infancy.

Sean was outraged at these interpretations and he felt that this therapist had not even begun to understand what was really going on. He therefore refused to communicate any further with the therapist, who had promptly interpreted this attitude as a confirmation of his previous diagnosis. Sean's drug treatment was considerably increased after this and he felt great despair at this obvious miscarriage of justice.

The episode, however, made a great impact on him and he had been trying to figure out ever since whether this therapist had perhaps been right. Starting to address this issue by reading about psychoanalysis and discussing his inner experience in the light of his reading gave him a first hold on reality. He could now start to formulate what had been confused and contradictory. He was not analysing himself; on the contrary, he was using psychoanalytical notions to sharpen his awareness of what he needed to clarify in his own terms.

He came to the conclusion that his need for solitary withdrawal, far from being regressive, was in fact progressive. He was not hiding away from the outside world. He was not afraid of it. He was not refusing its struggles. He was simply, as he put it, 'in existential training'. He felt quite strongly that in the last few years he had confronted life's problems and human difficulties more sharply than any smug therapists ever would in the comfort of their armchair theories. Now that Sean had something to come up against he began to act in a much more lively way.

He set out on a quest for knowledge that led to him avidly reading books on social psychiatry and alternative approaches to therapy. There too he found much to criticize and correct through his own experience. He particularly disagreed with the view that his behaviour must be the response to a false situation in his family. This also related to a bad experience he and his parents had had during a couple of sessions of family therapy whilst he was hospitalized. He thought that this experience had much contributed to his parents' decision to support him in discharging himself from the hospital.

The clear assumption in these family sessions had been that something was basically wrong with his relationship to his parents. Again it had been suggested that there must be symbiotic ties between him and his mother or that he was being encouraged in some other way not to grow up. Sean felt that this therapeutic intervention had been an interference with the task he was trying to accomplish instead of a help.

All the people who had been trying to help him professionally had automatically assumed that his behaviour was wrong. They had tried to show it to be a symptom of some underlying pathology. No one had ever considered the possibility of his behaviour being correct and willed. Because his behaviour made him suffer everyone assumed that made it wrong. What he had wanted instead was for someone to not only encourage him in his behaviour, which for the moment was the only right attitude, but for that someone to enable him to be more effective in it.

He had indeed had a close relationship with his mother, but saw that as an asset, not as something pathological. He was quite certain that it was his parents' great sensitivity to his inner world that had enabled him to become so self-aware. He had no doubt that this had made it harder to get on in the outside world in the ordinary superficial manner that seemed to be expected. He had also no doubt that this was not a great loss. He felt strongly that if he could make sense of all this in himself in his own way, he would then be better equipped than many others to go out and do something constructive if he decided this to be worthwhile.

The only moment that he had doubted his own sanity was when his parents let him be hospitalized and treated as a mentally ill person. If they could no longer make sense of his need for isolation it was much harder to continue believing in himself. His exposure to the various therapies had then added to his confusion by providing intellectually credible models of explanation for what was the matter with him. That had nearly made him lose his hold on his inner reality. That was, he thought, why he had needed over two years to get back to a normal level of confidence in himself. The only way in which it had been possible to safeguard his sanity had been through spending this much time by himself. He had simply not been ready to assert his truth against the whole world before his truth was clear to him. Any interference from outside set him back; total withdrawal was the only solution.

With the tutorial relationship strengthening through these explorations and discoveries, Sean felt ready to acknowledge its therapeutic dimension. Once he felt sure that his inner world would not be ridiculed, questioned as pathological or reduced to fit a theoretical framework, he asked for assistance in clarifying various issues that he was still puzzled about.

During the year and a half of these tutorials Sean's confidence in his ability to relate to himself adequately and intelligently increased steadily. Eventually he felt sure about what he wanted there to be at the centre of his being: an ongoing dialogue with himself so clear and true that he would be able to convey it clearly to others as well.

Without consulting his therapist he placed advertisements in several newspapers proposing himself for philosophy tutorials (he did after all have a philosophy degree and his own experience of life). Within another year and a half he was settled in a rented room and making a (be it sparse) living for himself. He was also looking into doing a masters degree. His phase of withdrawal was over.

Sean continued to see his therapist for some time and the issues that he needed most to come to terms with now were his relationships to other people. It was only after he had clarified things in himself that he was ready to tackle the next hurdle. After the going inwards, having gained safe ground inside, it was time to move outwards. Now that he had created an inner reality and knew how to re-create himself whenever necessary, he was ready to confirm his existence through action in the outside world and in being with others.

Action and commitment

Once clients have gained access to a safe quietude and inwardness, their action and engagement with the world can become much more rewarding. Instead of making blind choices on the spur of the moment, it will now be possible to make well-informed decisions in tune with inner motivation.

Obviously in reality the picture is far less idyllic than this for most clients. For years after they begin to take stock of their situation they will still find themselves entangled in conditions they feel oppressed by. Becoming aware of the possibility of taking direction of one's own life does not automatically lead to ideal conditions. First of all, there is usually a vast area of past conditioning and sedimented habits, which cannot be instantly discarded. Second, the process of taking charge is usually riddled with contradictions and setbacks, often in the form of the opposite motivation for dependency and oblivion. Third, even for those who do take the autonomous way of life most seriously, choices are inevitably always limited.

No person, however free and autonomous, will ever be able to live the perfect life. No one will be able to lead a life that is skilfully modelled on individual intentions and ideals. Life is much more powerful and indomitable than anyone's personal willpower. Eventually even the most determined person will have to acknowledge her limitations.

It is possible to view these limitations imposed by the human condition as dreadful and depressing circumstances. It is also possible to view them as a given framework, within which it is possible for an individual to create her personal life as a work of art. Just as every artist has to come to terms with the limitations imposed by the medium she works with, every person has to come to terms with the given conditions of her life. It is in fact only through a process of recognition of these imposed boundaries that she will be able to take account of the unexploited possibilities existing within this framework (Camus, 1942; Tillich, 1952).

Any action a person initiates is marked by the given facts of her situation. The extent to which she is able to make a new mark on that situation by her action and attitude depends largely on the awareness with which she embarks on the action.

There is very little point in encouraging clients to undertake any action for which they are not prepared to make any sacrifices. Though a client may comply with explicit or implicit demands for action made on her by the therapist, she will eventually resent her own compliance. At this point she may either experience distaste with her life or herself or she may protest and decide to revolt. Most clients start from a position of disgust with their current lifestyle; disenchantment with the world is where existential work originates not where it should terminate.

Naturally, every person will have much to disapprove of in her situation and her daily activities; few, if any, will ever find the ideal situation and commitments for themselves. Therefore no client who pretends to have got it all right this time round will in all likelihood have reached the stage of self-awareness in action that the existential approach aims for. Such self-awareness is characterized by the ability to see clearly what dangers lie ahead and which negative consequences one's actions are likely to have. It is also exemplified by a certain amount of self-doubt. Nothing is gained if the existential approach purely incites to one-sided idealistic engagement in some cause. Blind fanaticism, however satisfying it may be, is not preferable to blind fatalism. The reverse is of course equally true.

Most clients who come for existential therapy find themselves somewhere in between the extremes of fatalism and fanaticism. Mostly they regret the way in which their life seems to be turning out, without having a clear idea how far this is their own doing or how far they are to be pitied as helpless victims of circumstances. They often feel that they ought to be able to do better for themselves and they come to a counsellor or psychotherapist so as to find out what moves to make in order to get ahead in life.

Clients like to think that the practical results of therapeutic work will be instantaneous. They are often greedy for material and situational changes in their lives, either because they have just lost what they used to have or because they want to get rid of it. In both cases the emphasis is often on the desire for a quick replacement. Fleeing towards new commitments clients frequently ignore the opportunities open to them to found their existence on a more solid base than that of action for the sake of action. What's more, many counsellors are part of the problem by their own longing for quick and concrete results.

The balance in our society is so much in the direction of action and speed, away from contemplation and calm, that though most people feel pressurized by this, they nevertheless measure themselves by this standard. People are often only content if they have achieved some concrete results in demonstrable action. Their sense of accomplishment is directly proportional to the amount of things they have actually done in a day. The sense of accomplishment gained from right action, from the savouring of a specific engagement well chosen, well undertaken and well carried out, seems to have become an increasingly rare experience.

If the existential therapist is to provide an atmosphere of peace for genuine reflection and understanding, she must carefully watch out for her own and the client's attempts to comply with society's expectations in this area. She must remember that what she is assisting the client with is becoming able to create meaning for herself in action. It is not to create action in the hope that this will satisfy in itself. Action must be self-initiated to make sense. Any action undertaken with genuine commitment and intention will bring great satisfaction, independently of its results.

Creating a meaningful life is about finding the right attitude and becoming absorbed in that process. It is not purely goal-oriented or significant only through the results obtained. Existential therapists, like their clients, should not be overly concerned with outcome. Focusing on finding the right attitude and maintaining it through a process of inward reflectiveness will be far more to the point. The fact that positive consequences will flow from this kind of attitude makes the process so much more worthwhile.

Of course it must be kept in mind that for some people the ability to initiate action capable of securing their survival is sufficiently rewarding in itself. Therefore they might be momentarily content with the simple ability to survive no matter what the conditions of their existence. But this is not true for many others. Most clients are engaged in action, which they find hardly rewarding or meaningful, sometimes to the extent that they wish they would no longer survive.

As was made abundantly clear in the preceding section, the first requirement for movement forward in this situation is for the client to come face to face with herself, in the ruthless honesty of inner silence. Without this nothing constructive will occur. As long as the client perceives and describes her situation through the eyes of an external observer no contact can be made with her internal source of motivation. She will be full of value-judgements about her own predicament. It will be evident that she considers herself as having a particularly hard time or as particularly weak or inadequate. In any case she will be making some kind of negative assessment of herself and the situation she finds herself in. Frequently during this time she will seek to convince herself and the therapist of her basic misfortune in finding herself in appalling conditions or in being such a nasty person. Many early tears in sessions are an expression of such self-pity.

The most effective attitude for the therapist to take in the face of this initial self-indulgence is neither to disapprove nor to approve. Exhortations to pull oneself together are as ineffective as empathetically (or pathetically) offered handkerchiefs. Instead the practitioner takes a firm and comfortable attitude. She must expect this situation, as she will recognize the ordinary human response of complacency and the need to collapse and fold from her own experience and self-reflection. She will know that people are best served if they are allowed to reach the conclusion for themselves that things are of course rarely as terrible as they seem and that they generally possess the inner strength to cope with whatever happens to be their lot.

While there is nothing wrong with a little complacency to smooth the edges of existence, there is greater passion to be gained in confronting the real issues than in some second-hand emotions related to the way in which things appear externally. The therapist avoids relating to the client's public world assessment of her own situation. Instead she may point towards the client's effort to disengage from an unsatisfactory situation or self-image.

When the client expresses her distaste with herself for being stuck in an uninteresting job for instance, the therapist construes this as an indication of the beginning of a process of taking stock of life choices. She will help the client then to make this disenchantment into an opportunity. She will enable the client to recognize her regrets as a source of awareness of what she does feel motivated to make of her life. With reflection the client may of course discover that it is a different attitude that she needs and not a different job. On the other hand, she may find that she does need to change jobs and that she has prevented herself from getting ready for a better job through moaning about this one instead of taking constructive action.

Whatever the eventual outcome, the practitioner ensures that the client examines her situation carefully first. Becoming aware of her present attitude towards her commitments is the first step in this process. This usually involves the complete existential exploration as described in the previous chapters. Action can only become synchronized with one's most intimate intentions if these are acknowledged and understood.

Taking stock of action specifically requires that some light is thrown on the client's longings and aspirations. Every action, however inadequate it may be, aims to provide the person with something. In triumphant action the person obtains through her own efforts and initiative what she not only deeply desired but also felt entitled to.

This notion of entitlement is quite a crucial one when considering action. Much disheartened or defeated action has become so for lack of conviction in the possibility of success. Much lack of conviction is due to a lack of sense of entitlement. This simple and self-evident notion is clearly illustrated in the plight of a dominated group or individual. It took the American blacks longer than perhaps necessary to begin their fight for freedom, partially because a great number of them felt a sense of gratitude for their slightly improved conditions and thus did not realize their entitlement to absolute freedom.

Many women do not want to be associated with the women's movement, partly because they do not desire some of the privileges struggled for and partly because they do not feel entitled to them. It took nearly two years of work in counselling for Julia to move from a pure longing for privacy to a recognition of her entitlement to have her own room in her own house. Julia was a forty-five-year-old-housewife. She considered her privileges of being a mother and a wife so great in terms of security and love given to her that she was afraid to claim her rights for personal space. She intuitively understood that claiming her right in this personal area would change her entitlements to absolute power and security in the rest of the house. She also feared she would lose her husband's and children's devoted gratitude if she withdrew her total availability.

For Julia, claiming her rights meant giving up other privileges, as it invariably does. She made some half-hearted attempts at liberating herself. Then she realized that she would have to think through the consequences of her actions before she could be sure that she wanted to make the choice to change. As soon as she had made up her mind she gained a conviction and a readiness to accept the logical consequences of her action, which allowed her to obtain what she wanted in a very effective manner.

Similarly Jill, who complained incessantly about her boring job, came to recognize how her complaints expressed doubt about her entitlement to anything better in her professional life. In her complaints Jill was attempting to obtain reassurance from other people about her right to be disenchanted with a dull job. She wanted some sort of confirmation from others that she was entitled to want more out of her professional life than she was getting. In herself she disbelieved that she was entitled to such success. She longed for it and she saw how she might implement it, but she did not have the conviction that it was her right to claim it.

When she first recognized this lack of conviction in her entitlement she was, as most people are, inclined to find explanations for this in her upbringing. It was her father's sternness and her mother's telling her not to succeed professionally that must be the cause of her lack of belief in herself, she thought. It took over a year before Jill could begin to see how her sense of not being entitled to a different job had a lot more to do with her intuitive understanding of the consequences involved.

She realized that attaining a different status in the company for which she was working would inevitably lead to her becoming much more isolated from her colleagues. Although she aspired to the public power that would come with a promotion, she dreaded its consequences for her personal life. She would be envied rather than supported, as she was now. She feared that she was not ready for this alienation from her peers. In fact she started to realize that she quite enjoyed the privilege of disenchantment with her work, in so far as it provided expressions of compassion in those around her.

She soon discovered that her constant complaining about her tedious work had given her the reputation of being over-skilled for her job and that the social status amongst her peers that this brought her was most pleasant. Looking at it from this angle made her also see the possibility of her current power being based on illusion and manipulation. For the first time she began to be serious about testing her own ability to go for promotion.

While she was taking a management course, preparing for a move, she got more and more evidence that her parents were in fact extremely supportive of her ambitions. She began to realize that her lack of feeling entitled to a better job had not stemmed from her education. After working through her fears of the duties that a new role would entail there was little left to hold her back. Jill set out on a new professional career, aware of her desire to remain in touch with her motivation for success and determined to remain lucid and not to fail in her duties.

The explicit formulation of entitlements and duties that come with commitments is the only way to gain access to conscious decision-making. Engagements undertaken in the knowledge and understanding of the possible consequences and implications are consistently more fulfilling than haphazard ones. It is still possible to make mistakes of course, even when a commitment is made with full and free choice. It will, however, be far easier to recognize such a mistake in time to make the necessary adjustments.

Naomi thought that she had made the most of her life's decisions with a clear awareness of her options and that she had generally been able to make good and profitable choices in this way. Naomi was twenty-two and she prided herself in her well-above-average intelligence and her maturity beyond her years. She came to counselling because she thought that she might be interested in becoming a counsellor herself eventually. She described herself and her life in a way which demonstrated her insights and her understanding of other people.

She was particularly acutely aware of the conflicts that her parents had been going through for several years. She gave a sharp analysis of the mistakes they were making. She also recounted how they had throughout her life tried to guide her in the right direction and how she had been able to accept their guidance without letting it dictate her decisions. As an example of this she related how she had opted for the study of a language at university rather than opting for reading law, as her parents had wished. She had not gone against them as she originally intended by going to art school or by reading philosophy. She understood how realistic her parents' concerns about her future employability were. She had not given in to their choice for her, but had been able to integrate their advice on keeping career opportunities in mind.

It was only when she was asked whether she was actually enjoying her studies, which were clearly chosen as a compromise rather than out of genuine interest, that she began to show a less self-satisfied image of herself. She did not in the least enjoy her studies and this was precisely why she thought she might look for an alternative career to that of language teaching or translating.

Even when admitting her lack of satisfaction with her current achievements, Naomi still seemed in full control of her destiny. She introduced the subject of other satisfactions, which made up for the lack of interest in her studies and mentioned how she had been living with her boyfriend Adam for the past few years. Here again followed a self-congratulatory reference to the way in which she was in full charge of her own existence. She had refused to get married. She knew exactly how much closeness was good for her and how much of it would suffocate her. Of course her parents and Adam's parents mildly disapproved of the situation, but that was just the effect of the generation gap and it only made the situation interesting.

She mentioned in passing how she had not had time to do any artistic work for ages, because of her intense relationship with Adam and because of the time spent studying or going to the movies. That, she said, was the one thing she regretted. She knew that she had to find time to do more art again. When she was asked what it was she missed in not doing more art, her expression changed dramatically. She was suddenly scraping her throat and looking away from the counsellor. She spoke with difficulty and hesitation about her love of beauty. When the counsellor pointed out to her how reluctant she appeared to talk about this, she replied that she was not sure that the counsellor could understand. The counsellor's question whether she was unused to being understood in this brought sudden tears to her eyes.

In the silence that ensued, Naomi cried soundlessly but passionately. It was as if she was pouring out all the tears that she had been storing underneath her external composure for many years. She cried for nearly fifteen minutes, without being able to find any words to explain her pain and without the counsellor attempting to intervene in any way.

There was a brief exchange at the end of the interview. Naomi said that this obviously meant that she needed a counsellor instead of needing to become one herself and she asked to begin as soon as possible. In the ensuing two years of work Naomi retraced her own attitude towards her life. Everything that she had originally presented as evidence of being in charge of her own life turned out to be evidence of her submission. She discovered that most of the choices that she had made had been entirely based on disillusionment.

Naomi did not believe that any action or engagement was worth fighting for. Her view of the world was almost totally sceptical. She had given up most things that she had once longed for. She had decided that she ought to grow up and leave her childhood dreams behind or be eaten alive. The only thing she held on to tightly was her secret belief in her own superiority over the crazy world around her. This superiority, she thought, was the result of her intelligence and her ability to adapt to any conditions without giving up her inner freedom. It never occurred to her that she was enslaving herself to the very things she despised through giving up fighting for what she did value.

She had studied something that she was uninterested in, believing that she had come to a perfect compromise with her parents. She hardly realized that though her parents had had to give up their influence over her in her refusal to read law, she had nevertheless herself given up her first choice too. Her artistic work had been far more important to her than she had even let herself know. She prided herself in having outgrown her childish love of painting in watercolours. She told herself that she was far too intelligent to let such an immature interest spoil her career opportunities. She loathed the whole idea of teaching, though she had had fantasies of becoming an artist. Now she was stuck with teaching a language as the most likely career option. She was starting to feel trapped in the outcome of her own decisions and choices.

What she had thought to be realism turned out to be a very negative and restricting approach to life. This was even more evident in her relationship with Adam. She admitted to not loving Adam. She had decided that love was not a feasible option in this world and that she would be far better off if she stopped looking for it. At first she had simply dismissed the idea of marriage and she had retained the idea of loving cohabitation with someone until it became clear that the relationship had come to an end. But, after living with Adam for a few months, she had come to the conclusion that even short-term love was an illusion.

With every illusion that she surrendered Naomi felt that she was growing older and that there was less of a future left. It seemed to her that the more one understood about life the less anything seemed worth living for. Life was just one long disillusionment. She longed to grow older and tougher so that she would not feel the pain and soon have done with all this nonsense.

Naomi felt entirely responsible for her own life. She believed that she had made her choices with absolute insight into the available options and that she had generally made the right choices. Therefore there was no hope left. If making the best choices led to this kind of wasteland she could well imagine what life would be like for people who felt at its mercy.

It took a long time before Naomi was able to recognize that she had in fact only ever made one positive choice so far. She had only opted for one definite attitude, which she was committed to with conviction: her cynical scepticism. All the other choices had been compromises or renouncements. There had been no engagement in any creative action with her full commitment other than that of her pledge to disbelieve that anything was worth fighting for.

Once Naomi could see her own attitude from this perspective it was possible for her to examine her lack of a feeling of entitlement to believe strongly in something. She came to the conclusion, first hesitantly, then with some enthusiasm, that she must be afraid of having to give up some other privilege if she were to commit herself to some really worthwhile cause. In this way she came to see her only commitment as a commitment to cowardice. She had actively adopted a consistent attitude of avoidance of conflict and confrontation. The result was that she had narrowed her world in such a way that she felt that there was hardly any room left to breathe. In fact at the age of twenty-two she was already waiting for her life to end.

It was easy for Naomi to see what she was afraid of losing. It was the security of a comfortable middle-class lifestyle that she had been willing to abandon her ideals for. It was really no wonder that she had felt all motivation slowly drain out of her life. She had never put her own youth and vitality to the test. She had accepted the privileges of a way of life, which was in essence not very dissimilar to the lifestyle of her parents, which she thought she had rejected. All her energy had gone into strategies that would enable her to maintain this lifestyle, albeit in an alternative mode, whilst satisfying her own insights into its limitations through increasing scepticism.

There was only one thing for it; she had to draw the conclusions of her own insights and decide whether there was anything worth fighting for. It was plain to Naomi that this was a foregone conclusion; she had in some ways already recognized such a cause in her previous commitment to withdrawal and scepticism. It was her own integrity; her own ability to stand up in a world where everything appeared to be difficult or unsatisfactory that was closest to her heart. Her previous attitude had in fact been an attempt to keep herself standing in the only way she knew how: through holding on to her comfort and her intelligence at the same time.

Time had come for a more daring approach now that she had come to the conclusion that there was not much to be gained from the cowardly or sceptical mode. Naomi experienced an intense sense of relief when she had reached this stage. At once life seemed possible again. She decided that if she had been able to stand the aridity of life's most negative and absurd aspects she must be really quite strong. This gave her the conviction in her own ability to cut out a more constructive life for herself and it gave her the taste for the quest for a more meaningful life.

When she had reached this point in her explorations Naomi had already resumed her watercolour painting for several months. She now decided to enrol for an oil-painting course, which she had wanted to apply for years ago. Her new engagement with something that she highly valued, had pleasure in and was good at changed her life dramatically. She met different people at her painting classes and she discovered how empty her relationship with Adam had been. Within six months of this discovery Naomi moved to a small bedsit, where she spent much of her time painting. She went back to art school for various other courses and within another six months she had, together with a new group of friends, put together an exhibition of their work.

The exhilaration of realizing herself capable of actually making money doing what she enjoyed doing was tremendous. At the same time Naomi was well aware that the few hundred pounds that she had earned selling two paintings were no guarantee of her making a living. Her past experience of scepticism and compromising stood her in good stead this time and she successfully and purposefully investigated various alternative options for making a living in this field.

Naomi realized that now that she was moving in the direction that was right for her, it did not matter whether she had to compromise a little. As long as her compromises did not forfeit her main commitment they were supportive rather than undermining actions. She felt great satisfaction in thinking of herself as a struggling artist. She was proud of being able to support herself without any leaning on her parents' charity. Her discovery of the possibility of engaged and committed action had thus brought her independence as well.

Naomi's experience illustrates the necessity of consulting the source of one's inner motivation before making commitments. It is one thing to believe oneself to be in total charge of one's life and to make all decisions according to a clever interpretation of external reality. It is quite another thing to listen carefully to the voice of one's deepest inclinations and learn to make choices of action according to what makes inner sense.

Naomi could have had an externally successful life and all the comfort in the world without ever gaining any real sense of vitality and meaning from it. The only way forward for her was to find out what it would be worth making sacrifices for and redirect her life's choices accordingly.

Naomi was fortunate enough to come to the realization of how she was wasting her life at a very early age. Many people build most of their adult life on misconceptions about their own entitlement to happiness. People all too often confuse their longing for security with the notion that challenge and meaningful engagement must be a threat.

Yet human life is never so insecure as when we pursue security. The most certain way of achieving satisfaction is not by striving after pleasure or comfort, but by going all out for something for which we would not mind giving up our security. Engaged action produces a sense of satisfaction as certainly as disengaged action produces boredom. Engaged action, in the last analysis, is possible only through personal inward reflection about one's sense of the goals that are capable of making life meaningful.

If it is true that people are no more than the sum of their actions (Sartre, 1946), it becomes crucial that action is taken with reflective inwardness. Purpose and meaning can only be created if we are prepared to make those commitments that our conscience dictates. Only engagements made from such a stance will be honoured and carried through. It is only from this attitude of intentional commitment that actions can be experienced as a movement towards greater attainment. Instead of simply complying with externally imposed obligations you can live your life as a personally enriching fulfilment of inner duty. Duty is now understood as something that is due to oneself.

External circumstances very often determine the sort of commitments that an individual is likely to make. Through small but frequent choices for transformation these circumstances can be affected considerably. The choice to submit to your circumstances entirely almost inevitably leads to dissatisfaction and existential guilt. Existential guilt is in this way a reminder of what you owe to yourself. Only to the extent that you take up this existential challenge will you experience a strong sense of being in charge of your own life. Commitment to creative action brings with it this sense of being in possession of yourself and your life. This sense increases with continuing reflective intentional engagement. It stands in contrast with the sense of being in charge of the situation, which merely indicates the effort of remaining in control of the external world. There is a big difference between the quest for external power and that for inner strength and vitality. The latter in existential literature is often referred to as resolution (Macquarrie, 1972).

The aim of existential therapy is to enable clients to engage themselves in resolute action. This is based on an authentic appraisal of their life's purpose. In finding the right commitment people discover a vital energy and aliveness, which they did not believe themselves capable of. This courage to live by their own convictions and ideals often allows them to accept sufferings otherwise unthinkable.

It is crucial for the therapist to remember that nobody can determine what another person's commitment ought to be. Two people in similar circumstances might feel moved in opposite directions. Suggesting positive action to a client will be likely to forestall her own exploration of her present situation and it will thus set her back rather than move her on. The role of the therapist or counsellor is to make sure that the client takes all the time she needs to take stock of her life before she undoes previous commitments and embarks on new ones. Sometimes a change of attitude is all that is needed. Sometimes the client needs to find the inner source of strength capable of fuelling her with enough energy to start a revolution. Either way reflection will need to be thorough before appropriate and self-initiated action can be undertaken.

Communicating and relating

Most clients see their difficulties as being centred on problems in relating to other people. It is rare that a series of sessions does not include some reference to a basic unease in relationships. It is important to address any issues that the client is concerned with. It is, however, even more important to go to the root of the client's problems rather than be content with a superficial treatment of the obvious.

The unease people experience in their relationships often stems from a more basic unease with themselves and with life in general. Those who are confused about their own direction and purpose are bound to feel overwhelmed by the presence of others who appear to want to push them along in various directions. Blaming their difficulties on negative relationships with others is rarely correct or useful. Indicating that problems in living are entirely determined and caused by destructive and traumatic experience in childhood relationships to their parents is even less useful and probably no more correct.

People are undoubtedly basically social creatures and it is unlikely that anyone who is living a full and fulfilling life will be incapable of positive human relationships. However, pushing them to focus on improving their relationships without giving them a chance to learn to relate to themselves first is a waste of time.

Many counsellors and therapists make the mistake of translating all their clients' experience in terms of their transactions with other people. This is, of course, an attractive way of looking at things as the therapeutic relationship itself provides first-hand and direct experience of the client's difficulties in this domain. It is far more difficult to allow the client to discover her internal presence to herself than it is to force her to become aware of her present relationship to the therapist. It might be argued that the latter is a reflection of the former. It might even be argued that the client can model her relationship to herself on the relationship she experiences with her therapist. It is obvious that people do model themselves on others and that they are constantly integrating new attitudes absorbed from others.

The question remains whether this kind of passive absorption and conditioning is what therapy is all about. The existential approach as much as possible distances itself from such deterministic practice. What is looked for is the opportunity for the client to find in herself the space to decide how she wants to relate to others or how indeed she does not want to relate to others.

The existential therapist is therefore neither directive nor non-directive in her relationship to the client. She is simply available to the client with the intention of considering her influence over the client and she aims to enable the client to become equally aware of the interaction between them. The objective is to help the client in finding her own feet. This means allowing the client to discover her own centre of gravity, rather than encouraging her to lean on others or get others to lean on her.

In this sense it is autonomy that is aimed for rather than dependence or independence. Other people will be recognized in the same way as self is recognized, in their striving for their autonomy and their detours through dependence, independence and counterdependence. From an autonomous position relationships can take on a new meaning. Instead of feeling directly threatened by others or feeling obliged to threaten them in order to defend oneself, it becomes conceivable to co-operate and respect others as well as being respected by them. This position is one of reciprocity, of mutuality, of interdependency.

It is interesting to note how relationships can be seen as taking place both on the public and the private dimension. Those relationships that are located exclusively on the public dimension can be considered as conforming to Buber's I–It mode of relating (Buber, 1923). On this level people attempt to use and affect each other in the same way that they would use and manipulate objects.

As we have seen earlier, Sartre (1943) describes three variations of this sort of human relationship. In the first place there is the option of manipulating and enslaving the other, in a basically sadistic or dominant mode. In the second place it is possible to give one's own freedom up to be used by the other, in a basically masochistic or submissive mode. In the third place there is the option of withdrawing from this type of human relationship altogether for fear of losing one's self in the process. This is the option of indifference or denial of the feasibility or interest of human relationships.

It has already been suggested that there are two forms of this withdrawal from public dimension relationships. Passive withdrawal, in fear of being absorbed by others, may have extremely isolating and ultimately destructive consequences. Active withdrawal for renewal and return to a source of inner counsel may on the contrary be the only way forward towards a different type of human relationship. In order to attain private human relationships, a close contact with the inner world is obviously essential.

Buber's I–You relationship is always clearly entered into from a position of intense subjectivity. In relating to others in this mode, their subjectivity is recognized in the same way in which one's own is. I–You relationships are thus relationships with others that can be included in one's private sphere. Intimacy is here based on a recognition of each other's personal world and a respect of each other's needs, desires and dislikes.

The existential therapeutic relationship strives to monitor its inevitable public dimension as closely as possible. It also aims at being open to the intimacy of I–You recognition of subjectivity in the client. It further aims at enabling clients to build an I–You relationship with themselves.

Beyond these two dimensions of interpersonal relationships a third level can be recognized. It is the level of the I–Me relationship, or the perfect merging of two beings who totally identify with each other and who operate in absolute self-forgetfulness, aiming at something that transcends their separateness and thus binds them together. This sort of relationship is of course to be located on the spiritual dimension. It signifies the human ability to aspire to something beyond the sphere of concrete human reality. It opens the possibility for relationships that are imaginary and absolute. In this type of relationship the individual surrenders her aspirations to selfhood and strives for something greater than herself instead.

Any close couple relationship has moments where it moves towards this dimension. Sexual release and abandonment is only possible if the partner, at least temporarily, is perceived as one with oneself. This oneness then becomes a path towards the infinite. In the ecstasy of sexual union there is a pure sense of belonging to an absolute and superior world: one feels in seventh heaven.

On a different plane this type of total absorption can also be experienced in a couple's absolute commitment to one another. For a while neither of the partners recognizes the other as a separate human being. There is a definite sense of belonging together, a sense of being one person in two bodies. Neither tries to enslave or be enslaved by the other. Neither tries to be open to the other's subjectivity, both are just together in the harmony of unity. Almost invariably such experience coincides with a joint project, which is highly desirable to both and for which each would be willing to cease to exist as an individual if this were necessary. Of course one of the most common unifying I–Me projects is that of procreation.

In procreation the union is in effect realized and the separateness of the two individuals is transcended in the most tangible and concrete way. For many couples the raising of their offspring allows them to remain in touch with this sense of wondrous union and commitment to something greater than themselves. For many other couples the procreative union has not even begun to be experienced in this light. Childrearing is then more likely to be experienced as a reminder of the obligations of the physical dimension rather than as a door into the ideals of the spiritual world.

To a certain degree the existential therapeutic relationship aims at the mode of operating of the unifying I–Me relationship. The therapist and the client will usually experience this coming together of their project at the moment when the work is progressing towards an honest appraisal of the client's aspirations. Therapist and client will at such a moment recognize that they share the concern for discovering the truth about human motivation and for coming closer to understanding the meaning of life. The unity momentarily experienced is not that of identification or recognition of sameness. The latter is closeness of the I–You kind. It is usually referred to as empathy. Of course it also plays an important role in the therapeutic relationship.

In the unity of the shared project individual differences become unimportant for a moment. All that stands out is the awareness of an underlying motive, which binds people together. The energy and enthusiasm generated in such a moment of merging with an absolute notion of one's own destiny can be considerable. Many religions, especially more primitive ones, build their ceremonies around this type of experience. Healing rituals do the same thing. Healers, shaman or priests on these occasions allow themselves to merge with their protégés in a movement towards God, nature or some other power identified as superior to people and thus as capable of absorbing their distress and replacing it with renewed strength.

Many forms of therapy and counselling mention nothing about this type of experience. Yet many experienced practitioners are capable of allowing this merging to occur at some stages during a series of sessions. There is little doubt that this is the bit extra thrown in on top of the usual approach, which can make the outcome suddenly so miraculously positive.

While it is important to recognize the potency of such catalytic experience there is no point in attempting to make it happen through a specific technique or other artifice. The strength of the therapeutic merging is relative to the quality of honesty in the mutual engagement with the pursuit of truth. Counselling and therapy can be valid without this spiritual component. It is, however, rare that the client will feel deeply moved and inspired to make life into something new and more complete without this sort of experience.

Julia (who was mentioned in the previous section) began her own counselling sessions when one of her children went through an episode of schizophrenia. At first she had worked with a counsellor whom she felt was far too directive and who tried to make her behave differently with her son. She sought advice from the consultant treating her son and it was decided that a different approach should be tried. Julia was well able to get on with the second counsellor, who worked basically from a client-centred perspective. She felt that this new counsellor was able to understand her and support her in her distress about having failed as a mother. All the same she thought that something was missing still. She sensed that it must be possible for her to go beyond her current emotions. She felt that her counsellor did not even begin to address the issues that were somewhere hidden in the background of her mind. There was, she thought, some idea that she was trying to get a hold of, and rather than stewing in her dissatisfaction she would like to get some help in coming to grips with this elusive and vague longing.

Her counsellor, who was very young and still in supervision, brought these issues to her supervisor and to the consultant. After a joint meeting with Julia the team agreed that it might be beneficial for Julia to switch to working with an existential therapist.

Working from an existential perspective with Julia involved assisting her in re-examining her relationship to her son (Mick, aged eighteen). It also involved helping Julia to trace back for herself what she had intended to achieve for her son and what she had tried to be for her son. This obviously meant that she would examine what it was she had wanted to make of her own life, especially of her life as a mother. This implied assisting her in the investigation of her own convictions rather than simply making an inventory of what had gone wrong.

It was especially important to do this as all previous counselling experience had involved the implication of Julia's responsibility for her son's problems. The first counsellor had actually told her what she was doing wrong and had made her practise alternative strategies. Julia had co-operated for a while but she felt mortified at the alleged wrongness of her whole life's experience and behaviour. She had also disapproved of the proposed alternatives and experienced even greater alienation from Mick when she attempted to relate to him as was being suggested to her.

While the second counsellor had certainly respected her feelings, she had also obviously assumed that somehow Julia had been wrong and that letting her stew in her guilt feelings for long enough might bring her to better her ways. Or at least this is how Julia had perceived the situation.

It was soon evident that Julia felt intense guilt about Mick's hospitalization, but not directly about his way of behaving. She felt guilty because she had let him down by giving up taking care of him herself. She felt no guilt whatsoever about the appearance of his symptoms. So far everybody had assumed that she felt guilty because she recognized her son's illness as her own responsibility. For Julia, on the contrary, the illness (or rather the madness) was something that only Mick was responsible for. She herself had only fallen short when she had been incapable of handling him the way he now was.

Up to this point Julia had not thought that it was possible to get anyone to see that she had been good as a mother. She did not know why she was so certain of having been good and she wanted to try to understand her own internal reasoning. When she had previously mentioned to counsellors that her intentions had been all good, they hurried to explain to her the difference between intentions and effects. If her son had become ill, it was implied that her mothering must have been wrong or bad, however good her intentions may have been.

The situation was a bit like that of the investigation of a crime. Julia had been branded the guilty party and she had nearly succumbed under the pressure and she had nearly begun to believe in her own guilt herself. Yet, in the interest of justice and her own (if not her son's) sanity, she was now consulting an independent investigator who might be able to assist her in proving her innocence and in the process also clarify the crime itself.

Julia adored this account of the situation. Immediately it put her and the therapist on the same side. They were thrown together by circumstances, as allies in the pursuit of truth. It mattered little whether this was a slightly melodramatic representation of the situation. It mattered even less whether this was the only truth of the situation. It was a unifying image which allowed Julia for the first time in years to feel confident about her own intentions and actions. She felt now not only capable of taking a hard look at herself, she was sure that it would be quite safe to do so and that it was the only way out of her current predicament.

Julia felt committed to something beyond counselling and psychotherapy; she felt committed to discovering the truth. She felt therefore open to herself in a way she had not been before. She began to volunteer information freely. She wanted to co-operate as much as she was able to. In fact, she said, she now felt that at last there was another person again who was prepared to share her own intimate convictions and elucidate them.

The therapist was able to maintain this close collaboration towards the goal of establishing the truth. She was well aware of the risk of collusion associated with such an attitude. It was necessary to remember that only the motive and the goal were shared. The attitudes, moods, emotions and thoughts of Julia still needed to be examined with the greatest clarity. The participation with Julia in her crusade for personal freedom did not imply approval or agreement with Julia's way of being. Being aware of that made it possible to recognize the times when Julia herself was diverted by self-indulgence or side-tracked by a blind need for approval.

The combination of absolute alliance and ruthless discipline in case of dishonesty had a powerful effect on Julia. So far she had mainly described herself as preoccupied with the well-being of her children. Mick, the hospitalized son, was the youngest of three. All three, though aged eighteen, twenty and twenty-two, were still living at home. Julia saw this as a proof of her being a good mother. She had always had conflicts with the two elder children, especially with her daughter, Didi, the middle child. She thought that her eldest child, Norm, would probably want to remain at home for as long as possible. Didi might get married. Mick, who had always seemed the most promising child, because of his original ideas and hobbies, might turn out not to be capable of leaving the nest after all.

She had always particularly loved Mick and they had had a closeness that was very special. Yet she had always known that she would have to let him go and she did not feel that she had been possessive of him as people often suggested to her. She had been far more possessive of Norm, the elder son, she thought. Norm, she said, was much more like her husband (also named Norm) and he would not have wanted it any other way. He enjoyed being taken care of by her and he was quite capable of putting her in her place if she hassled him too much over something like dirty shirts or socks with holes. She felt almost used by him, treated like a maid. She recognized how she had herself encouraged this kind of relationship, since she so much enjoyed just mothering him.

Her relationship to her elder son was in many ways modelled on her relationship to her husband. Both adored her and let her 'mother-hen' them. Yet both were safe in their own world, where she could not reach them. They were a real team together, going to football matches and for drinks, laughing at her concern for them. They were devoted to her and she was devoted to them. She was not sure whether they did not exploit her a little, even though they pretended to be in the palm of her hand.

Her relationship to her daughter, Didi, had always been marred by the awareness of Didi's preference for her husband over herself. Didi had always been a daddy's girl, vying for Norm's attention with her. There had been competition between Julia and her daughter for as long as she could remember. This is why she fully expected Didi to move out of the home before long. In fact, she thought this might well be the best solution, because she had almost daily rows with Didi. The rows were mostly about small matters such as whether it was necessary to wax floors several times a week or not.

She had, however, also had arguments with Didi about Mick, particularly just before Mick was hospitalized. Didi claimed that her mother was being far too accepting of Mick's bizarre behaviour. She urged her to consult a doctor rather than bring him food in the garden shed where he had been living for months. Julia now felt that she should perhaps not have let Didi influence her decision about Mick. She regretted having let him be hospitalized as it had turned out to have only bad effects on him and herself. It seemed to her that Mick might now be lost to her forever.

Losing Mick was the profoundest experience of deprivation for Julia. He had been, and still was, the most precious of them all. She saw him as an extension of herself. He was most like her of all her children, yet he had a strength and a power all his own. She said that she wanted to believe that what had happened to Mick had been the effect of some physical illness. She could not understand how such a brilliant and excellent child could have become so unlike himself and so distant from her.

Julia had let Mick develop more and more crazy behaviour without interfering, because she hoped it was just his way of going through adolescence. The other two had made her life difficult in other ways and she hoped that Mick's behaviour would soon pass. He had installed himself in the garden shed, sleeping on old rags, claiming it to be the safest place in the house. At first, during summer, it had hardly bothered her. Then he had refused to move back into the house in the autumn and she began to try to persuade him to change his mind.

The more Julia pleaded with him, the worse things became. Soon he was refusing to come into the house to eat or take baths. In fact he started to use the back of the garden as a toilet. Neighbours began to ask questions and Julia increased her efforts to try to influence Mick and get him to resume a normal life. Now Mick, who had so far been fairly reasonable and placid, began to yell at her and had several times referred to her as a witch. Julia began to suspect that something serious was happening, as she knew that Mick was in earnest when he called her a witch. He was not just insulting her, he was accusing her of practising witchcraft.

Yet she had still been prepared to put up with all of this as long as he still spoke to her. She hoped that he would recover from the strange episode and return to normal once winter drove him out of his hiding place. When winter came, Mick remained in the shed. He refused to discuss his reasons for doing so. Then one night, when it was freezing, Julia went to the shed and when she saw that Mick was blue with cold, threatened that she would call the doctor unless he returned to the house.

When Julia returned to the house Mick came running after her screaming in a rage that he would kill her. He threw handfuls of his own excrement at her and then went on to throw them at windows after she had taken refuge in the house. The doctor was called now at last. Mick was hospitalized. Though she had not been able to communicate truly with him since this she felt strongly that there must be something her son had been trying to say to her. While everybody else talked about Mick's delusions, she felt sure that his thoughts about witchcraft had some other significance.

Julia realized that most people had inferred that Mick might be expressing his horror of her abusive and smothering witch-like behaviour. She knew that her previous counsellors believed her to be the origin of her son's madness. She had thought so at moments herself as well. She was afraid that Mick might also end up believing this to be the only explanation of his behaviour. Deep down she was convinced that things might be a lot more hopeful than that.

Being able to talk about this openly without fear of being made to conform and without fear of being allowed to think herself into madness, enabled her to formulate her own theory of events.

Julia thought that the reason Mick had always been the most precious to her was that he and she shared a similar outlook on life. Whatever had happened she had always known that Mick was her ally. He would sometimes give her a wink or a smile that clearly signified his loyalty to her. She thought that without this sort of loyalty she would not have been able to keep her own sanity. Gradually it became evident how hard Julia had found it to live in closeness with four other people without losing her own sense of autonomy. It was only her intimacy with Mick and their unspoken loyalty to the same cause that allowed her to stand up in altercations with the others.

A much less nice picture of Julia's position in the household gradually evolved. She described how often she felt weak and insignificant when her husband and Norm took sides against her. They treated her as a commodity, someone to be flattered sometimes in order to keep her at her job of providing comfort and security for them. But definitely, with all the devotion they expressed, they appeared to despise her as a lesser human being. Whenever she tried to take part in their discussions about football or politics they would treat her as if she were a small and ignorant child. They would come and go as they pleased and yet each had more space to himself in the home than she, who was always there, would even dare to claim as her own.

The theme of dominance and submission was clear; her relationship with the two Norms was definitely on the I–It level. Moreover, it had been fixated in a stable position of their domination over her and her submissive acceptance of their needs and demands on her. There was no recognition of either of the Norms as a full person with a subjective world and there was no sense of her own subjectivity as important to them. Julia wondered how she would be able to establish some autonomy so as to be able to disengage from the current power imbalance and re-enter the relationship from a position of awareness of her own centre of subjectivity.

This issue became exemplified by her longing for some space to herself, where she could withdraw from the family life and find herself again. She had yearned for such privacy. She felt sure that she would be able to understand them better and relate to them better if she was not so absorbed in her role as housewife and mother. Yet she dared not think in terms of claiming anything for herself, for fear of losing their love. Love in this case meant need. Julia was terrified of the two Norms not needing her any longer. She felt sure that they would not want her there unless they needed her. This again was evidence of her I–It relationship with them. Her personality was not important in the relationship; she counted only in as much as she provided a concrete, objective service.

It was a very long time before Julia began to feel brave enough to tackle the issue concretely and to start thinking in terms of actually changing the house around so as to accommodate her own desire for personal space.

The motivation for her eventual courage to change came from the recognition of the similarity of her own frustration at not having room for herself and that of Mick, who had affirmed his need for space by moving into the shed. She was shocked and moved when she came to realize this similarity. Although it seemed obvious, Julia had never admitted her own longing in any explicit way and she had therefore been blind to the significance of Mick's actions. Now she understood why she had felt so tolerant of Mick's strange living arrangements. It was hardly surprising that he wished to have a room to himself: he had always shared a room with Norm. That room was full of Norm's things and left little personal space for Mick.

Julia at once knew what Mick had meant by his attacks on her. He must have felt abandoned by her, she thought, because she had not directly supported his efforts to establish himself independently. She had usually seen eye to eye with Mick but she had ceased to be able to do so when his new need for autonomy became too great for her to keep up with. Keeping up with his acknowledgement of a desire to live apart from the usual goings-on in the household would have meant that she would have had to declare her position openly. She had not felt ready to do so and she had thus in a sense opted for loyalty to the others over loyalty to Mick. No wonder that she had felt guilty for his hospitalization. It was her betrayal of their close union that had forced him into his extreme and isolated position. In doing so he was acting out her own isolation.

After Julia had come to this insight into her relationship with Mick, she felt ready to approach him in a different manner. He was still in hospital and he had his own therapeutic counselling sessions as well as psychiatric treatment. Even though Mick was fairly withdrawn and uncommunicative in his behaviour on the ward and with his counsellor, Julia was able to talk with him for the first time in months.

She felt certain that Mick was going to be all right now that she had been able to tell him how sorry she was for having let him down. Instead of expressing concern and compassion for him, as she had done previously, she now voiced her admiration for his daring behaviour. She told him how she had been hurt and scared, especially because he had attacked her personally. She said that she had simply not been able to understand what he was trying to say. She told him that she was trying to sort things out for herself now and that she was beginning to see a glimpse of light. She said she would need him to clarify quite a lot for her as well when he felt ready to do so.

Even though Mick was more withdrawn than ever during the week or two following this conversation, it was evident that he was thinking instead of being frozen as before. Ten days later Mick wrote a letter to his mother. In it he declared himself unable to relate to his mother, since she had chosen to devote herself to witchcraft rather than to truth. When and if she would discard her black magic and poisonous concoctions he might be able to talk to her again. He would be waiting to see a sign. Until then he would have to reserve himself out of self-protection. Unlike her, he stated, he had 'no skin of crocodile or viper blood to shield him'.

Julia was on the edge of despair when she received this letter. She had thought that everything would return to normal and the evidence was that it would not. Mick still held a grudge against her and she did not understand why. She was however eager to find out and put some more pieces of the puzzle in place. At least there was some communication, so there must be hope.

In her explorations of what Mick's words evoked for her, Julia began talking about her relationship with Didi, her daughter. She believed that Mick must be referring to the way in which she recently had tried hard to get closer to Didi. For many years there had been mostly disagreements between them. Over the last few years she had tried to win Didi over. In doing this she had sometimes pretended to like things that she really disliked, such as pop music and hair-dyeing. She remembered how Mick's first reference to her as a witch had been when she had been helping Didi to dye her hair green, three years previously. Though it had been a joke then, there was plainly some connection with her getting involved in feminine trickery together with Didi.

Once Julia opened this line of investigation memories flooded in. It was increasingly evident to her that Mick must have experienced her behaviour over the past few years as a declaration of war, or at the very least as a desertion. She had tried so hard to get close to Didi because she was afraid that she would lose her forever. She wanted to be close to her only daughter before it was too late. She also could not stand the idea of Didi preferring the Norms to her. To a certain degree she had been successful in wooing Didi. She got some respect from her; Didi recognized her as a real human being by telling her things that no one had ever told her before. Even though she had not liked what Didi said, she knew that at least Didi was concerned about her. Even if she criticized her for slaving away, at least it indicated that she saw what her mother was doing with her life. Didi acknowledged her as another person in a way that the Norms had not for a long time.

But as much as Julia valued this new dimension of relating gained with Didi, she was now painfully aware of the cost at which she had obtained it. In order to gain Didi's attention for herself, she had sometimes disregarded Mick entirely. She remembered laughing about his bizarre hobby of collecting earthworms, even though she had well known what it meant to him. She had ridiculed him in front of the whole family, because it would please Didi. She ignored his hurt, telling herself that he needed to grow up and that she could not always protect him. Now Mick was saying to people that he was an earthworm himself. He was even suggesting that she had made him into one, so that people could tread on him and fracture him.

Julia thought that Mick's accusations of her being a witch were based on his observations of her scheming to be let in on the secrets of feminine wiles with Didi. She had never been much like that and he had of course been sensitive to the difference, because he had known her so well previously. She now felt shame at her own desire for female power. She was able to trace this back to a deeper longing for respect and recognition by other people. It was as if, noticing that she seemed unable to obtain for herself the sort of autonomy and strength in relationships that she craved, she had settled for an attempt at gaining power in less honest ways. Suddenly it seemed no longer absurd to compare this to resorting to witchcraft.

Julia understood more and more of the logic of Mick's attitude by simply considering her own relationships carefully. She began to see that Mick had been in some ways closer to her than she had been to herself. That was why he had been able to pick up the dissonance in her attitude. She began to wonder whether his behaviour had been an attempt to save her as well as himself. His warnings of danger, his condemnation of her witch-like behaviour, could all be seen as an endeavour to call her back to the more truthful attitude with which she used to be capable of relating to him. His moving out to the shed then was like setting an example to her. He might have been telling her that she too needed some space. She needed to put some distance between herself and those people for whom she was willing to betray herself and him.

It had taken months before Julia had reached this perspective. During this time she had not seen Mick much. He was stable and still in hospital and he did not care to see anyone of his family until the 'signs were right'. The other members of the family dismissed this as another symptom of Mick's illness. Julia now took it extremely seriously. She thought that she knew what Mick meant. More than that she had begun to feel on his side again. Even though she deplored his way of affirming his point of view, she recognized it as a point of view that made sense. She felt personally involved, rather than simply concerned about his problems.

Julia felt that she needed to take some action. If Mick had been brave enough to move to the shed and nearly freeze to death in order to protect her and his integrity, she could stand up and be counted as well. From now on Julia undertook to become honest with herself in her relationships with Norm, her husband, Norm, her son, and Didi, her daughter. She decided that she must speak her mind and ask for her own space. Moreover, she must dare affirm her own opinions, about football, politics, hair-dyeing or anything else, without fear of reprisals. Months went by before a true beginning was made on the implementation of this new attitude. Julia became aware of just how far she had gone in her attitude of compliance.

It was more and more plain to her that without Mick to support her, she felt so little and so unprotected in the face of other people's apparent assurance, that she felt as vulnerable and naked as an earthworm herself. Even though she still had no opportunity to talk through all this with Mick, she had now reached a point of total acceptance of Mick's seemingly delusional behaviour. She not only had peace with what he had done and said, she was grateful for it. She experienced his mad behaviour as a sacrifice. She wondered if she would ever have been able to understand herself so much and begin to fight to become strong, without his challenge of her complacency. Mick had been one with her. He had seen right through her in a way that she herself had not even been capable of until now. She was grateful to him. She was also horrified at the thought of his loneliness. He had carried a heavy burden for the two of them. She had deserted and left him to carry on by himself, when she had seen an opportunity for gaining protection from others, stronger than he.

She wrote him a long letter to explain her new understanding once she felt sure enough about herself. She gave a copy of this letter to each of the other family members. The effect was dramatic. At first there were many heated family discussions. Julia was told several times that she had gone mad like her son. She kept going. Her way of expressing herself became gradually less confused and more to the point. In therapy sessions she had to be reminded constantly to trace her own attitude back to her intention of integrity and truth. She had to fight with herself in order not to blame her husband or Norm or Didi. She had hurt many feelings in her various outbursts of misplaced self-pity or Mick-crusading. But in spite of all this a new form of communication was being established in the family.

The first tangible consequence was Didi's announcement that she was moving out. She settled into a flat with a boyfriend. Within a month of this Julia reassigned Didi's room as Mick's room. She moved his possessions into it and let Mick know that he was welcome home. Mick declined, but began to be interested in seeing his mother at the hospital again.

A very important phase now began during which Julia had regular conversations with Mick, which she then tried to explore and understand in her therapy sessions. It was apparent that Mick had himself grown up and changed. His experiences transformed his own outlook on his relationships. He felt quite bitter towards Julia for having used him as an extension of herself, then having discarded him the moment she did not think she would need him any longer. Slowly their conversations led to a stage where it was possible for Julia to begin to talk about her own weakness to him. Then it became possible to start to explore the positive aspects of their former closeness. Instead of dismissing it as all abusive and symbiotic, it became possible to signal its value and its strength.

It was during this time that Julia became sensitive to the different ways of being one with another person. The one way of being close stemmed from a longing for escape from the dangers of other human relationships in the safe harbour of unison with a similar soul. The other way of being close was that of a mutual recognition of oneness of purpose and commitment. Her oneness with Mick had had both aspects. They had both needed one another for protection. Yet there had also been an element of shared dedication to sincerity and truth. It was only when the latter had dissipated and the former still remained that the situation became intolerable to Mick.

Mick, who had understood his mother's weakness before she had herself, protected himself from her disloyalty in the only way he knew how: by living like an earthworm. Now that it was becoming possible to talk about these things with one another, Mick felt eager to rebuild closeness to his mother. He did not feel ready to face living close to her, however, until they had both become strong enough to stand alone.

Julia was again impressed by the strength of Mick's determination and the clarity of his understanding. She realized that she herself would have been ready to abandon all her insights if she had been allowed to move back into the safety of being close to her son. She knew that now that Didi was no longer there it would have been possible to have a peaceful and absorbed closeness with Mick, had he returned. Again she felt grateful for his pushing her back to herself. She now negotiated with each of the family members (including Didi) to use Didi's old room for herself so that she could have her own space.

The move signified much in terms of Julia's seriousness about establishing her own autonomy and her willingness to reconsider all her relationships to the other family members. She was engaging in a grappling for equality with her husband. She was risking the loss of her elder son's reliance on her as a silent and always present mother. She was presenting herself as a full human being, wishing to relate to others as completely as possible. She gained much respect from Didi for the change in her attitude. The difficulties with the Norms were only just beginning now.

After some weeks Mick asked if he could come home for a weekend. Julia was overjoyed but made sure to let Mick stay in what used to be the dining room, rather than give up her newly gained territory to him. Mick appreciated the significance of her ability to stand strong in her own domain. He felt ready to leave hospital and go home permanently in these circumstances. It was Julia's coming to terms with herself that allowed him to begin relating to her again in an ordinary way.

In the following months Julia's relationships were far richer than she had ever believed possible. She discovered that it was possible to be close to Mick again without losing herself in the process. There was an I–Me relationship, without the I or the Me drowning. She also discovered how it was now possible to respect and love Mick as a different and other person, understanding his inner world if only a little and leave him free.

She began to have a similar I–You relationship with Didi, who was now gaining her independence in living no longer with her boyfriend but alone. It was the fighting with Norm and her husband that seemed most difficult. While I–Me and I–You relationships were rewarding, she still had trouble asserting herself, without spite, in an I–It mode. This was evident also in her avoidance of this sort of confrontation with Didi or Mick.

The next step for Julia would clearly have to be in the direction of a greater confrontation with outside world, I-It relationships. She needed to focus on relationships outside those of her immediate family. Julia began to consider the possibility of undertaking some work outside the home. She was encouraged in this direction by her conviction that only if she were able to show such initiative would she be able to maintain her new autonomy. She thought this must be crucial in terms of her leaving space for Mick as well as for herself.

Julia's struggle was almost entirely situated in the domain of relationships to other people. She seemed at first entirely dominated by passive I–It relating. Her longing was for the oneness of I–Me relationships in which she would feel understood and strengthened by a connection with another person. Finding a counsellor who would allow such a relationship was a first necessity. Understanding the negative as well as the positive aspects of the I–Me relationship she had had with her son was the next step.

The tasks Julia undertook after this were those of disengaging herself from negative I–It relationships and learning to take a resolute stance with others. She was able to do this only through an acknowledgement of her own efforts to dominate and please others. When she began to face herself in this way she became capable of seeing others in a new way as well. Before long she realized the freeing effect that her new attitude was having on other people. A more mutually appreciative I–You relating now became possible. At the same time she discovered the feasibility of I–Me closeness with her son. She continued to work in counselling sessions on her still fearful attitude towards the potential dangers of I–It relating. One of her goals now became that of becoming capable of I–You and perhaps one day even I–Me relating to her husband. She was however well aware that for this to become possible her husband would also have to be willing to reconsider her in a different way. She felt certain that he would do so only if she continued her transformation, becoming capable of less submissive behaviour.

Julia's husband would undoubtedly have to do quite a lot of work on his side of the relationship if things were to shift dramatically between them (for instance reconsidering his own closeness to his son Norm). In the sessions with Julia this was not considered as a likely option. The focus remained consistently on what Julia could do herself, rather than waste time speculating about her husband's mistakes or responsibility. The assumption throughout was that Julia would have to make the most of her relationships, without expecting any help from others to ease her progress. In this way the temptation to blame and find excuses was kept at bay. From this position every positive development became a bonus and an encouragement to Julia.

While relating naturally involves another person, the only way to improve a relationship is by solitary reconsideration of one's personal part in the relationship. One partner willing to do this thoroughly may be able to transform the set pattern. Two partners willing to do this will become capable of great mutual understanding and collaboration.

Living in time

Progress, from an existential perspective, is seen as leading to the ability to live in time. Living in time is that mode of existence where people are aware of their own inevitable progression from birth to death. This progression is not avoidable and therefore change and transformation are not avoidable. Progress is therefore defined as the gracious reception and active governing of one's process of ageing and transformation. Progress is awareness of one's ability to shape the givens of the past into an acceptable present, thus creating new prospects for the future.

Clients may be considered well in charge of their own progress in so far as they are able to find strength in their recollection of the past and hope in their vision of the future. A steady progress is marked by a capacity to appreciate and enjoy the present without harking back to the past or fleeing from it. It is in addition characterized by a resolute facing of whatever may lie ahead. Progress may be hampered by fear of the future and holding on to present illusions of ease. It may be equally hampered by a wish to hurry on towards the future, which is invested with the imaginary powers of salvation and release of any further troubles and efforts.

Existential therapy and counselling aims at enabling clients to abandon false hopes of a smooth and perfect life, where the past would be all achievement and the future all promise. The existential therapist does not promise a nirvana of accomplishment in the savouring of an always fully and deeply experienced here and now. The client is on the contrary helped to come to terms with the reality of life as a constant challenge. Savouring moments of peace is only possible against the background of the recognition of their temporary nature. Relishing the adventure of an actively undertaken life is only possible if striving for everlasting security is firmly dismissed as unattainable.

An awareness of eternity as the ground of time may be at the horizon of one's perception of existence. But even then the immediate surroundings will still be temporal. While a belief in an after-life and God may have a pacifying influence, it can never fully replace the need to come to terms with the apparent absurdity and relentlessness of earthly existence. As simple mortals faced with a limited time to spend in this world, one of the inescapable tasks is to reconcile oneself to having to create a meaningful existence, in which not too much time is wasted and where some sense is made of what could seem nonsensical.

With the disappearance of spiritual guidance from church and creed, more and more people spend much of their lives living haphazardly. It is often only towards the time that they start considering their death as a concrete possibility that the urge to make sense of their life is felt. Many people report how they did not really have a sense of time going by or running out until it was nearly too late. It is fairly easy in Western culture to lose oneself in time by living with a full schedule and little serious awareness of the actual passing of time.

In the same way in which money has become a commodity, replacing its essential and important essence of indicator of value, so time too has become a commodity, measured in minutes and hours rather than in depth of experience. To regain the sense of one's personal time is undoubtedly one of the goals of existential work. This involves recollection of one's past and projection of one's future. It involves a thorough reflection on the way in which one is currently designing one's world and life for the future out of the materials of the past. Learning to live in time means taking an active part in the authorship of one's existence. Awareness of the nothingness that one came from and the nothingness one is heading for will be a constant reminder of the relative freedom of the moment.

Throughout the therapeutic sessions clients will refer to their pasts as the cause of their current troubles. They will present themselves often as moulded by certain events or experiences. At first it will be simply necessary to draw their attention to the way in which they are presenting themselves to the world in doing this. Presentation is precisely this process of bringing certain aspects of the past into the present; the way in which one presents oneself or represents oneself is an active process of selection of past experience.

In this representation some elements of past experience are emphasized and reiterated, others are omitted and perhaps even effaced. The way in which a client carries her image of herself forward into the present can therefore have as strong an impact on her as any other form of present experience. The client who repeatedly tells herself that she has had a deprived childhood and that there is little hope for her ever to overcome such trauma is actively, in the present, realizing this trauma for herself. The suffering experienced in such actual reliving of real or imagined past experience can be as intense as that experienced through exposure to new trauma.

There is nothing weak or unreal about such reliving of the past. Many clients have succeeded in creating and re-creating strong and convincing story lines for themselves, which they stick to faithfully, and which are well integrated with external reality. However most people are not aware of the active authorship that they are involved in. Living with one's past and creating the images of the present comes as naturally as breathing. With an existential approach the counsellor or psychotherapist does not suggest to the client to breathe or create certain images in a particular manner. All the practitioner does instead is to draw the client's attention to the way in which she is at present already breathing and creating life images.

There is no need to insist that the client take responsibility for her active part in the construction of her reality. She has a perfect right not to take responsibility as long as she does not want to do so. The client is simply shown how she can observe her own recollecting of herself, her own re-creating of her self-representation

The emphasis in working on past experience and memories is therefore not just on the way in which the memory is being relived in the present but on the awareness of the fact that it is this particular memory that stands out. To help the client to pay attention to her selectiveness in remembering is as important as the realization of the impact of the memory itself.

Out of the millions of experiences, real and imagined, that a person has during her lifetime, only certain ones are picked as representative. Some facts are collected from the past and turned into a live and determining present. Some facts are left behind for later recollection. Some facts are so rarely gone back over that they fade into the distance entirely. While it is probably possible to retrieve anything ever experienced and polish it up for further use in the present, it is clearly those elements that are kept under regular scrutiny that have the strongest influence.

Conscious awareness of those aspects of the past that one is retaining most strongly is not necessarily a criterion for this recollection. Psychoanalysis has given abundant evidence of the way in which people can remember and act on certain aspects of their past experience without full awareness of these aspects. An existential approach does not consider these aspects as being unconscious. It prefers to think of them as non-reflective intentions (van Deurzen-Smith, 1997).

Intentions are the way in which people direct themselves towards the future with their own particular way of recollecting themselves from the past. Intentions are always expressed in some way, but they are not always reflected on or transparent to the person. Intentions are the way in which people carry forward their representation of themselves. They are often confused with wishes and expectations. Wishes are those things people would like to see as part of their future. They are in a sense entirely cut off from the past. Expectations are those things people imagine will happen next as a logical consequence of what has happened previously. They are in a sense disconnected from the future. Wishes and expectations are both passive experiences. When wishing or expecting the person is waiting for the world to unfold.

In the process of intending, on the contrary, the active link is made between past and future. Coming to terms with one's active intending is therefore the way towards living in time. As has been shown already, wishes and expectations are often in contradiction with one another. In this way they interfere with the process of one's intending. They stand in the way of the act of self-creation undertaken with one's intention.

If one's essential intention is, for example, to be in charge of one's life, there may be a past recollection of failure to be in charge and thus an expectation of impotence. At the same time, there may still be a wish for total control, regardless of the likelihood of ever achieving this. A client, for example, may say: 'I want to be in control,' whilst thinking 'and I never will be of course.' Achieving a life in tune with her intention, in this case, would mean for this client to cease escaping into future illusions about unlimited power, or being paralysed by expectations derived from her past. It would mean that she would connect herself instead with the real evidence of her intention of being in charge in her past and present experience. It would mean the recognition of limitations on being in charge, rather than a striving for absolutes. It would mean paying attention to the ways in which she is already now developing her being in charge. It would finally mean learning to detect the effect of her intentions and therefore becoming more tuned in to the actual possibilities or impossibilities of being in charge. This would lead to an increased sense of continuity of the process of intending. Once the client recognizes how she is realizing her intention while she is in the process of doing so, she can start to make fine adjustments in her attitude, enabling her to express her intentions more fully.

Living in time thus implies living in tune with your intentions, making the connection between expectations and wishes. Living in tune with your intentions means expressing them in action with awareness of their effects on the world, on yourself and on others. Thus the process of correcting errors of expression can automatically take place, ensuring that every action and commitment is geared towards the goals intended. Living in time thus creates a sense of great reality and authorship of your own destiny.

When Maud came for counselling she felt anything but in charge of her own destiny. She was more or less forced by her social worker to try counselling sessions. Maud had had serious problems with her children. She was a single parent with two children under five. She was suspected of child battering and she was being scrutinized carefully. Maud was fully informed of the gravity of the situation after her youngest child had had to be treated several times for injuries that suggested physical mistreatment. It was made clear that her counselling sessions were separate from the assessment procedure of her case and that there was to be no communication between the counsellor and those involved in the assessment.

After Maud made sure that the counsellor would indeed respect confidentiality, she immediately admitted her frequent rages against the children. She acknowledged her exasperation at the situation and her despair of ever being able to manage any better. She realized that she had sometimes been quite beyond herself and that she had at times shaken the children violently or thrown them in their cots in such a way that they got hurt. She was terrified of the health visitor and social worker who might take the children away from her into care. She swore that she loved her children more than anything else in the world and she could not envisage them being taken away from her. Yet she thought that if the authorities knew just how bad things would get sometimes they would not hesitate to act.

All efforts to ease her material situation and give her the maximum support in terms of benefits and assistance with the childcare had made little difference to Maud's behaviour. In fact she thought that the more people tried to help her the worse the situation seemed to get once she was on her own with the children. She had some hope that a counsellor might be able to sort her out and tell her how to improve things. What she really could not understand was how she could love her children so much and have such good intentions for them and yet treat them so badly. There seemed to be a gap in her experience of time. One moment she was trying really hard to keep things nice and she felt sure that she would be good with them and the next moment she would suddenly lose her temper and find herself beating a child without quite knowing why.

Clearly all Maud's past experience was leading her to expect not to be able to manage; she could see no reason to find strength in herself or trust herself. At the same time she had the desire to be in control and she liked to imagine herself as in total control of the situation. The more she acted in accordance with her wish for control the less she seemed capable of exercising any control. Her wishes for the future and her recollections of herself from past experience did not connect in any way. She tried to bridge the gap by getting angry or by seeking help from others. In this way she got more and more evidence of her own impotence and less and less experience of her own positive intending and ability to express and realize her intention.

Maud had no doubt whatsoever about what her intention was: she wanted to be a good mother and stay generally in control of the situation. At the same time it was difficult for Maud to formulate what being a good mother meant. She knew that it meant not beating and shaking her children as she often ended up doing, but she had no constructive ideas about what it would consist of in a positive sense. She talked about love, but she felt discouraged at the idea that in spite of her generous love of her children she would still hurt them. Her apparently needy approach to the counselling sessions was based on her genuine sense of feeling at a loss. She really did want someone to tell her what she was doing wrong.

So, in examining her dependent position with regard to the counsellor, it transpired that what Maud was after was an understanding of her own mistakes. She was not searching for an authority who could take over her life and childcare for her. She simply wanted to know how to do it herself. Once she was reassured that there would be no further need to doubt her own intentions for the moment, it became easier for her to give truthful accounts of her actual interactions with the children. She was much relieved at the chance of trusting her own intentions again. She had begun to doubt herself completely after the social worker had suggested that she might have unconscious longings to hurt her children. Although this seemed absurd to her, she had felt that it might explain her sudden aggressiveness at times when she was most trying to be good.

Now that it was possible to recount such instances without dreading to expose her own unconscious cruelty, Maud could start looking at her reactions with the sole purpose of examining the ways in which her good intentions would misfire.

Maud reported an instance of putting the younger child to bed while the elder one was playing. At first she felt confident enough about being able to get the baby to sleep before the three-year-old started claiming her attention. Yet, feeling in a rush to get the baby down, when she heard the elder child starting to whine for her, she did not take the time to put the baby down as gently and tuck him in as thoroughly as she normally would have. Leaving the baby's room to go attend to the elder child, who by now was crying because he had hurt himself, she already knew intuitively that the baby would also start crying in a minute. She swore to herself that she would behave like 'a good mother' and be patient and she ran to her other son to soothe his pain, already prepared for the crying of the baby. As soon as the baby did start to howl she felt panic rise and she tried hushing the bigger one without feeling any sympathy for his pain.

In the next five minutes she went back and forth between the two children without being able to calm either down. Still she was intending to be a good mother. She was also experiencing a sense of great failure because she felt totally out of control. It was this sense of being ruled by her children's distress that made her suddenly resentful. Their crying reminded her of her own impotence, her own helplessness. Before she knew what she was doing she now lifted the baby out of his cot and threw him onto her older boy in a rage. Realizing full well what she had just done from the increased intensity of the double screams of the children, she anxiously picked up the baby and took it back to its cot. She then raced back to her now hysterically crying three-year-old and started beating him in order to regain control over him. She was aware of the sense of satisfaction that she gained in doing so. It was shame at this satisfaction that made her stop before any physical harm was done.

Going over the actual sequence of this event had an incredible impact on Maud. Never before had she done so. She had always tried to forget such events, because she felt so ashamed of herself and she wanted to pretend that it had not really happened. What stood out for Maud was the way in which she knew on some level (intuitively, as she called it), that a negative cycle was beginning. At first this knowledge seemed entirely mysterious. Before long, however, Maud began to see how it was evident from her own way of behaving with the children that she would fail to convince them of the need for sleep and calm. It occurred to her how she was creating an atmosphere of unrest and dissatisfaction with her frantic going back and forth. It was her own intention of being a good mother that was misfiring and that became the origin of her later bad behaviour.

It was, however, clear that her intention at that very moment was not simply to be 'a good mother'. She recognized herself that her intention or her preoccupation at this time was more precisely to remain in control. Being a good mother at such a moment consisted before anything else of remaining in control of her children. Feeling ruled by them and used by them then became experienced as failure and was soon turned into resentment and punishment. Even there, she recognized her mistreatment of the children not as a direct punishment, but rather as an instinctive and violent expression of her desire to regain control.

While still ashamed of her bad treatment of those dearest to her, Maud could now see how her basic intention, even at the worst time, was still only that of remaining in charge, or of regaining control after having lost it. The next step was to explore the ways in which she would lose control in the first place. It was not difficult for Maud to see that this mostly happened through her fear of losing control. It was precisely because she tried to get the children to bed quickly, or because she would try to make them comply with the imaginary standards of good mothering, that she would begin to panic, when realizing her efforts were going to remain vain. She was in fact creating her own failure through her own unreasonable expectations. This was a totally new perspective for Maud and it was a particular relief to her to consider her experience from this angle.

Maud was not failing because of some basic defect in her. She was not secretly and deviously sadistic or aggressive towards children. She was not the victim of her own lack of mothering abilities. Nor was she failing because she could not cope adequately with her difficult circumstances. She was failing because she was trying too hard. She was failing because she loved the children so much that she wanted to be a perfect mother. She was failing because there was too much at stake. She was failing because she doubted herself too much. In her efforts to live up to her intention of being a 'good mother' she was setting herself a standard that was unrealistic. Her constant failing to satisfy her wish made her expect her own defeat. It was when she could see her own defeat looming before her once more that she would start to panic. Her panic was a way to find a last resort out of failure. Her panic entitled her to aggressive and controlling anger, which for a moment would give her a taste of control.

Maud recognized how easy it would have been to get addicted to the 'kick' of beating her children. The sheer relief of the illusion of being in charge again through this experience of dominance over them had a certain appeal. Once she could recognize the attraction of this way of gaining control, it was also possible to look for ways less damaging to the children and more satisfying to herself for the experience of such a sense of being in charge of them rather than controlled by them.

Maud began to experiment with variations on the theme of applying mild control before the situation got out of hand. She would admonish the elder child to stay in his room with a safe toy while she would take time to put the baby to bed slowly. She would tell herself that he could do without her for a bit, even if he whined, and that he would be better off without her panic than with her getting angry at him. Later she managed to tell him, as well as herself. Once she had fully attended to the baby, she would leave him alone and again refuse to feel the need to run back to him if he whimpered. She would tell him too, while feeding him his bedtime bottle, that she would not be able to attend to him for a bit after putting him down. She felt sure that the children understood her new tactics, for within weeks of her initiating these changes, bedtime routines were established which left her free of the temptation to resort to violence.

Maud concluded that the children were able to understand her now that she was able to understand herself. She felt that all that had been needed was for her to give herself the credit of her good intentions and bridge the memory gaps about her own behaviour. Thus living through her experience in a consequential way, with awareness of her own progress, opened up the possibility for making new connections. Where there had been a disconnection between her desire to be good and her expectation of being bad, it became feasible to implement her intention in a way that enabled her to be better than she had ever thought herself capable of being.

Once freed of her need to hide her own motivations, actions and intentions to herself and others for fear of failure, Maud discovered that she was capable of great consistency and continuity in her behaviour as a mother. As soon as she began to feel a bit of a success as a mother a new enjoyment in mothering was discovered. The children responded to this joy with much more rewarding behaviour. A positive, rather than a negative, cycle was engaged on.

Maud's story illustrates how useful it can be to contemplate the direct logic and continuity of a person's experience and of the way in which she models and organizes her world. Doing this involves the translation of the meanings a person reads into her perceptions of the world. The client takes her perception and interpretation of the world usually totally for granted. Therefore the therapist needs to help her in clarifying and thinking through the implications of her current process of shaping her existence.

It is of course particularly gratifying when it is possible to assist a client in revising the way in which she is shaping her own future while there is still time to correct the course of events. But all too often people come to therapy only after the fact. They conduct their lives in the way that seems right at the moment, often without much consideration of different options available. They live as if they had no choices in the matter whatsoever and one day they wake up to find that everything that seemed to make their choices self-evident and necessary has suddenly ceased to exist. Counselling or psychotherapy is then opted for as a last resort to try to make some sense of what now appears to be a wasted and absurd life.

Redundancy counselling or bereavement counselling often have this sort of starting point, where everything previously valued suddenly appears bleak to the client. Depressions following a separation or a divorce as well as those marking the loss of a position at retirement or after children leave the home are usually the product of the complete questioning of a person's previous identity and lifestyle. In some cases people simply regret the loss of a valued period of their lives, and given time and new engagements they will be able to move on and go forwards again. In some other cases the situation is rather more complex. The loss may indicate that the past lifestyle was senseless or at least the person may for the moment experience it as such. Then the person's entire life may seem devoid of meaning, as if it had been lived for nothing in an absurd waste of energy and time. The consequence of such an appraisal of life is frequently to wish for life to finish or on the contrary to wish that one could start anew.

When Martin arrived for his first therapy session, after having been given early retirement at the age of fifty-nine, his opening statement was 'I don't know what I am doing here. I have nothing of interest to say to you. My life has been entirely wasted. Everything that I have touched has turned to dust. I expect I would save myself a lot of trouble if I did the same.'

In speaking about the way in which this turning to dust had happened, Martin developed three main themes. Most importantly there was his work, in a big firm in the City, for which he had given most of his life, and certainly most of his energy and time, for the previous forty years. He had not attained the position that he had hoped for in spite of all his efforts and over the last few years his life had become unbearable because a younger colleague had been given the promotion that he himself had longed for and felt he deserved. Now under this colleague's authority, he had withdrawn his engagement from his work and his professional life had become torture.

In response to this Martin had become increasingly sour at home as well as at work. His wife, who had always complained of his lateness and frequent absences, now began complaining about his presence. Their marriage had been marred by continuous disputes ever since the children had left home, but that had been a fact of life. It seemed to him that it came out of the blue when his wife had left him to live in Spain with a friend. He felt betrayed and incredulous of what was happening to him. His performance at work as a result of this became so poor that he understood why the firm had encouraged him to accept early retirement. This came as a relief at first, but turned into another cause of disbelief when he realized what exactly was being proposed to him in terms of financial arrangements. Again Martin felt betrayed and cheated out of the rewards for the work he had done with devotion for many long years. His younger colleague had had a hand in this state of affairs, he felt sure, but at the same time he blamed himself for not having been astute enough to keep this fellow in check.

Instead of feeling anger at his colleague, he felt pity for him, because he could see him copying all his own errors and devoting himself entirely and ruthlessly to the firm. This sense of superiority of insight into human mistakes was by far the most positive aspect of Martin's initial account of himself. It was duplicated in his attitude towards his children. Both his children had entirely disappeared into the distance and had remained so for quite a number of years. His daughter was married and lived in the USA with a husband even more ambitious than he himself had ever been. He knew from his wife that his daughter was unhappy in a childless and loveless, well-to-do marriage. He felt sorry for her, but unable to communicate with her or her husband.

His son had had some difficulties with the law ten years previously and Martin was unsure about his means of making a living for himself. He had not spoken to his son for six years and did not know where he currently lived. Some time during the therapy sessions it became known to him that his son was living in Spain, near his wife and her friend. This closeness between his wife and his son became a new experience of betrayal.

Betrayal and a lack of loyalty were what Martin expected to get from anyone who was his peer or his superior. For his younger colleagues and for his children he felt pity and envy. He thought that they did not know what they were doing with their lives and that they would only discover the truth after it was too late for them as well. One of his favourite expressions was: 'If only one could be their age again and know what one knows now.' When asked what it was that he did know, he replied that he was not sure at all. He was however quite interested in pursuing this line of enquiry. It appealed to him particularly in so far as it seemed his best chance at retrieving something of value out of all these years of wasted life. At least if he had learnt something in the process there might have been something gained after all.

The moment Martin understood that all might not be lost yet, his attitude towards therapy shifted from dismissive to interested. He became more receptive to his inner experience and he began to wonder why it was that he had always been so disparaging about people who wished to cultivate an inner life. It seemed to him now that this was about all one could rely on. At least, he said, no one could take your thoughts away from you. Establishing a sense of inner comfort and belonging made it possible for Martin to begin to contemplate his life in a different light. He discovered that he was able to view his past from a multitude of different angles. He could describe his own life in terms of a series of failures and errors. He could also read into it the history of a spoiled child who was prepared by his parents for a fate of ruthless ambition and mindless activity. On the other hand he could trace back his own attitude as formative of the situation that gradually developed around him. Then again that left him with the option of blaming himself and taking full responsibility for his destructive behaviour or blaming it on others or on circumstances.

Gradually it started to sink in that there was another possibility: steady and serious enquiry into all of these different elements, leading to an investigation of how he could make his past make sense for him. In other words, Martin discovered the secret of creating meaning for himself, not only meaning in the possibilities of the future, but meaning in the apparent absurdity of the past.

Martin's learning to live in time, instead of wanting to hasten its course or undo its marks, was made easier by the occurrence of a new crisis. The colleague who had outdone him at work abruptly died of a series of heart attacks. As this colleague had been more than ten years younger than Martin, he felt a sense of unexpected achievement in having perhaps saved his own life by failing while there was still time to reconsider.

It was now conceivable that what had seemed like failure before could be construed as the beginning of a far greater success than that of commercial ambitions. At least he had had time to rethink his life before it was too late. At least there was still time left to change his course. At last Martin became entirely serious about considering what he would want to make of his life or at least of what was left of it. For a while he was preoccupied with the idea that he had missed an opportunity to sort things out with his colleague before the latter's death. This was precipitated by the message he got at his colleague's funeral. His colleague had asked his wife to tell Martin 'to forget and forgive and count his blessings'.

In the end it was of course up to Martin's own imagination to interpret the message. He decided that his colleague wanted his pardon for their fierce competitiveness and that he had obtained it directly by working himself into his grave. He was still preoccupied with the notion of having to count his blessings as he so clearly had lost everything worth living for. It occurred to him, however, that what his colleague must have meant was that for him, Martin, there was still the blessing of time left to spend alive. He had time on his hands and knowledge and experience to guide him in the use of it. When asked how he would have imagined wanting to spend that time if it were he in hospital, dying, rather than his colleague, the answer was definite and clear.

Martin decided that the first task that he still needed to accomplish was to take time to talk with his children and with his estranged wife. No matter what the outcome would be (and he had indeed little expectation that it could be positive), he owed it to himself at least to have tried to let them all know how he was different now and keen to hear from them.

He set out on a number of journeys, interspersed with a few therapy sessions here and there. The very activity of his travels and the exposure to new situations and old relationships had a strange mellowing effect on him. He was visibly changed each time. He was exposed to many arguments and sad realizations of his own past mistakes. The bitterness against him in the people who had been closest to him made him sometimes despair, but increasingly reflective and more open to a humble consideration of his life's errors and missed opportunities.

After much disappointment with the apparent actual lack of possibilities to re-establish any closeness with either his wife or his children, he settled down in a routine at home by himself. It was when he had already come to terms with the need for him to start relinquishing the past entirely that his wife approached him with an invitation to come and spend some time with her in Spain. When Martin eventually decided to go to her, it was with the most serious intention of wanting to hear her as well as speaking his own mind to her. First it was a disappointment to realize on his arrival in Spain that she had asked him over because she felt incapable of handling their son who was in legal trouble. He accepted this situation soon as the logical consequence of his previous relationships with them and he welcomed the opportunity to start making a concrete contribution to correcting what was still possible to correct.

Before long Martin engaged in a complex legal battle. He was grateful to be able to redeem himself in such a practical way. In spite of the stresses that he became exposed to in the course of his new commitment, he gained great satisfaction in having found a way of making sense of his own mistakes. He had found a means of redressing the balance of his life by concretely addressing the issues resulting from his own past errors.

Martin wrote to his therapist that even though it was proving increasingly difficult to efface the past or to change the course of his own history dramatically, he had discovered the inner peace that comes with the knowledge that one is doing the right thing. Obviously Martin was becoming tuned in to his inner sense of truth. Instead of despairing about time lost or time running out, he was living in time. He had abandoned his old illusions of gaining total control over his own destiny. He had overcome his fears of being at the mercy of fate's inevitable destruction of everything.

In full recognition of his own limitations Martin had begun to make peace with the challenges of living life existentially. He no longer desired great rewards or proofs of his own merit. He was simply determined to make the most of even the worst. For Martin it had been the consideration of his not too distant death that had made such a new and resolute attitude possible. Without being actually worried about the prospect of dying, his experience of loss of his existence had been acutely real through the loss of all those things and people that had thus far meant life to him. With hindsight Martin felt that fate had done him a favour by depriving him of artifices. He had never before felt as real and truly himself as he did now.

Martin had secured for himself the secret of living in time. It consisted in surrendering to the inevitability of death and realizing himself as creatively as was possible given the circumstances that he had already brought about. He replaced his regrets about the past with consistent efforts to redress the balance where possible. He replaced his panic about the future with a steady progression towards the end of a life well lived. He was now participating in his own destiny instead of proclaiming himself either the victim of an unfortunate causal chain or the master of his life with full control and devastating responsibility. The knowledge that he was doing his best with passionate commitment procured him the steadfastness and vitality of a life well spent.

Learning to live in time with oneself thus signifies finding those things in oneself that the old saying demands to be granted from God: serenity to accept the things one cannot change, courage to change the things one can and wisdom to know the difference.

Chapter summary

1. The self is the centre of gravity of the world relations that an individual is involved in.

2. Existential therapy is a process of enabling a person in achieving greater awareness, understanding and governance of her world relations and therefore of her own changing self.

3 The therapist functions as an alter ego and a reminder of the client's voice of conscience and inner truth.

4 The principle of kinship encompasses the old notions of projection, introjection, identification and projective identification. People's interactions are often based on a desire either to unify and merge or differentiate and separate.

5 Existential therapists encourage their clients to become increasingly self-reflective about their interactions with the world and in particular with others.

6 The objective is not to analyse, but to describe, become aware of and understand oneself, whilst constantly verifying one's position in the world in relation to external reality and different points of view.

7 Bringing to light what is in the dark, revealing what is covered up and paying attention to what is actually there are all part of this process of becoming self-reflective and exploring hidden world dimensions.

8 This process inevitably involves a confrontation with the limits of the human condition and a coming to terms with one's own limitations and possibilities.

9 Any assistance given to people who are distressed or lonely needs to be truth-seeking and non-patronizing.

10 Confusion only leads to madness if it cannot be understood and made sense of.

11 When finding one's own truth it can be hard to hold one's own against the assaults form the outside world, yet in order to find real truth multiple perspectives have to be taken into one's view.

12 When action is led by self-reflection about what matters we can engage with the world in a well-informed way and live in harmony with our own vision and motivation.

13 We are only free within the limits of the given situation. Our conditions form a framework within which we can exercise our own choice and creativity.

14 Blind fanaticism is as unproductive as blind fatalism: self-aware living always involves a certain amount of doubt as well as a resolute commitment to a particular set of values and objectives.

15 The existential therapist does not confront self-pity and self-indulgence directly. Instead she makes an alliance with the client's aspiration to a better life and encourages a sober process of taking stock.

16 Actions can only become synchronized with one's most intimate intentions if these are acknowledged and understood.

17 Much defeated action has become so for a lack of conviction of possible success. Much lack of conviction is due to a lack of a sense of entitlement.

18 Claiming one's rights always means giving up some previously established privileges. The value of something is determined by the number of things one is willing to give up for it.

19   Engagements undertaken in the knowledge and understanding of the possible consequences and implications of one's choices are consistently more fulfilling than haphazardous ones.

20   Trying to avoid loss is a bad principle to live by, though most people do. People all too often confuse their longing for security with the notion that challenge and meaningful engagement must be a threat.

21   Engaged action produces a sense of vitality and satisfaction as surely as disengaged action produces a sense of apathy and boredom.

22   Existential guilt is a reminder of what you owe to yourself. Only to the extent that you take up this existential challenge will you experience a strong sense of being in charge of your own life.

23   The aim of existential therapy is to enable clients to engage themselves in resolute action which is based on an authentic appraisal of their life's purpose.

24   The unease people experience in their relationships often stems from a more basic unease with themselves and with life in general.

25   Beyond the I–It and I–You forms of relationship there is the possibility of the I–Me relationship, which consists of complete union and merging with someone we feel we belong with. This is always a temporary state.

26   Living in time is that mode of existence where a person is aware of their inevitable process of transformation and progress from birth to death. They know that change is something unavoidable and inexorable, rather than something that is hard to bring about.

27   Progress is to shape the givens of the past into an acceptable present, creating new prospects for the future.

28   Resoluteness consists in neither fear nor idealization of past or future, but a steady facing of what lies behind and ahead of one, whilst realistically assessing what one is surrounded by right now.

29   Striving for security is not a feasible option and life's challenges need to be accepted, welcomed and faced up to. Human life is never so insecure as when we pursue security.

30   Time like many other things has become a commodity in our world. Recovering a sense of personal and meaningful time is part of reclaiming authorship of one's life.

31   Through our intentions we carry forward our own representations of the world and of ourselves in an active manner, rather than passively as we do with wishes or expectations.

32   Wishes and expectations are often in conflict with each other.

33   Living in tune with your intentions means expressing them in action with awareness of their effects on the world, yourself and others.

34   Doing one's best with commitment and awareness of self, world, others and ideals is often enough to make for a life well lived.

7

Conclusion

In the preceding pages a method of counselling and psychotherapy has been described which aims at emphasizing a person's life rather than just the person. Instead of proposing a rigid technique it outlines a framework from which interactions with the client can be created, monitored and understood.

Basic therapeutic skills such as an ability to listen rather than guess, to hear rather than to prescribe, to reflect rather than to distort the client's meaning and to reassure rather than to confuse the client are assumed. At the same time the manner in which such skills are applied is reconsidered. Rather than promoting another method to enhance empathic understanding, make interpretations or prompt behavioural change, the existential approach reminds therapist and client to reflect on life's basic issues.

Existential counselling and therapy have therefore been described as a way of broadening one's perspective. The emphasis is turned away from high technology and strategic interventionism. Instead counsellors, therapists and clients of all denominations are shown that they will probably benefit from taking a closer look at their own view of the world.

It has been argued that such a reappraisal of one's way of perceiving and experiencing life can guide the therapeutic process towards sometimes surprising outcomes. Instead of adjustment to the norm, what may ensue is a life inspired by the aspiration to personal values and ideals. Instead of pursuing change for the sake of change, people may rediscover their own inevitable process of transformation and come to terms with limitations and possibilities in a way not thought of before. They may find themselves able to create new meaning where life had become apathetic and listless. They may be delighted to reveal a new depth to themselves and their lives that leads to passionate rather than depressed living. They may recover their own spirit of adventure and faith in themselves and the world around them.

Clearly, from an existential position clients are encouraged to come to terms with their own view of life, but in doing so they will also be confronted with some of the facts of living they had previously ignored or not recognized. Existential therapy is firmly rooted in philosophy and ethics. The message conveyed implicitly to clients is a message about life rather than primarily about themselves. The message reads as follows.

People are not basically so very different from each other. There are some fundamental issues that every human being has to struggle with sooner or later. Recognizing those issues and grappling with them is a necessity for any human being. While individual differences may give people a diversity of starting points and positions, the issues themselves are not all that different.

What may seem like negative conditions initially may turn out to contain the promise of much positive learning and experience. There are no lives without positive possibilities. However badly a person has suffered, there is always the potential for finding some creative opportunities in the situation.

Apart from some extreme and rare exceptions, on the whole people can rely on getting their share of assets and opportunities. They can equally rely on getting their share of shortage and challenge. Opportunities and challenges come in many different shapes. Learning to recognize them is essential. An experienced existential therapist will see a way through most human problems and adversity and hone a person's talents and assets to deal with it.

Finding meaning and purpose in life and a consistent course in that direction must be one of the most enriching and satisfying ways to live. Being able to get on with oneself is the first achievement in this direction. Being able to handle external situations effectively is the next. Being able, first, to cope with the challenges of relationships with others, then to discover the possibility of unity and harmony is another level of this exploration.

Reflection on the human position in the universe may also be a significant element of the search for meaning and truth. We all rely on the basic structures and laws of the universe and on such principles as the passing of time or movement in space. We do not have to be religious or believe in a god or other higher being to know that there is more to life than meets our eyes. Wondering about what is and why it is leads to a healthy attitude of doubt, but also of respect for what transcends us. Anybody's personal guess or belief about this is therefore as valid as she or he wants it to be.

However, the design of the wider universe or scientific principles of causality can never be sufficient explanation for any occurrence. Nothing can be entirely blamed on god or on fate, on culture or on one's parents. On the other hand there is no use for a damning and heavy sense of personal responsibility. Recognizing the interplay between our active and re-active participation in the givens of existence can be a good start to finding a safe position in the world. Acknowledging our own limitations as well as our own merits is another important step in the right direction. Coming to know both our duties and our entitlements is equally significant. Yet the attitude to life that might be most in line with this ability to include opposites and contradictions, paradoxes and polarities is one of passionate engagement with a purpose beyond that of mediocre averageness. For it is possible to become too sensible and do too much sober balancing and weighing.

In the end, people are usually incited to act in accordance with what is deep down of real significance to them. There is an undeniable implicit exhortation in an existential approach for people to stand up for what they feel ready to make sacrifices for and to claim their rights to live a life as full as humanly possible. The mature existential therapist will be able to moderate such passions in a realistic manner. Still, people will be encouraged to feel entitled to the best. They will also be reminded of the need to be prepared for the worst and to expect their share of both good and bad. With all that, the word is: whatever will be obtained will be laboured for and what is worth labouring for must be worth one's best effort.

In the last analysis the existential approach reclaims the merit of spirit. The art of human living without vitality and purpose, without will and commitment, would be stale, mechanical and boring. As one of the rare approaches that does not assume an essential or conditioned self in the person, the existential approach's final motto could be Nietzsche's famous saying: 'Will a self and you will become a self.'

Retracing the path of the willing of that self and projecting and designing its course for the future is what existential work is all about. The existential therapist uses her influence over the client in such a way as to lead her progressively from confusion to resolution. She does this by applying an essentially Socratic method of firm encouragement of exploration of the client's personal version of the truth. The counsellor or psychotherapist assists the client in first recognizing this partial truth, then in articulating it so that its inherent contradictions can be examined. Finally, she assists the client in expanding her truth in the direction of a wider and more universal truth, which is already implied.

The measure of success of the existential method is therefore the extent to which both therapist and client experience a sense of progressive tuning in to a truth that can encompass apparent contradictions. The proof of its validity is the extent to which it can be lived with so as to make sense of human experience and to substitute meaning and understanding for chaos and perplexity.

Only when people stop trying to be cured of life or to change it do they become truly alive. Only then, when they begin to be ready for the recurrent challenges, crises and troubles, do they start to be open to the depth of experience and reality that comes with a true commitment to existence. It is then that they discover, with surprise and wonder, that in spite of all their distress, worry and suffering, life is ultimately full of promise and eminently worth the effort of living it.

The most gratifying task of the existential therapist is to assist people in their struggle to live such a worthwhile life. In this process both therapist and client will constantly be reminded that earth is a place somewhere between heaven and hell, where much pain and much joy is to be had and where some degree of wisdom can make all the difference.

References

Binswanger, L. (1944) 'The case of Ellen West', in R. May, E. Angel and H.F. Ellenberger (eds), *Existence*. New York: Basic Books, 1958.

Binswanger, L. (1946) 'The existential analysis school of thought', in R. May, E. Angel, and H.F. Ellenberger (eds), *Existence*. New York: Basic Books, 1958.

Binswanger, L. (1963) 'Heidegger's analytic of existence and its meaning for psychiatry', reprinted in J. Needleman (ed.), *Being-in-the-world: Selected Papers of Ludwig Binswanger*. London: Souvenir Press, 1975.

Boss, M. (1963) *Psychoanalysis and Daseinsanalysis* (tr. I.B. Lefebre). New York: Basic Books.

Buber, M. (1923) *I and Thou* (tr. W. Kaufmann). Edinburgh: T&T Clark, 1970.

Camus, A. (1942) *The Myth of Sisyphus*. Harmondsworth: Penguin.

Deurzen, E. van (1998) *Paradox and Passion in Psychotherapy*. Chichester: Wiley and Sons.

Deurzen-Smith, E. van (1984) 'Existential psychotherapy', in W. Dryden (ed.) *Individual Therapy in Britain*. London: Harper & Row.

Deurzen-Smith, E. van (1997) *Everyday Mysteries: Existential Dimensions of Psychotherapy*, London:Routledge.

Frankl, V.E. (1955) *The Doctor and the Soul*. New York: Vintage Books, 1973.

Frankl, V.E. (1967) *Psychotherapy and Existentialism*. New York: Washington Square Press, 1970.

Heidegger, M. (1927) *Being and Time* (tr. J. Macquarrie and E.S. Robinson). New York: Harper & Row, 1962.

Heidegger, M. (1957) *What is Called Thinking?* (tr. J. Glenn Gray). New York: Harper & Row, 1968.

Jaspers, K. (1931) *Psychologie der Weltanschauungen* (tr. M. Franck and A. Newton), in M. Friedman, *The Worlds of Existentialism*. Chicago and London: University of Chicago Press, 1964.

Jaspers, K. (1951) *Way to Wisdom* (tr. R. Manheim). Newhaven and London: Yale University Press.

Kierkegaard, S. (1844) *The Concept of Dread* (tr. W. Lowrie). Princeton, NJ: Princeton University Press, 1944.

Kierkegaard S. (1845) *The Point of View for my Work as an Author* (tr. W. Lowrie). New York: Oxford University Press, 1939.

Kierkegaard, S. (1846a) *Concluding Unscientific Postscript* (tr. D.F. Swenson and W. Lowrie). Princeton, NJ: Princeton University Press, 1941.

Kierkegaard, S. (1846b) *The Present Age* (tr. A. Dru). New York: Harper & Row, 1962.

Laing, R.D. (1960) *The Divided Self.* London: Tavistock/Harmondsworth: Penguin, 1970.

Laing, R.D. (1961) *The Self and Others.* London: Tavistock/Harmondsworth: Penguin, 1971.

Macquarrie, J. (1972) *Existentialism: an Introduction, Guide and Assessment*. Harmondsworth: Penguin.

May, R. (1950) *The Meaning of Anxiety.* New York: Norton.

May, R. (1969) *Love and Will.* New York: Norton.

Midgley, M. (1981) *Heart and Mind.* London: Methuen.

Sartre, J-P. (1938) *Nausea.* Harmondsworth: Penguin, 1962.

Sartre, J-P. (1939) *Sketch for a Theory of the Emotions.* London: Methuen, 1962.

Sartre, J-P. (1943) *Being and Nothingness: an Essay on Phenomenological Ontology* (tr. H. Barnes). New York: Philosophical Library, 1956.

Sartre, J-P. (1946) *Existentialism and Humanism* (tr. P. Mairet). London: Methuen, 1948.

Szasz, T.S. (1961) *The Myth of Mental Illness.* New York: Hoeber–Harper.

Tillich, P. (1952) *The Courage to Be.* Glasgow: Collins/Fontana.

Tolstoy, L. (1886) *The Death of Ivan Ilyich* (tr. L. Solotaroff). New York: Bantam Books, 1981.

Valle, R.S. and King, M. (1978) *Existential-Phenomenological Alternatives for Psychology.* New York: Oxford University Press.

Von Uexküll, T. (1921) 'Unwelt und Innenwelt der Tiere', in R. May, E. Angel, and H.F. Ellenberger (eds), *Existence.* New York: Basic Books, 1958.

Yalom, I. (1980) *Existential Psychotherapy.* New York: Basic Books.

Recommended Reading

Novels and plays

Anouilh, J. (1951) *Antigone*. London: Methuen.
de Beauvoir, S. (1954) *The Mandarins*. Harmondsworth: Penguin.
de Beauvoir, S. (1966) *A Very Easy Death*. Harmondsworth: Penguin.
Camus, A. (1947) *The Plague*. New York: Knopf, 1948.
Dostoevsky, F. (1864) *Notes from the Underground*. Harmondsworth: Penguin.
Dostoevsky, F. (1866) *Crime and Punishment*. Harmondsworth: Penguin.
Dostoevsky, F. (1880) *The Brothers Karamazov*. Harmondsworth: Penguin.
Eliot, G. (1872) *Middlemarch*. Harmondsworth Penguin, 1999.
Fynn (1974) *Mr God, this is Anna*. Glasgow: William Collins & Co.
Goethe, J.W. von (1774) *The Sorrows of Young Werther*. Harmondsworth: Penguin, 1989.
Green, H. (1964) *I Never Promised You a Rose Garden*. New York: New American Library.
Hesse, H. (1919) *Demian*. London: Granada.
Hesse, H. (1924) *Steppenwolf*. New York: Holt, 1947.
Horwood, W. (1987) *Skallagrigg*, Harmondsworth: Penguin.
Kafka, F. (1926) *The Castle*. New York: Knopf, 1954.
Miller, A. (1953) *The Crucible*. Harmondsworth: Penguin.
Peake, M. (1953) *Mr Pye*. Harmondsworth: Penguin.
Sartre, J-P. (1938) *Nausea*. Harmondsworth: Penguin, 1962.
Sartre, J-P. (1943) *No Exit* and *The Flies*. New York, Knopf, 1947.
Shute, N. (1950) *A Town like Alice*. London: Pan Books.
Steinbeck, J. (1939) *The Grapes of Wrath*. London: Pan Books, 1975.
Tolstoy, L. (1886) *The Death of Ivan Ilyich*. London: Bantam Books.
Turgenev 1. (1862) *Fathers and Sons*. Harmondsworth: Penguin.

Philosophy

Blackham, H.J. (1982) *Six Existentialist Thinkers*. New York: Harper & Row.
Buber, M. (1923) *I and Thou* (tr. W. Kaufmann). Edinburgh: T.T. Clark, 1970.
Camus, A. (1942) *The Myth of Sisyphus*. Harmondsworth: Penguin, 1975.
Friedman, M. (1964) *The Worlds of Existentialism*. Chicago and London: University of Chicago Press.
Heidegger, M. (1927) *Being and Time* (tr. J. Macquarrie and E.S. Robinson). London: Harper & Row, 1962.
Howard, A. (2000) *Philosophy for Counselling and Psychotherapy*. Basingstoke: Macmillan Press.
Jaspers, K. (1950) *The Way to Wisdom* (tr. E. Paul and C. Paul). London: Routledge & Kegan Paul, 1951.
Kaufmann, W. (ed.) (1956) *Existentialism from Dostoevsky to Sartre*. New York: Meridian.

Kierkegaard, S. (1846) *Concluding Unscientific Postscript* (tr. D.F. Swenson and W. Lowrie). Princeton: Princeton University Press, 1941.

Kierkegaard, S. (1844) *The Concept of Dread* (tr. W. Lowrie). Princeton: Princeton University Press, 1944.

Mace, C. (1999) *Heart and Soul: The Therapeutic Face of Philosophy.* London:Routledge.

MacMurray, J. (1957) *The Self as Agent.* London: Faber & Faber.

MacMurray, J. (1961) *Persons in Relation.* London: Faber & Faber.

Macquarrie, J. (1972) *Existentialism: an Introduction, Guide and Assessment.* Harmondsworth: Penguin.

Merleau-Ponty, M. (1945) *Phenomenology of Perception* (tr. C. Smith). London: Routledge & Kegan Paul.

Midgley, M. (1981) *Heart and Mind.* London: Methuen.

Nietzsche, F. (1878) *Human, All too Human: a Book for Free Spirits* (tr. R.J. Hollindale). Cambridge: Cambridge University Press, 1986.

Nietzsche, F. (1882) *The Gay Science* (tr. W. Kaufmann). New York: Random House, 1974.

Nietzsche, F. (1883) *Thus Spake Zarathustra* (tr. A. Tille). New York: Dutton, 1933.

Olson, R.G. (1962) *An Introduction to Existentialism.* New York: Dove Publications Inc.

Plato (1938) *Portrait of Socrates.* London: Oxford University Press.

Ryle, G. (1949) *The Concept of Mind.* London: Hutchinson.

Sartre, J-P. (1939) *Sketch for a Theory of the Emotions.* London: Methuen, 1962.

Sartre, J-P. (1943) *Being and Nothingness* (tr. H. Barnes). New York: Philosophical Library, 1956.

Sartre, J-P. (1946) *Existentialism and Humanism* (tr. P. Mairet). London: Methuen, 1948.

Scott, N. (1978) *Mirrors of Man in Existentialism.* New York: Collins.

Spinoza, B. (1677) *Ethics* (tr. R.H.M. Elwes). New York: Dover Publications, 1955.

Warnock, M. (1970) *Existentialism.* Oxford: Oxford University Press.

Practical application

Bateson, G. (1973) *Steps to an Ecology of Mind.* St Albans: Paladin.

Bettelheim, B. (1962) *Dialogues with Mothers.* New York: Avon Books.

Bettelheim, B. (1987) *A Good Enough Parent.* London: Thames & Hudson.

Binswanger, L. (1963) *Being in the World* (tr. J. Needleman). New York: Basic Books.

Boss, M. (1957) *Psychoanalysis and Daseinsanalysis* (tr. J.B. Lefebre). New York: Basic Books, 1963.

Boss, M. (1979) *Existential Foundations of Medicine and Psychology.* New York: Jason Aronson.

Cohn, H. (1997) *Existential Thought and Therapeutic Practice.* London: Sage.

Collier, A. (1977) *R.D. Laing: Philosophy and Politics of Psychotherapy.* New York: Pantheon Books.

Deurzen-Smith, E. van (1984) 'Existential psychotherapy', in W. Dryden (ed.), *Individual Therapy in Britain.* London: Harper & Row.

Deurzen, E. van (1998) *Paradox and Passion in Psychotherapy.* Chichester:Wiley and Sons.

Deurzen-Smith, E. van (1997) *Everyday Mysteries: Existential Dimensions of Psychotherapy,* London:Routledge.

Du Plock, S. (ed.) (1997) *Case Studies in Existential Psychotherapy.* Chichester: Wiley and Sons.

Field, J. (1936) *A Life of One's Own.* Boston: Houghton Mifflin.

Frankl, V.E. (1946) *Man's Search for Meaning.* London: Hodder & Stoughton, 1964.

Frankl, V.E. (1955) *The Doctor and the Soul.* New York: Knopf.

Frankl, V.E. (1967) *Psychotherapy and Existentialism.* Harmondsworth: Penguin.

Freud, S. (1916) 'Introductory lectures on psychoanalysis', *The Standard Edition of the Complete Psychological Works of Sigmund Freud* (tr. J. Strachey), Vol. 15. London: Hogarth, 1961.

Freud, S. (1930) 'Civilization and its discontents', *Standard Edition,* Vol. 21. London: Hogarth, 1964.

Freud, S. (1932) 'New introductory lectures on psychoanalysis', *Standard Edition,* Vol. 22. London: Hogarth, 1964.

Fromm, E. (1949) *Man for Himself.* London: Routledge & Kegan Paul.

Jaspers, K. (1964) *The Nature of Psychotherapy.* Chicago: University of Chicago Press.

Laing, R.D. (1960) *The Divided Self.* Harmondsworth: Penguin, 1970.

Laing, R.D. (1961) *The Self and Others.* Harmondsworth: Penguin, 1971.

Laing, R.D. (1967) *The Politics of Experience.* Harmondsworth: Penguin, 1970.

Lomas, P. (1981) *The Case for a Personal Psychotherapy.* Oxford: Oxford University Press.

May, R., Angel, E. and Ellenberger, H.F. (eds) (1958) *Existence.* New York: Basic Books.

May, R. (1967) *Psychology and the Human Dilemma.* New York: Norton.

May, R. (1969) *Love and Will.* New York: Norton.

May, R. (1969) *Existential Psychology.* New York: Random House.

May, R. (1983) *The Discovery of Being.* New York: Norton.

May, R. and Yalom, E. (1985) 'Existential psychotherapy', in R.J. Corsini (ed.), *Current Psychotherapies.* Itasca, IL: Peacock.

Oatley, K. (1984) *Selves in Relation.* London: Methuen.

Rogers, C.R. and Stevens, B. (1967) *Person to Person.* London: Souvenir Press.

Ruitenbeek, M. (1982) *Psychoanalysis and Existential Philosophy.* New York: Dutton.

Schafer, R. (1976) *A New Language for Psychoanalysis.* New Haven and London: Yale University Press.

Smail, D.J. (1978) *Psychotherapy: a Personal Approach.* London: Dent.

Strasser, F. and Strasser, A. (1997) *Existential Time Limited Therapy.* Chichester: Wiley and Sons.

Szasz, T.S. (1961) *The Myth of Mental Illness.* New York: Hoeber–Harper.

Szasz, T.S. (1965) *The Ethics of Psychoanalysis.* New York: Basic Books.

Tillich, P. (1952) *The Courage To Be.* New Haven: Yale University Press.

Valle, R.S. and King, M. (1978) *Existential Phenomenological Alternatives for Psychology.* Oxford: Oxford University Press.

Yalom, I. (1980) *Existential Psychotherapy.* New York: Basic Books.

Yalom, I. (1996) *Lying on the Couch.* New York: Basic Books.

Zinker, J. (1977) *Creative Process in Gestalt Therapy.* New York: Vintage Books.

Index